Explore the World

NELLES

# AUSTRALIA

**Authors:**
Peter Hinze, Paul Chadwick, Fiona Gillies,
Gary Walsh, Carol Stuart, Anne Biging,
Marc Marger, Andrea Brown, Ulf Marquardt,
Wolfgang Koch, Uwe Seidel, Lesley Darlington

*An Up-to-date travel guide
with 133 color photos
and 29 maps*

**Dear Reader:** Being up-to-date is the main goal of the Nelles series. Our correspondents help keep us abreast of the latest developments in the travel scene, while our cartographers see to it that maps are also kept completely current. However, as the travel world is constantly changing, we cannot guarantee that all the information contained in our books is always valid. Should you come across a discrepancy, please contact us at: Nelles Verlag, Schleissheimer Str. 371 b, 80935 Munich, Germany, tel. (089) 3571940, fax (089) 35719430, e-mail: Nelles.Verlag@t-online.de

**Note:** Distances and measurements, including temperatures, used in this guide are metric. For conversion information, please see the *Guidelines* section of this book.

# LEGEND

| | | |
|---|---|---|
| ★★ Main Attraction (on map) | Broome *(Town)* Park *(Sight)* Places Highlighted in Yellow Appear in Text | National Border |
| ★★ (in text) | | Provincial Border |
| ★ Worth Seeing (on map) | International Airport | Expressway |
| ★ (in text) | National Airport | Principal Highway (hard/loose surface) |
| ❽ Orientation Number in Text and on Map | National Park, Nature Reserve | Highway (hard/loose surface) |
| Public or Significant Building | \ 13 / Distance in Kilometers | Other Road (hard/loose surface) |
| Hotel, Lodge, Camp | Beach | |
| Market | **Bluff Knoll** 1096 Mountain (altitude in meters) | ✪✪✪ Luxury Hotel Category ✪✪ Moderate Hotel Category ✪ Budget Hotel Category |
| Pedestrian Zone | | *(for price information see "Accomodation" in Guidline section)* |
| ✝ Church | Railway | |

**AUSTRALIA**
© Nelles Verlag GmbH, 80935 München
All rights reserved

Fourth revised edition 2001
ISBN 3-88618-216-9
Printed in Slovenia

| | | | |
|---|---|---|---|
| **Publisher:** | Günter Nelles | **English Editor:** | Sidaway Sollinger / |
| **Editor in Chief :** | Berthold Schwarz | | Transwords |
| **Project Editor:** | Peter Hinze | **Cartography:** | Nelles Verlag GmbH, |
| **Editor:** | W. Gartmann | | München |
| **Lithos:** | Priegnitz, München | **Printed by:** | Gorenjski Tisk |

- S09 -

# TABLE OF CONTENTS

## TRAVEL INFORMATION

## *MAP LIST*

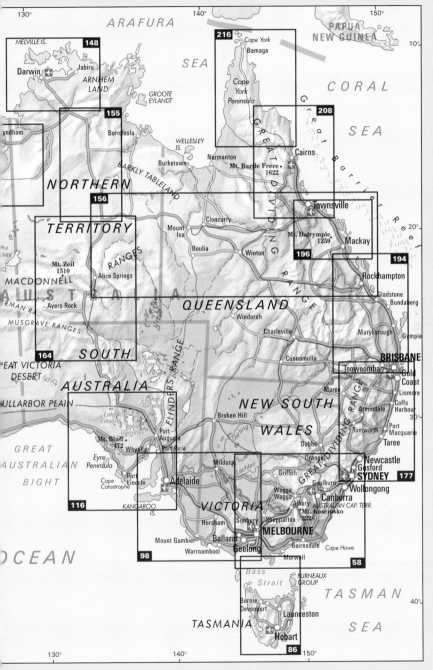

# HISTORY
# OF AUSTRALIA

## HISTORY AND CULTURE

### The First Australians

Human settlement of Australia probably began about 40,000 years ago and today the descendants of those first settlers are called Aborigines. The Aborigines are Asiatic in origin and seem to have arrived in Australia via New Guinea in three waves of immigration during a time when both countries were still linked to Southeast Asia by a chain of numerous small islands. Not until the melting of the great ice cap in the northern hemisphere and the accompanying rise in water levels did this land bridge finally disappear, leaving the Aborigines virtually cut off. The Australian continent had become an island.

The first Australians, as the Aborigines are often called, did not arrive as one large homogeneous group. Historians believe that after settling they split up into some 600 tribes, speaking approximately 200 different languages. They lived by hunting small animals, fishing, and gathering berries and herbs. They seldom built huts or shelters: only in the south as protection against the cold, and in the north against heavy rainfall. The Aborigines owned very few material possessions. This was partly because of their nomadic lifestyle, in which baggage would have been a hindrance, but more importantly it symbolized their particular philosophy of life. They believed that the Earth in her natural state was sufficient and that nothing needed to be added to

*Previous pages: A bevy of lifeguards keeping an eye out on things. The Outback in New South Wales. Uluru (Ayers Rock) in the evening light. Left: Aborigine art in the Katherine Gorge region.*

her. Mythical ancestors were believed to have created the world and all its animal and plant life during the "dream time" and to have defined the rules by which the tribes people must live.

The various tribes remained in close contact with each other, and people living in border areas were multilingual. Intermarriage was permitted, and tribal disputes were settled at meetings (corroborees). There was no hostility or warfare as we know it. Birth control was practiced in order to avoid overpopulation. The land was divided up by "dream paths" along which certain tribal groups had right of way. Along these routes sacred sites were established, some of which can be seen to this day.

There was hardly any contact with the world outside the Australian continent, and what little there was was restricted to the northern part. The inhabitants of New Guinea probably visited, and, sporadically, Malayan fishing boats may have landed, but it was not until the discovery of Australia by the Europeans that profound (and irreversible) changes took place in the lifestyle of the Aborigines.

### The Coming of the Europeans

Despite centuries of speculation over the existence of a terra australis incognita, a land mass in the southern hemisphere, Australia was not discovered by Europeans until relatively recently. Fernão de Magalhães (Magellan) sailed close by when he discovered Timor in the 16th century. The same thing happened to Luis Vaez de Torres, who passed between Australia and New Guinea. Finally a Dutchman, William Janus, became the first European to land in northern Australia (Cape York) in 1606. In 1642 Abel Tasman approached from the south and landed on the island that now bears his name, Tasmania. He assumed, however, that Tasmania and Australia formed a single land mass.

Although the landscapes and appearance of Cape York and Tasmania could hardly be more different, the Dutch were agreed on one point, that this strange continent, which they called New Holland, had an intolerable climate and was completely lacking in economic potential. They lost all interest in it and concentrated instead on Indonesia which they found to be much more lucrative. History granted Australia a further period of grace when, half a century later, William Dampier, an English pirate, confirmed the commonly held opinion that Australia was of no economic interest.

Captain James Cook, however, took a different view. Sailing from Tierra del Fuego, via Tahiti and New Zealand, he was the first European to land on Australia's east coast, in a bay that seemed like paradise. It proved to be an ideal anchor-

*Above: Captain Cook reached Australia on the 28th of April, 1770. Right: The cartographer Peter Goos had already "discovered" the country in 1666.*

age, and he called it Botany Bay because of its profusion of plant life. Not until three days had passed did the sailors see any signs of human life. Captain Cook wrote in his diary, "Sunday 22nd: We steered alongshore N.N.E. and were so near as to distinguish several people upon the beach. They appeared to be of a very dark or black colour."

Cook's ship, the Endeavour, sailed northward from Botany Bay and ran aground on a coral reef in the area of the present-day Whitsunday Islands. While repairs were being carried out, Cook and his crew explored parts of the coast of this strange continent and met some of its inhabitants. Cooktown in Queensland is a reminder of those early explorations. Captain Cook concluded his mission in the same way as he had done elsewhere, by officially proclaiming the eastern part of the continent a British Crown Colony, to be called New South Wales.

This was to prove a most advantageous step for Britain. When the United States proclaimed independence five years later, in 1776, Britain no longer knew what to do with her troublemakers, petty thieves and murderers, who had hitherto been banished to the American colonies, so New South Wales became a new site of deportation. The name Botany Bay soon lost its aura of enchantment, and became an object of dread in England, as the refrain of an old folk song strikingly reminds us:

*My awful sentence is pronounced,*
*I am bound for Botany Bay.*

In 1788, after a voyage lasting eight months, the eleven ships of the famous First Fleet, commanded by Captain Arthur Phillip, dropped anchor in the mouth of the Parramatta River. Captain Phillip called the bay Sydney Cove, after the British Home Secretary of the time, Lord Sydney, and founded the first settlement of the new colony in Parramatta, now a

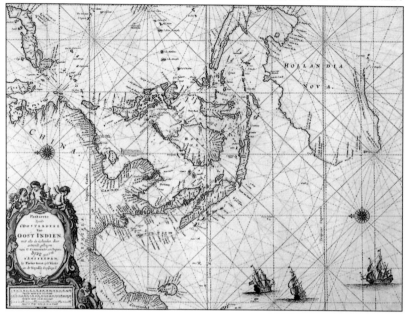

suburb of the city of Sydney. January 26, 1788, is considered the official date of the colony's foundation.

The First Fleet had 191 female and 568 male convicts on board, all guilty of a great variety of offences. However, this new country offered them all the same opportunity, namely to become free settlers after obtaining a pardon. For their own protection, the prisoners were accompanied by soldiers, mostly rough characters who had themselves been troublesome in the army, and who had thus been conveniently banished by their home country.

The first years in the colony were tough. Corruption and violence were the order of the day. Officers and even soldiers could lay down the law and many used their positions to further their own interests. The convicts, on the other hand, had to work very hard and often suffered from malnutrition and disease. In addition there were constant and bloody fights with the Aborigines. Although there were some early free settlers alongside the con-

victs, the army officers ruled the colony entirely and, furthermore, it was they who took over the important rum trade. This contingent of men entered history as the "rum corps."

In spite of such trials, the colony grew. William Bligh, one of the best-known naval officers of his time, who had already survived one mutiny on HMS Bounty, tried to establish law and order in New South Wales but was deposed by rebellious soldiers. It was left to his successor, Governor Lachlan Macquarie, to stamp out corruption among the officers by bringing his own loyal troops with him from Britain.

Under Macquarie, New South Wales blossomed for the first time. New settlements were founded and three explorers, William Wentworth and two of his companions, were the first Europeans to risk a journey beyond the Blue Mountains and then further into the interior where they discovered fertile grazing land. The canny Captain John MacArthur, a British army officer who settled in the colony

and who had many progressive ideas for its development, laid a cornerstone for Australia's later prosperity by introducing merino sheep to the continent.

By 1810 New South Wales already had a population of 10,000. As the colony prospered, land was no longer to be had so cheaply.

Cattle farmers, known as squatters, moved onto unexplored land without acquiring legal property rights. They lived in the bush under the most arduous conditions, braving snakes, bushfires, heat and drought in the summer and extreme cold in the winter. These tough characters were quite unimpressed by government officials and their concerns. And then, in 1836, the use of grazing land became regulated by law, and the squatters suddenly became a respected group within Australian society.

*Above: In the Pioneer Museum at Normantown, Queensland. Right: One of the most famous Australian paintings – "Shearing the Rams," by Tom Roberts (1890).*

Under the leadership of John Macquarie, Sydney soon grew into a thriving town. The new colony became a major exporter of fine merino wool. Settlements such as Newcastle, Bathurst, and Port Macquarie quickly developed into small towns.

William Charles Wentworth, already mentioned above, was the son of freed convicts (also known as "emancipists"), and was keen to be rid of the social taint of his background. He had considerable success in the fight for the constitutional right to self-government by all citizens of Australia (meaning, of course, all white male citizens). This was partly because his demands met with a sympathetic response from Governor Macquarie himself. The latter, an old-style soldier who had studied law, was experienced enough to realize that people who had served their sentences should not remain stigmatized for the rest of their lives. The government offered the emancipists cheap credits to enable them to buy their own land. As free farmers, they contributed to the growing prosperity of the colony. Towards the end of his period as governor, in 1822, Macquarie was able to observe with some satisfaction that he found New South Wales a prison, and left it as a colony. It was also thanks to Wentworth that the colony attained greater independence from Britain and that the governor had a legislative council at his side which put an end to the sometimes brutal autocracy of the governors.

### Further Colonies Founded

New South Wales was the first colony, but by the beginning of the 19th century further colonies were being established. This was seldom due to the vision of the first settlers, however. More often than not, outside influences were the deciding factor.

When French ships first began cruising along the coasts in 1803, the British

founded a military stronghold at the location of present-day Hobart on the island of Tasmania.

Tasmania, which had been named Van Diemen's Land in 1642 by its Dutch discoverer Abel Tasman, offered excellent conditions for successful farming.

Soon convicts and free settlers from New South Wales began to arrive on the island. Unfortunately, the convicts were treated in such a brutal fashion that many soon died. The ruins of Port Arthur are a reminder of that terrible period. Even worse, and a fact almost completely forgotten today, was the treatment of the Aborigines by the military, whose aim was to exterminate all of the island's original inhabitants – a shameful goal, that was accomplished within a few short, tragic years. Geographical isolation, which made any kind of control from Sydney, still less London, extremely difficult, can hardly be offered as an excuse for such atrocities. In 1825, Van Diemen's Land was granted political independence from New South Wales, and Hobart was de-

clared its capital. Colonel George Arthur became the first governor. Not until 1853 did the colony acquire its present name, Tasmania, as a tribute to its discoverer, Abel Tasman.

After Tasmania, Queensland was the next colony to be founded. In 1824, the site of present-day Brisbane was merely a convicts' camp. These early days were made especially difficult for the few freed farmers among the settlers by a prolonged period of drought. The wool trade did not flourish as expected, but they persevered. Queensland remained part of New South Wales for a long time, and did not achieve independence until 1859, when it also received its present name in honor of Queen Victoria. Britain's fear of French imperialism played an important part in the foundation of Western Australia. In 1829, as a precaution against French territorial ambitions, Captain Fremantle declared the entire west coast to be British Crown Territory. 400 volunteer settlers who had sold up all their land and possessions in Britain, emigrated to the area. On their ar-

*Above: Chinese immigrants trekking into Victoria's goldfields (1853).*

rival, however, they found that the promises made to them of a great future were empty: the country was dry and infertile. In addition, there was a severe lack of laborers and very soon grain had to be imported from Van Diemen's Land. After several lean years that saw hardly any improvement in the situation, the settlers were finally forced to ask London to send out convicts to help work the land.

South Australia was also founded by free settlers but its foundation had its origins – following true Australian tradition – in a prison. In distant London, Edward Wakefield, serving a sentence behind bars for seducing minors, was gloomily contemplating his future and thinking about Australia. He came up with the idea of selling land in the colonies to free settlers, preferably young British married couples. The proceeds from this could then be used to pay for the passage to Australia of people willing to work there.

This proved to be a brilliant idea which soon caught on after Wakefield's release from prison, and which, after some modification, was enacted by Parliament in 1834 as the South Australia Act.

In 1836 the first immigrants landed in South Australia. Within a very short time, due to an incomprehensible and unnecessarily long-winded surveying and purchasing system, they became embroiled in real estate speculation on a vast scale. Many new settlers lost all their savings, while others became wealthy property owners overnight. Governor Geoffrey Gawler finally put an end to this intolerable situation. First, he speeded up the system of allocating land, in order to encourage settlement further away from Adelaide. Second, he initiated the construction of an extensive road network. Both these policies were successful but, unfortunately, Gawler immediately had the new roads "embellished" with imposing buildings, which left the city's coffers empty, so that, consequently, his successor was forced to embark on a rigorous policy of cutbacks and saving which led to unemployment and depression. This period of economic stagnation finally ended when copper deposits were discovered in Kapunda and Burra Burra.

As absolute religious freedom had been firmly enshrined in the founding charter of South Australia, many members of religious minorities emigrated there from Britain and Germany. The Germans were Old Lutherans who arrived in South Australia as complete village communities, including their pastors. They earned their livelihood by growing vegetables and planting vineyards. In the Barossa Valley (north of Adelaide) you can still sample the traditional, delicious German Bienenstich cake ("bee-sting cake"), the recipe for which includes honey and almonds.

The founding of the colony of Victoria proceeded less happily. The very first settlers, who had established themselves as early as 1803 in Port Phillip Bay, were forced to abandon the settlement very soon, worn down by the grim conditions and badly served by their community leaders. They searched elsewhere and soon found a better life on the nearby island of Tasmania. It was not until 1835 that settlers John Pascoe Fawkner and John Batman risked a second, this time successful, attempt. In 1837 the city of Melbourne was founded, and finally, in 1851, Victoria was established. However, it was to be something quite different that thrust the new colony into the newspaper headlines across the world.

### Gold Fever!

The 1851 gold rush hit the region like a tidal wave. The place where it all began was Ophir in New South Wales and the effect of subsequent events on the whole of Australia was so great that the gold rush can be said to have heralded a new era. Edward Hargraves, who had just returned from the gold fields of California,

triggered this gold rush, when his expert eye spotted the signs indicating gold. As soon as the news of any new strike became public, whole convoys of prospectors, known as "diggers," would set out. Gold was particularly abundant in Ballarat, Castlemaine, and Bendigo in Victoria, and was found later on in Queensland and western Australia too.

Ships carrying new prospectors arrived daily from Britain, as well as from continental Europe, America and China. The diggers lived in tent villages around the prospecting sites, and later founded numerous new towns. Adventurers from all over the world streamed to the fifth continent, drawing in their wake, among other dubious characters, ladies of easy virtue. Even the famous Lola Montez, whose dancing had once bewitched King Ludwig I of Bavaria, now arrived to entertain the diggers. Her reward was appropriate to the venue: gold nuggets were thrown onto the stage when she finished her show!

The British government finally abolished the transportation of convicts, because with everyone now dreaming of going to Australia, it was no longer considered a punishment to be sent there. The roughneck diggers were able to make a lot of money for their new country, and decided that they wanted to have a say in politics and public life. However, the colonial government persisted in seeing them only as a source of revenue. This state of affairs provided a fertile breeding ground for the conflict that soon followed. When the government tried to raise taxes on gold finds, one result was a pitched battle between the diggers and the police in a town called Eureka. Although the diggers were defeated on that occasion, the government finally had to give in. The gold prospectors fought for, and were granted, a voice in the country's affairs. The gold rush thus helped Australia on its way to becoming a democracy. Only the Chinese, who had also followed

the lure of gold in large numbers, continued to face prejudice and racism for a long time to come. Nowadays, of course, it is impossible to imagine any Australian city without its colorful Chinatown.

## The Federation of Australia

The six colonies flourished. Their growing prosperity and the increase in population that followed the gold rush helped to steer the country's economy into a real Golden Age. The division of the continent into separate colonies began to be seen as a hindrance as it restricted economic expansion. For example, each of the six states had a different postal system, and each imposed high import duties on the others. Even the railways had been built with different gauges. Entrepreneurs

*Above: Ned Kelly, the Australian "Robin Hood", who brought excitement and terror to the High Country at the end of the 19th century. Right: The very first session of the Australian Parliament.*

in particular felt hampered by this somewhat chaotic situation and demanded the economic alignment of all the colonies. For their part, the workers united to form the Australian Labour Federation, which developed into the present-day Labour Party.

These federal ambitions suited the British, who were already nervous about the military defense of Australia and realized that only a united Australia could be secure. The Prime Minister of New South Wales, Henry Parkes, finally put into words what everyone had been thinking: "Let's have a united Australia!" A constitution was drafted, refined, and put to the vote in two referenda in 1898 and 1899. The newborn constitutional assembly sat temporarily in Melbourne. However, as Sydney and Melbourne fought constantly over which city had the better claim to become the capital, a compromise was sought. It was decided to set the seat of Parliament halfway between the two cities, and thus was born the present-day capital of Canberra. In 1900 the constitution was laid before the British House of Commons and signed by Queen Victoria. On 1 January 1901, Australia became officially known as the Commonwealth of Australia.

## Australia, the New Federal State

Australia had become a nation and Edmund Barton was its first prime minister. By this time, over 80 per cent of the population had been born in the country, which meant that a genuine Australian way of life had developed. Further immigration was still encouraged, however, so that Australia had a population of about 5 million by the First World War, but there was still a feeling of "keeping ourselves to ourselves." In 1901, Parliament passed a bill, the famous White Australia Policy, which was designed particularly to prevent Asians from immigrating. Unpopular Europeans were also discouraged. For

example, Catholics were not seen to be as desirable as Protestant immigrants. Especially undesirable immigrants were forced to do a dictation to test their spelling. The trick here – a Kafkaesque system – was that the test could be given in any European language! So, for example, in 1936, German author and pacifist Egon Erwin Kisch had to take a dictation in Scottish Gaelic, and, of course, failed! The Labour Party experienced a phenomenal rise in popularity during the years before the First World War, thanks to the support of strong unions. Soon Australian politics without the Labour Party was scarcely imaginable. The country was flourishing and the building of Canberra, 300 kilometers (207 miles) from Sydney, became an expression of this new prosperity and confidence.

### The First World War and its Consequences

On 5 August 1914, Australians enthusiastically cheered the news of Britain's declaration of war on Germany. This meant that Australia, too, was at war. It seemed as though the young nation was almost impatient to enter its first fray. Volunteers streamed into the cities and signed on at military barracks.

Australia's involvement in the war really began when she occupied the then German colony of New Guinea. After that it was a matter of defending the Empire in Europe. By then Turkey had entered the war on Germany's side and was threatening Britain's supremacy on the Suez Canal – Britain's lifeline to the Empire. Australian and New Zealand troops assembled near Cairo in Egypt and formed the Australia and New Zealand Army Corps (ANZAC). A force of 30,000 men then joined the British attempt to land on the Gallipoli peninsula in northwest Turkey.

However, due to inadequate planning by the British High Command, and the numerical superiority of the Turks, the army was driven back into the sea, with enormous loss of life. The disastrous

Gallipoli campaign was a turning point in Australian history. On this dusty battlefield, far from home, Australians realized for the first time that Britain's interests might not always coincide with their own. That moment of truth was to give Australians a new sense of direction.

When the terrible news finally reached their distant homeland, the number of volunteers dwindled rapidly, especially as more bad news was arriving from the front in France as well. Australian Prime Minister, William Hughes, tried to introduce conscription, but this caused a public outcry. The Labour Party threw Hughes out and, for the most part, stood out against the introduction of conscription. "Little Digger" Hughes then founded the National Party which soon won the confidence of many of the people. There were many Catholics among the ranks of the Labour Party, mostly Irish and Scottish workers, who did not feel so committed to the idea of the British Empire, and were no longer willing to fight for it. Finally, two referenda produced a decision not to introduce general conscription.

In the slaughter in the trenches of Flanders, Australian dead totaled around 60,000, with 150,000 injured. At the end of the war, Hughes traveled to Europe in order to take part in the peace negotiations in Versailles. He refused to be intimidated by the great powers and insisted, in his own loud and unsophisticated fashion, that Australian interests must be considered. He demanded full reparation of all war costs, an early return of all prisoners, and the cession of Papua New Guinea to Australia. His table-thumping oratory, however, very soon got on the nerves of the other victors, who then contrived to exclude him from further conferences. At home, however, he was hailed as a hero. During the 1920s, life in Australia was

*Right: Sydney Harbour Bridge was completed in 1932.*

good once again. From Italy there came a huge wave of immigrants, fleeing from poverty in their own country. They grew fruit and vegetables in Victoria and cut sugar cane in Queensland under a scorching sun. Commerce flourished in the cities. Luxury goods from Europe appeared in the shops and museums boasted valuable exhibits. So that the workers could also share in this prosperity, the unions fought for a 44-hour working week, and, to national rejoicing, the new Parliament buildings were opened in Canberra. Unfortunately, however, the country was now definitely living beyond its means. Two days before "Black Friday" (24 October 1929), when the US Stock Exchange collapsed on Wall Street, the Labour Party replaced the Country Party as the governing fraction, and found to their horror that the treasury was empty.

Dragged down by the international economic crisis, Australia's export trade collapsed. As throughout much of the world, the thirties were a grim period for Australia. Prices for wool and wheat, Australia's most important exports, plunged, resulting in widespread unemployment. It was unfortunate that at this very time the Australian Minister of Finance was absent for months in London, taking part in conferences aimed at putting the Commonwealth countries on an equal footing with Britain.

In 1932, just as the prime minister was officially opening Sydney Harbour Bridge, a man came galloping up on a horse, pushed him aside and slashed the ribbon with one blow of his sword. The horseman was a member of a small group of Hitler supporters, who saw fascism as the solution to the country's economic plight. In the face of the growing menace of Nazi Germany, official policy in Australia was largely based on pious hopes and wishful thinking: If no one provoked Hitler, he wouldn't become dangerous. Much greater dismay among Australian politicians was aroused by the brutal and

24

unjustified invasion of Manchuria by Japan. After all, this conflict was practically on their doorstep.

### The Second World War

In September 1939, Britain declared war on Germany. In a speech to the nation, Australian prime minister Sir Robert McKenzie, made it clear that Australia was now also at war. This time, however, the outbreak of hostilities found Australia quite unprepared. The entire Australian navy consisted of two cruisers and the army's airplanes were thoroughly antiquated. Industry had to be converted as swiftly as possible to armament production. Very soon, Australians were fighting in North Africa, in the Mediterranean and in Greece. The brave Desert Rats, who fought General Rommel and his troops in North Africa, are famous to this day.

But who was defending Australia? From the moment Pearl Harbor was attacked in December 1941, the war was no longer confined to Europe, but had arrived in the Pacific. The Japanese made lightning strikes on British ships in Singapore, and took Hong Kong. When Britain did not seem to react to this, the fear of invasion spread through Australia. Prime Minister Curtin felt abandoned by the British and in his hour of need he turned to the USA. Australians' fear of their formidable Japanese opponents turned to panic when Japanese bombers reduced the town of Darwin to rubble in February 1942.

The American Commander-in-Chief, General Douglas MacArthur, then took over the defense of Australia, and, in return, deployed Australian troops in the malaria-ridden jungles of New Guinea. The Japanese were beaten back only after heavy Allied losses.

The Second World War also changed everyday life for those at home. Everyone suffered under the high wartime taxes, and many basic supplies, such as tea and fuel, had to be rationed. When the war finally ended on August 15, 1945, Australia joined in a worldwide sigh of relief.

## After the Second World War

Australia had learned a lesson from this war, namely that in matters of foreign policy she should in future lean toward the USA and improve relations with neighboring countries. Strict immigration controls were to be liberalized, especially toward Europeans. Prime Minister Joseph B. Chifley set up a federal department of immigration, which encouraged settlers from all over Europe. Twice more, foreign policy obligations forced Australians to become involved in wars: first in 1950 in Korea, and then in 1963 in Vietnam, which was controversial. Conscripts were called up through a lottery system. This random way of selecting people to fight stirred up feeling just as it had long before during the First World War. All over the country students protested against taking part in the war.

*Above: Young Australians in particular have a sceptical attitude towards their country's economic future.*

## Economic Problems

In the "boring fifties" Australia seemed to be a very male-dominated society. "Dinkum Aussies" of Anglo-Saxon descent dominated the general scene. Women had no place in public life; they were supposed to look after the home and children. Aborigines and Asians were treated as second-class citizens, as, to varying degrees, were all other non-Anglo-Saxons. There was little variety of goods in the shops, and the Australian diet consisted mainly of white bread, fish and chips, and steak. The great change in direction, signs of which had begun to appear after the Second World War, did not really take place until the 1970s under Gough Whitlam, the Labour politician who became prime minister in 1972. A new wind immediately began to blow through Australian politics, sweeping away outmoded attitudes and laws. Whitlam began to tackle the racism which had hitherto characterized Australian domestic and foreign policy.

The Aborigines were granted rights of self-determination. Their Land Councils began claiming back sites of religious importance and giving them heritage status. The colony of New Guinea was granted independence, relations with Asian countries were improved, and contact was made with Communist countries for the first time. Immigrants from all over the world began to settle in Australia, bringing their cultures and colors with them. Multi-culturalism was the term used to describe this new type of society. Women began campaigning for equal rights as well.

The country was booming – culturally as well as economically. The first Australian to receive a Nobel Prize for Literature was Patrick White in 1973. His best-known novel, Voss, was based on the life of a German immigrant, Ludwig Leichardt, a dedicated explorer of the interior who never returned from his final expedition in Australia. They were exciting times indeed - and again many people spent more money than they really had. Whitlam secretly borrowed petrodollars, a fact that soon became known. A political scandal rocked the country, and some representatives of big business even plotted to topple him. In the end, Governor General Sir John Kerr, Britain's highest representative in Australia, sacked Whitlam by using Britain's traditional right of veto. Malcolm Fraser, Whitlam's successor and a member of the conservative Liberal Party, tried his best to halt inflation, but the cost of living continued to rise. In 1983, the Australians changed allegiance again and elected Robert "Bob" Hawke of the Labour Party, a popular "mate" and a long-time union member.

When Australia celebrated the bicentenary of European settlement in 1988, Queen Elizabeth II was greeted by representatives of the Aborigines at the opening of the new Parliament building. In the 200 years that lay between this encounter and the arrival of James Cook in Botany Bay, much had happened. Yet the difficulties between Aborigines and the white settlers have still not been resolved. In the future, Australia will have to offer the original inhabitants of the continent a way of life that is more worthy of human beings than anything offered to them before.

Although some tentative steps in this direction have been taken in recent years, relations between Aborigines and white Australians are still tense. Confrontations occur constantly, especially in the cities. However, politicians of all parties are now much more committed to achieving a settlement between the two population groups. At the same time, the present strong wave of immigration from Asia is threatening to create new ethnic tensions. Australia will have to overcome her geographical isolation, which has proved such an attraction to outsiders, if she is to survive economically. This will only be possible if the country improves relations with her Asian neighbors. Australia, as a Constitutional Monarchy, is a member of the British *Commonwealth of Nations.*

The British sovereign is the head of state, represented by a Governor-General in Australia. Since the mid-1990s, there have been weighty discussions concerning Australia's leaving the British crown and establishing an Australian Republic. Many Australians, especially the post–war immigrants from Europe and Asia, feel this step away from the former colonial fatherland is long overdue. However, the monarchists cling to the old structures and traditions. During a referendum in 1999, the majority of the Australians chose to remain in the Commonwealth with the Queen as head of state.

The nation experienced an upswing with the Olympic Games in September 2000. The extensive preparations and events allowed the Australians to show the world just how proud they really are of their country at the end of the world "down under."

Darwin
Cairns
Broome
Townsville
Rockhampton
Alice
Springs
Kalgoorlie
Brisbane
Perth
Adelaide
Canberra
Sydney
INDIAN OCEAN
Melbourne
TASMANIA
Hobart

# SYDNEY – AUSTRALIA'S SECRET CAPITAL

**EARLY DAYS**
**THE ROCKS**
**DOWNTOWN**
**DARLING HARBOUR**
**NIGHT-LIFE**
**AROUND SYDNEY**

*Sydney*

You could hardly find a more beautiful place to begin your trip through Australia than the shores of **Sydney Cove**. The best time to visit is at dusk, when the lights of Sydney Harbour Bridge show up clearly to the north against the red evening sky. To the east, the first opera goers will be on their way to the Sydney Opera House where the curtain will soon rise on the evening's performance.

The ferry to Manly will be setting out from Circular Quay, and among the pubs in The Rocks district, business people from nearby downtown will stand shoulder to shoulder at the Orient Hotel bar drinking the customary pint of beer after a hard day's work.

These summer evenings are not the only times when you could easily conclude that **\*\*Sydney** is one of the most beautiful cities in the world. Other occasions might be a trip on a harbor ferry, enjoying a hot day in the surf at one of the city's Pacific beaches, listening to a midday concert in Martin Place, shopping in the Queen Victoria Building, enjoying the night-life in Darling Harbour and King's Cross, or just quietly observing

*Previous pages: Devil's Marbles south of Tennant Creek. Elegant Sydney Harbour Bridge. Left: View of Sydney and Darling Harbour from AMP Centrepoint Tower.*

nature amid the tranquil space of one of the many national parks that are within easy reach of Sydney.

One other thing should soon become clear when you make any of these outings, and that is that the wild Outback and lonely interior, which is still the image Australia conjures up for many visitors, has nothing whatever to do with Sydney. In fact, Sydney has developed into an exciting, cosmopolitan city, so much so that many Aussies no longer feel truly comfortable there, because Sydney has become altogether too big (almost 4 million inhabitants), too loud, and too hectic for them. For the people who live in Sydney, however, this is just the way they want it. No wonder the inhabitants proudly call themselves Sydneysiders, which sounds a little like sunnysiders and is probably meant to. People living in Sydney do walk on the sunny side, enjoying life and nature to the full. For many people, the height of the waves for surfing is more important than the height of the share index. It is this very joie de vivre and lack of seriousness that make Sydney the ideal starting point of an Australian trip for so many tourists. However many thousands of kilometers you travel and however many weeks you spend in Australia, wherever you are, you will never forget Sydney.

*City map page 36, Guidepost pages 44-45*

## EARLY DAYS

The early history of Sydney was anything but happy. In January 1788, eleven ships of the First Fleet, under the command of Captain Arthur Phillip, landed in Botany Bay with a thousand convicts on board.

This was the bay in which Captain James Cook had dropped anchor in 1770. However, Arthur Phillip decided against remaining in the bay described so euphorically by Cook, and looked instead for another anchorage, which he soon found in a natural harbor a little way to the north. Later he called this place Sydney Cove. It was here, on the rocky western shore of the bay, still named The Rocks to this day, that the foundations of the city of Sydney were laid during the decades that followed.

*Above: Evening reflections of Sydney Harbour Bridge at Milsons Point. Right: Many of the buildings in The Rocks evoke colonial times.*

The early years were tough. The town was lacking in everything: clean water, roads, sanitation, garbage removal, building materials, and lighting. A total of only 165 gas lamps illuminated the town at night, and it did not help matters to have 106 of those same lamps lighting the way to the only hotel, which was of very little use to the greater part of the population. Obviously, there was a serious lack of funds. It was not until the population began to protest violently against these conditions that the British authorities were forced to agree to establish Sydney as a township on July 20, 1842, the official birth date of the city.

Now, more than 150 years later, times have changed. The Rocks district has become an inner-city attraction for tourists (especially after an elaborate restoration for Australia's bicentennial celebrations in 1988). When strolling through the old streets, you will probably be pleasantly surprised to find that the charm of the early days has survived in many places. And it's not only tourists you'll meet;

you'll often find yourself sitting at the same table with Sydneysiders in the restaurants and pubs. This mixture of old and new, foreign and ethnic, is what gives the quarter between Circular Quay and Sydney Harbour Bridge its special atmosphere, and a long walk around this area is well worth the effort.

## ⋆THE ROCKS

The **Park Hyatt Sydney** lies on the shore of **Campbell's Cove ❶**; it is one of the city's loveliest hotels, and the restaurants in the adjoining Campbell's Store offer good fare in pleasant surroundings (with a view of the harbor and opera house) This is not an inexpensive experience, but definitely well worthwhile.

Thus fortified, you are advised that the best place to start your tour around The Rocks is at **Cadman's Cottage ❷**, only a few meters from Circular Quay. The oldest existing building in Sydney dates from 1816 and it was once the quarters of the governor's boatmen, before former

convict John Cadman, with his wife and two children, moved in about the middle of the last century. They lived there for 19 years. Today the cottage houses the office of the **Sydney Harbour National Parks Information Centre,** and offers visitors a wide range of books and pamphlets about the flora and fauna of this metropolitan city. (For information about the city in general, head north to the *Sydney Visitors' Centre*, 106 George Street.) From the former **Sailors' Home** (1864), steps lead up to **George Street**, and here, among the frontages that include Unwins Stores, built in 1844, you will come across cafes and a few souvenir shops, almost hidden away, some of which are rather beautiful. At the left-hand end of the row of houses you will find the previously mentioned Orient Hotel (it frequently has good live music in the evenings). From here, **Argyle Street** will lead you to the upper section of The Rocks. After a few minutes' walk, you will pass, on your right, the **Argyle Centre** with its numerous shops, followed by

# DOWNTOWN SYDNEY

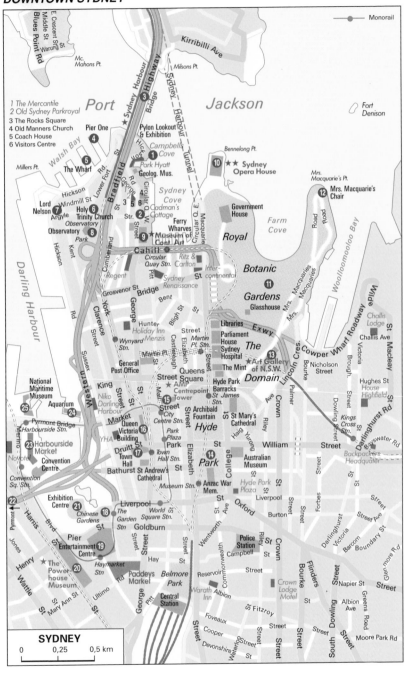

1 The Mercantile
2 Old Sydney Parkroyal
3 The Rocks Square
4 Old Manners Church
5 Coach House
6 Visitors Centre

Monorail

Port

Jackson

Fort Denison

E. Crescent St
Middle St
Warung St
Blues Point Rd
Mc. Mahons Pt.
Kirribilli Ave
Milsons Pt.

Sydney Harbour Bridge
Sydney Harbour Highway
Bradfield Highway
Sydney Harbour Tunnel

Walsh Bay
Pier One
Pylon Lookout & Exhibition
Campbell's Cove
Bennelong Pt.
Mrs. Macquarie's Pt.
Mrs. Macquarie's Chair

Millers Pt.
The Wharf
Park Hyatt
Geolog. Mus.
★★ Sydney Opera House

Lord Nelson
Holy Trinity Church
Sydney Cove
Government House
Farm Cove
Road Road
Woolloomooloo Bay

Hickson
Windmill St
Argyle
Observatory
Observatory Park
Cadman's Cottage
Cahill
Circular Quay Stn.
Ferry Wharves
Museum of Cont. Art
Royal

Botanic

Gardens
Glasshouse

Challis Lodge
Challis Ave
Wide

Darling Harbour

Regent
Ritz & Carlton
Inter-continental

Cumberland St
Lower Fort Rd
George St
Circular Q.W.
Pitt
Macquarie
Mrs. Macquaries Road
Cowper Wharf Roadway

Grosvenor St
Bridge St
Bent St
Macleay St
Victoria St
Brough St

Hunter St
Holiday Inn Menzies
Libraries
Parliament House
Sydney Hospital
The Mint
Art Gallery of N.S.W.
The
Domain

York St
Clarence St
George St
Street
Bligh St
Castlereagh
Elizabeth
Martin Pl. Stn.
Martin Pl.
Lincoln Cres
Bourke
Nicholson Street

Wynyard Stn.
General Post Office
Queens Square
Hyde Park Barracks
St James Stn.
Hughes St
Highfield

King St
Niko Darling Harbour
AMP Centrepoint Tower
Archibald Fountain
St Mary's Cathedral
Kings Cross Stn.
Darlinghurst Rd
Bayswater Rd

National Maritime Museum
Aquarium
Market Street
City Centre Stn.
Queen Victoria Building
Park Plaza
Hyde
Park
Australian Museum
William Street
Backpackers Headquarter

Pyrmont Bridge
Harbourside Stn.
YHA
Druitt St
Town Hall Stn.
Andrew's Cathedral
College St
Crown
Yurong
Haig
Riley
Forbes

Harbourside Market
Novotel
Convention Centre
Convention Sq. Stn.
Bathurst St
Museum Stn.
Anzac War Mem.
Hyde Park Plaza
Liverpool Street
Oxford
Burton

Exhibition Centre
Chinese Gardens
The Garden Stn.
Liverpool
World Square Stn.
Goldburn
Wentworth
Police Station
Campbell St
Crown
Bourke
Flinders
Darlinghurst
Victoria
Barcom
Boundary St
Glen more Rd

Pier Entertainment Centre
Haymarket Stn.
Hay St
Reservoir
Street
Crown Lodge Motel
Napier St
Albion Ave
Greens Road

The Power-house Museum
Paddeys Market
Belmore Park
Waratah Albion Inn
St Fitzroy
Moore Park Rd

Central Station
Foveaux
Cooper
Devonshire
Waterloo
South Dowling

SYDNEY
0   0,25   0,5 km

a row of beautiful terraced houses and the statue called First Impressions, on The Rocks Square. Past the Argyle Centre, steps in Cumberland Street lead up to **★Sydney Harbour Bridge ❸**, which has long been a national emblem for the whole of Australia. Because of its distinctive shape, Sydneysiders affectionately call the bridge the coat hanger, and there are no two ways about it: they prefer to continue to use the bridge rather than the new Sydney Harbour Tunnel. You should definitely follow this lead if only because of the view you get of the skyline!

The foundation stone of the bridge was laid on March 26, 1925, and after the structure had been tested for stress by the passage of 72 steam locomotives, and had passed with flying colors, the inaugural celebrations were held on March 16, 1932. Today, it is well worth climbing the 200 steps to the **Pylon Lookout and Exhibition** (access above The Rocks). There, in a most unusual museum, you can learn everything about the history of the bridge and enjoy the magnificent view. The more daring will want to try climbing the bridge's arches. This new attraction is called **Bridge Climb**.

Although it has been reproduced on millions of postcards, the view of the bridge is always fascinating, whether you are looking from the Sydney Opera House, MacMahons Point, Mrs. Macquarie's Chair, or Taronga Zoo, or enjoying a refreshing dip in the public swimming pool at Milson's Point.

Continuing along Argyle Street, the visitor will reach the western part of The Rocks, which stretches round **Miller's Point**, and where a very un-touristy, though typically Australian, suburban atmosphere has been preserved. Bales of wool are still piled up to the roof in enormous warehouses.

**Pier One ❹** banked on more traditional tourist fare, with kitschy souvenirs and take-out food. It's quite run-down now. **The Wharf ❺** is also the home of the *Sydney Dance Company* and the *Sydney Theatre Company*, both famous for their experimental productions.

**Holy Trinity (Garrison) Church ❻** is worth a stop, as indeed is the **Lord Nelson Hotel ❼** in which beer has been served since 1842, and which, therefore, holds the title of the oldest hotel in Sydney. From the vantage point of **Observatory Park ❽** there is a fine view of the Harbour Bridge.

The **★Museum of Contemporary Art ❾**, (beside Circular Quay), displays contemporary art from all over the world. Right across from it, the **Aboriginal & Tribal Art Centre** (117 George Street) offers visitors a sample of works of art by Australian Aborigines in a variety of settings.

### Downtown

**Circular Quay** is also an ideal starting point for a walk through Sydney's interesting and lively downtown section. If you walk in an easterly direction along Sydney Cove's Circular Quay Promenade, you will come first to the quieter part of town. After a while, you will pass the Sydney Cove Oyster Bar, a place well worth remembering for your evening meal. This is a favorite spot where Sidneysiders relax at the end of the day with draft beer and live jazz.

Before that, however, you should take a look at the **★★Sydney Opera House ❿**, one of the best-known landmarks in Australia. This unusual building was begun in 1959 and finally finished in 1973. It was built at a cost of 102 million Australian dollars, the sum having been raised through a public appeal and lotteries.

The building was designed by Danish architect Jorn Utzon, although he resigned from the project during its 16-year construction period because the contractors would not agree to follow his designs in every detail. Controversial though the building once was, today Sydneysiders

Sydney

are unanimous in their enthusiasm for their very own opera house, which stands proudly on **Bennelong Point**. During a walk around the building you will discover its many original and fascinating aspects and enjoy beautiful views of the harbor and the Sydney skyline – unfortunately, an unimaginative apartment block (nicknamed The Toaster by the Sydneysiders) on Central Quay East, directly beside the opera, disfigures the view. If one of the several daily tours of the opera is not enough for you, you can always book tickets for one of the frequent evening events. Programs can be studied at leisure in the **Mozart Cafe** or in the **Concourse Restaurant**, on Bennelong Point, where you can sit outside, right beside the Opera House, and drink a cappuccino.

Only a few meters east of here lie the huge, 30-hectare **Royal Botanical Gardens** ⑪, with their beautiful rainforest

*Above: Sydney Opera House is one of the city's landmarks. Right: Darling Harbour offers numerous attractions.*

greenhouse. Behind a security perimeter is **Government House**, the official residence of the Governor of New South Wales.

A beautiful footpath leads round Farm Cove to Mrs. Macquarie's Point where **Mrs. Macquarie's Chair** ⑫ has been carved from the rock. In 1810, this vantage point was created for the wife of the then governor Lachlan Macquarie. From here she could enjoy the view and try to overcome her home-sickness for distant Europe.

Today the point has become a much visited tourist attraction, so you might wish to avoid it in the daytime. In the evening it will afford a wonderful and peaceful view of the illuminated skyline, including Harbour Bridge and the Opera House. Mrs. Macquarie Road runs along **Wooloomooloo Bay**, which is the home base of the Australian Navy. From this point, the path returns to the city center.

Here, in the popular city park, **The Domain**, the *★Art Gallery of South Wales* ⑬, which opened in 1885, features important exhibitions in which Australian painters and Aboriginal art are featured.

At the southern end of the park, **St. Mary's Cathedral** is silhouetted against the modern skyline. Nearby Queens Square forms the beginning of **Hyde Park**  with its beautiful **Archibald Fountain** – a favorite spot to spend a lunch break. **Macquarie Street**, which begins here too, is flanked by numerous sandstone buildings which recall Sydney's history.

**Hyde Park Barracks**, built by Francis Greenaway in 1819 to house convicts, later served as a residence for the less dangerous homeless of Sydney. Today it houses an exhibition which gives the visitor an idea of the harsh life of colonial times. In the courtyard of the Barracks is a pleasant cafe.

Next to the Barracks is **The Mint**, which became known as the rum hospital, so named because the builder was rewarded for his work with the rum trade monopoly. In the mid-1800s the Mint began to strike gold coins. Both the name and the present-day museum are a reminder of those days.

Behind Sydney Hospital is **Parliament House**, which has been the seat of the New South Wales government since 1827. Beside it lies the **Library of New South Wales**. It is worth going inside for a look at its oldest section, the Mitchell Wing.

Midday is a good time to wander along the pedestrian precinct of **Martin Place**, where concerts are regularly given in the open air theater at the western end. It's an entertaining place in the heart of Sydney.

If you would like a bird's eye view of all that Sydney has to offer, then the *AMP Centrepoint Tower* ⑮ is the place to go for an exhilarating and uninterrupted view of the city (the entrance to the Centrepoint is in Market Street). Then, you can either go window-shopping or just people-watching in the pedestrian precinct on **Pitt Street Mall**, where

there are numerous boutiques as well as branches of all the large Australian department stores and where the beautiful **Strand Arcade** recreates a glimpse of old-world shopping.

If you are not content to just gaze at expensive fashions, but actually want to buy something, you would be better off shopping in Castlereagh Street.

The former offices and warehouses of the **QVB Queen Victoria Building** ⑯ were originally built in 1889, but became redundant years ago. Finally, after a long period of renovation, the first new shops in this Victorian building were opened in 1986. Today the QVB is one of the most attractive shopping centers in the world.

All these attractions can be reached by the modern monorail. From the *City Centre* station you can quickly reach the Queen Victoria Building, Sydney Tower and Pitt Street Mall.

The monorail also stops directly at the **Sydney Town Hall** ⑰ (George Street, *Park Plaza* stop). This was built between 1866 and 1869 and renovated extensively

for the city's 150-year celebrations in 1992. Next door is **St. Andrew's Anglican Cathedral**, which certainly merits a visit.

## DARLING HARBOUR

On the occasion of the bi-centenary of the *First Fleet* in 1988, Darling Harbour – until a few years ago an area of dilapidated docks and warehouses – was restored for millions of dollars, and has now become a place for entertainment and enjoyment. The renovation continues, with new attractions constantly being added.

Over Pyrmont Bridge, the **Chinese Gardens** ⑱, with its pagodas and authentic planting schemes, calls up memories of distant China. The **Sydney Entertainment Centre** ⑲ is one of the most important entertainment venues of the city for pop and rock concerts.

*Above and right: Fish Market and shopping in the Queen Victoria Building.*

It is only a few feet to the heart of **Chinatown**. This is where the Chinese immigrants, who came to Australia in the wake of the 19th century gold rush, found their "new" homeland, along Dixon and Hay Streets.

Behind the Exhibition Centre, in the southern section of Darling Harbour, you will find the *★**Powerhouse Museum** ⑳ (500 Harris Street). Today, under the roof of what was once the Ultimo Power Station is one of the largest museums in the world. It concentrates mainly on science and technology, art and design. There is lots to see and touch – an ideal outing for families!

The buildings of the **Sydney Convention & Exhibition Centre** ㉑ are used for various events, for example, the Olympic contests for boxing, table tennis and weight-lifting. Early morning is the best time to set out on an expedition to **Pyrmont** ㉒, where every weekday over 100 varieties of seafood are sold at **Sydney Fish Market** on Blackwattle Bay. You can watch the auctions and develop an appetite which will be satisfied later. Sydneysiders boast about their fish restaurants, usually quite simple establishments, which nonetheless offer top quality food.

The heart of Darling Harbour is the **Harbourside** ㉓. This airy building houses the new **Gavala Aboriginal Cultural Centre**, where one can visit art expositions and dance performances, many shops, food courts, cafes and restaurants, all with a view of the harbor.

After a pleasant meal, you should feel sufficiently revived to explore the other attractions on the opposite side of Cockle Bay. **Cockle Bay Wharf** houses numerous cafes, restaurants and a pub. **Sega World** is a gigantic computer game center; at **Oneworld Sports**, 62 video monitors broadcast sports events from all over the world, and the **Panasonic IMAX Theatre** shows 3 D movies on its gigantic curved screens.

Sydney

For a trip underwater, try the **Sydney Aquarium**  on the other side of the harbor. A plexiglass tunnel allows visitors to view many different species of fish from a safe, dry vantage point. The **National Maritime Museum** ㉕ was opened in 1992. Stretching over ten floors, it offers insight into Australian and international seafaring history.

### NIGHT-LIFE

As night falls, if you seek the noise and bustle, then the **Mercantile Hotel** (25 George Street) and the **Glenmore Hotel** (96 Cumberland St, directly beneath the Harbour Bridge) offer themselves as two typically Australian pubs.

In **King's Cross**, the (red) lights don't go out until the early morning hours. Although The Cross has lost much of its former attraction, the neighborhood around Darlinghurst Road, Victoria Street, Bayswater Road and William Street is still one of Sydney's most lively night-life districts: pubs, restaurants, night-clubs and prostitution characterize the neighborhood. The Cross also merits a visit during the day, as does **Oxford Street** more to the south, center of Sydney's brisk homosexual scene.

### AROUND SYDNEY

Circular Quay is not the only ideal starting point for a trip through downtown Sydney, you can also discover Sydney in another very pleasant way, that is by water on a ferry. All of the ferries departing in a westerly direction (from wharfs 5 and 6) will include the spectacular trip underneath the Harbour Bridge and then explore the quieter parts of the city along Port Jackson and Parramatta River.

In the year 2000, the ferry to the **★Olympic grounds** ㉖ on **Homebush Bay** has recorded particularly heavy traffic. The route to **Darling Harbour** has

long been popular. Beautiful beaches within the harbor area are **Balmoral Beach**, **Nielsen Park**, **Camp Cove** and **Watson's Bay** (with good restaurants). For a true Sydneysider, though, there is only one trip worth taking from Circular Quay. This waterborne journey leads eastward to the wonderful beaches on the South Pacific Ocean.

The trip to **★Manly** ㉗ is a must. From the ferry terminal in Manly, a lovely old pedestrian avenue, The Corso, will lead you to Manly Beach, which is where you will appreciate the truth of Manly's motto, *seven miles from Sydney and a thousand miles from care.*

Other attractive beaches in the north are **Harbord** (18 kilometers), **Whale** (38 kilometers) and **Palm Beach** (43 kilometers, bus 190 from Winy and Park). Lifeguards stand watch over bathers and surfers in many spots. While Manly Beach has a sporty, active atmosphere, the main purpose of being on **★Bondi Beach** ㉘ is to see and be seen. Towards the east and south are the beaches of **Coogee** (9 kilo-

# AROUND SYDNEY

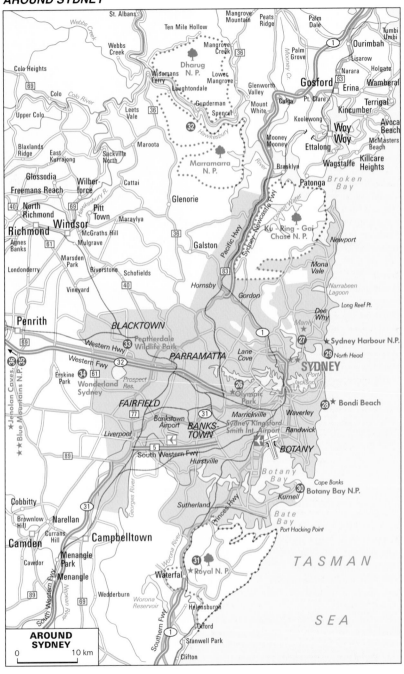

AROUND SYDNEY

0        10 km

42

meters, bus 373) and **Cronulla** (27 kilometers, train from Central Station). Beaches are not Sydney's only nature attraction. It also boasts numerous national parks within the city boundaries.

**Sydney Harbour National Park** ㉙ is an umbrella name for, amongst others, North, South, Dobroyd, Middle, George's and Bradley's Heads, Nielsen Park (with a beautiful beach), Shark, Clark, and Rodd Islands. **Manly Scenic Walk** can also be recommended, which takes you from Spit Bridge to Manly. **Botany Bay National Park** ㉚ lies south of the city and protects **Captain Cook's Landing Place**, the spot where the great explorer first stepped on to Australian soil at about 3:00 p.m, on April 19, 1770. A little further south lies the ★**Royal National Park** ㉛, Australia's oldest national park, founded in 1879 as the people's park. Francis Myers described the importance of the park as early as 1866, calling it a piece of wild land within reach of the civilization of a great metropolis. And nothing has changed to this day: there are 150 kilometers of hiking paths (the Coast Track is especially attractive); numerous beaches and good surfing are offered – only 36 kilometers away from Sydney. To the north of Sydney is ★**Hawksbury River** ㉜, a popular day trip. Along its banks lie the national parks of **Ku-Ring Gai Chase, Marramarra, Brisbane Water**, and **Bouddi**, with numerous facilities for bush walking, canoeing, and bathing. On the way to the Blue Mountains, it is worth detouring to **Featherdale Wildlife Park** ㉝ on Kildare Road, Doonside, (02-96221644), to visit the extraordinary collection of Australian animals. There are excellent photo opportunities, koala cuddling is free of charge, and the communicative wardens are very informative. Equally instructive is a visit to the Outback Woolshed, a part of the **Wonderland Sydney**

*Above: Bathing on Bondi Beach.*

㉞ amusement park. (Motorway M4, exit Wallgrove Road). The work of the sheep farmers, from the old days to the new, is documented here. ★★**The Blue Mountains National Park** ㉟ offers an enchanting wild landscape of rocks and forest (100 kilometers westwards; Great Western Highway). The following are well worth a visit: Wentworth Falls, lookout points at Echo Point and Govett's Leap, Katoomba with the Scenic Skyway and the Steepest Scenic Railway in the World (45-degree gradient), the Zig Zag Steam Engine in Clarence, between Lithgow and Bell, and Mount Victoria, at 1111 meters the highest point in the Blue Mountains, which take their name from the blue vapor hanging over the eucalyptus woods. The Blue Mountains are a favorite Sidneysider weekend excursion, (and for those enjoying extended hikes and riding).

The magnificent stalactite ★**Jenodan Caves** ㊱, 80 kilometers southwest of Katoomba in **Kanangra Boyd National Park,** are worth a visit.

## SYDNEY (☎ 02)

 **Sydney Information Booth**, Martin Place, daily 9:00 a.m.-5:00 p.m.. **Sydney Visitor Centre**, 106 George St, Tel. 92551788, daily 9:00 a.m.-6:00 p.m.. **Darling Harbour Information Centre**, under the freeway near the IMAX-Kino, Tel. 92860111, daily 10:00 a.m.-6:00 p.m. **NRMA** (Automobile Club), 151 Clarence St, Tel. 131111. **Manly Visitors Bureau**, Ocean Beach, North Steyne, Tel. 99771088, daily 10:00 a.m.-4:00 p.m. **Blue Mountain Information Centre**, Great Western Hwy, Glenbrook, Tel. 1800-641227.

**Airports**: international flights arrive at the International Airport Kingsford-Smith in the suburb of Mascot (10 km from the center), the domestic airport is 2 km further east. The NSW Travel Centre, which can assit in the bookings for transportation and accommodation in all of New South Wales, has a counter in the international airport. Tel. 96676050, daily from 5:00 a.m. until the arrival of the final flight.

It is easy to get to the city: The *Airport Express* (green or yellow busses) leave both airports every 20 minutes for Circular Quay (Route 300) or Kings Cross (Route 350), fare: $A 6; Tel. 131500. In addition, there is a *shuttle service* to the larger hotels. It is approxiamtely 30 minutes by taxi to the city center, and costs about $A 20.

**Car Purchase**: if you wish to cross Australia with your own car: at Kings Cross Car Market, car park corner of Ward Ave and Elizabeth Bay Rd (website: www.carmarket.com.au), you will find a broad range of offers. It is not only professionals who buy and sell here, backpackers also sell their vehicles here – at advantageous prices.

**Car Rental**: all the international car rental companies have several offices in Sydney. If you booked your car from home, order the pick up at the office closest to your hotel. *One way rentals* offered by some of the local car rental companies are quite practical, such as *Getabout*, Tel. 93805536 (website www.getaboutoz. com). New and used cars can be rented at very low rates from, among others, *Daytona*, Tel. 132480. Additional addresses can be found in the *Yellow Pages*.

**Explorer Busses**: The innercity is best discovered aboard the **Sydney Explorer**, the eastern suburbs and Bondi Beach are covered by the **Bondi & Bay Explorer**. Both busses begin their tour at Circular Quay and travel a predetermined route. The *Sydney Explorer* runs between 9:00 a.m. and 5:25 p.m. every 20 minutes, stopping at 22 important attractions, the *Bondi & Bay Explorer* runs every 30 minutes between 9:00 a.m. and 4:00 p.m. (in summer both busses might run

somewhat longer). A day ticket costs $A 22 for both lines. One can get on and off as often as one wishes. The *Sydney Pass* (valid for 3, 5 or 7 days) offers additional reductions; from $A 85. Information at all *State Transit* offices, Tel. 131500.

**Harbour Tours**: If you are looking for something other than the usual touristic harbour tours, then discover Sydney Harbour on one of the 11 public ferry routes. Departures from Circular Quay, information Tel. 131500.

**All Seasons Premier Menzies**, 14 Carrington St, Tel. 92991000. **Hotel Nikko Darling Harbour**, 161 Sussex St, Tel. 92991231.

**Intercontinental Sydney**, 117 Macquarie St, Tel. 9253900.**Manly Pacific Parkroyal**, 55 North Steyne, Manly, Tel. 99777666. **Old Sydney Parkroyal**, 55 George St, The Rocks, Tel. 92520524.

**Park Hyatt Sydney**, 7 Hickson Rd, The Rocks, Tel. 92411234. **Ritz-Carlton**, 93 Macquarie St, Tel. 92524600.**Ritz-Carlton Double Bay**, 33 Cross St, Double Bay, Tel. 93624455. **Rydges North Sydney**, 54 Mc Laren St, Tel. 99221311.

**Aarons Hotel**, 37 Ultimo Rd, Haymarket, Tel. 92815555. **Australian Sunrise Lodge**, 485 King St, Newtown, Tel. 95504999.

**City Beach Motor Inn**, 99 Curlewis St, Bondi Beach, Tel. 93653100. **Cremorne Point Manor**, 6 Cremorne Rd, Cremorne Point, Tel. 99537899.

**Crown-Lodge International**, 289 Crown St, Surry Hills, Tel. 93312433. **DeVere Hotel**, 44-46 McLeay St, Potts Point, Tel. 93581211.

**Lane Cove River Caravan Park**, Plassey Rd, North Ryde, Tel. 98889133. **Gemini Motel**, 65 Belmore Rd, Randwick, Tel. 93999011.

**Historic Hughenden Boutique Hotel**, 14 Queen St, Woohllara, Tel. 93634863.

**Periwinkle Guesthouse,** 19 East Esplanade, Manly, Tel. 99774668.

**Rooftop Motel**, 146 Glebe Point Rd, Glebe, Tel. 96607777. **The Mercantile Hotel**, 25 George St, The Rocks, Tel. 92473570.

**Backpackers Headquarters**, 79 Bayswater Rd, Kings Cross, Tel. 93316180. **Bernly Private Hotel**, 15 Springfield Ave, Kings Cross, Tel. 93583122.

**Billabong Gardens**, 5-11 Egan St, Newtown, Tel. 95503236. **Challis Lodge**, 21-23 Challis Ave, Potts Point, Tel. 92585422. **Coogee Beach Backpackers**, 90-96 Beach St, Coogee, Tel. 93158000.

**Glebe Point YHA**, 262 Glebe Point Rd, Glebe, Tel. 96928418. **Highfield House**,166 Victoria St, Kings Cross, Tel. 93269539.

**Montpelier Private Hotel**, 39a Elizabeth Bay Rd, Potts Point, Tel. 93586960.

**Sydney Central YHA**, 11 Rawson Place (across from Central Station), Tel. 92819111.

❌ **Badde Manors**, 37 Glebe Point Rd, a cosy, established cafe-restaurant, vegetarian cuisine. **Doyle's on the Beach**, 11 Marine Parade, Watsons Bay, Tel. 93371350, upmarket prices. **Doyle's at the Quay**, Overseas Passenger Terminal, West Circular Quay, Tel. 92523400. **Doyle's at the Fish Markets**, Arcade, Blackwattle Bay, Tel. 95524339. All three Doyle's Restaurants serve excellent fish, in all price ranges, and, of course, fish'n'chips. **Borobudur**, 123 Glebe Point Rd, Glebe, Tel. 96605611, Indonesian cuisine. **Hard Rock Café**, 121-129 Crown St, Darlinghurst, Tel. 93311116, represented the world over with the same atmosphere. **No Names**, in the Friend in Hand Hotel, 58 Cowper St, Glebe, Tel. 96602326, Italian, inexpensive. In the historical **Pumphouse Brewery / Tavern**, 17 Little Pier St, Darling Harbour (Mon-Sat from 11:00 a.m.; Sun noon-midnight) freshly brewed beer is served in a delightful ambience. Good music and beer is offered almost every evening at the **Orient Hotel**, The Rocks, George St.

As a general rule: the range of restaurants is so broad, that really everyone can get his money's worth. However, the range is meagre around Circular Quay.

⚡ **Events:** the Friday edition of the daily *The Sydney Morning Herold* provides a complete overview in the *Metro* supplement of all Sydney's events.

**The heart of the night-life** east of the city are Kings Cross (a red-light district in parts, some good pubs and discos) and Oxford Street (clubs and pubs – many catering to a homosexual / lesbian public). There are some good pubs with live music and numerous restaurants in The Rocks as well.

Good live jazz can be heard in **Soup Plus**, 383 George St, or in the **Basement**, 29 Reiby Place; close to Circular Quay. Those seeking to end the evening in a lively disco often head for the **Palladium** on the corner of Darlinghurst Rd / Rosslyn St, Tel. 93310127, or to the **Cauldron**, 207 Darlinghurst Rd, Tel. 93311523.

**Homosexuel Scene:** Sydney has become over the course of the last few years – on account of liberal city policies – one of the world's most vital gay centers. Meeting points are Kings Cross, Darlinghurst (The Albury, The Exchange, The Oxford, Midnight Shift) and Newtown (The Newtown Hotel).

🏛 **Art Gallery of NSW**, Art Gallery Rd, Tel. 92251744, daily10:00 a.m.-5:00 p.m.

**National Maritime Museum**, Darling Harbour, Tel. 95527777, daily 9:30 a.m.-5:00 p.m.

**Powerhouse Museum**, 500 Harris St, Ultimo, Tel. 92170100, daily10:00 a.m.-5:00 p.m.

**Sydney Aquarium**, one of the largest in the world, Darling Harbour, Tel. 92622300, daily 9:30 a.m.-9:00 p.m.

**Sydney Jewish Museum**, 148 Darlinghurst Rd, Tel. 93607999, Sat 11:00 a.m.-5:00 p.m., Mon-Thurs 10:00 a.m.-4:00 p.m., Fri 10:00 a.m.-2:00 p.m.

**Sydney Opera House**: Tours between 9:00 a.m. and 4:00 p.m., as well as opera and backstage tours. Tickets at Tel. 92507777, information Tel. 92507111.

**Taronga Zoo**: 12 minutes from Circular Quay by ferry. Visitors and the 3500 animals enjoy the view of the skyline of Bradleys Head Road in Mosman, daily 9:00 a.m.-5:00 p.m., Tel. 99692777. **The Australian Museum**, 6 College St, large natural science collection, Tel. 93206000, daily 9:30 a.m.-5:00 p.m. **The Museum of Contemporary Art**, Circular Quay West, Tel. 92524033.

🏳️‍🌈 **Mardi Gras**: The most strident and the most colorful parade for those who practice same-sex love runs every year through Oxford Street, Saturdays, mid-February – a must!

**The Festival of Sydney**: In January all Sydney dances – with open-air events, fireworks, concerts and culture from all over the world.

📷 **Olympia Grounds Homebush Bay**, 17 km west of the inner city, reachable by bus, train and ferry (State Transit, Tel. 131500). The **Olympic Explorer Bus** tours ($A 10) the grounds, daily from the *Visitor Centre* between 9:20 a.m. and 3:00 p.m. every 20 minutes. More information at the *Visitor Centre*, Tel. 97354800.

📷 **Markets**: Much to see and (almost) everything available to buy at the **Balmain Market**, St. Andrew's Church, Darling St, Balmain, Sat 10:00 a.m.- 4:00 p.m. **Glebe Market**, Glebe Point Rd, Glebe, Sat 10:00 a.m.-2:00 p.m. **Paddington Bazaar**, Oxford St, Paddington, every Saturday 9:00 a.m.- 4:00 p.m. **The Rocks Market**, Upper George St, The Rocks, Sat / Sun 10:00 a.m.-5:00 p.m.

📷 **Bondi Beach**: Not the cleanest of the city's beaches, but definitely the one with the most action! It is best to arrive by the bus lines 380, 382 and 389 from Circular Quay.

📷 **AMP Centrepoint Tower**: With its height of 304,8 meters, the tower (entrance from the fourth floor of the Centrepoint, close to the intersection of Pitt and Castlereagh Streets) is not only the highest building in Australia, but also provides the best views of Sydney. Tel. 92297444, Sun-Fri 9:00 a.m.-10:30 p.m., Sat until 11.30 p.m.

📷 **Sydney Harbour Bridge Pylon and Museum**, above The Rocks, Tel. 92473408, daily10:00 a.m.-5:00 p.m. **The Sydney Harbour BridgeClimb**, Tel. 92520077, website: http:// www.bridgeclimb.com. Daily 8:00 a.m. to sunset , *night climbs* are also available.

# FROM SYDNEY TO MELBOURNE

## – THE INTERIOR –
HUME HIGHWAY, CANBERRA, HIGH COUNTRY
## – ALONG THE COAST –
PRINCES HIGHWAY, SNOWY MOUNTAINS, SAPPHIRE COAST, WILSONS PROMONTORY

## – THE INTERIOR –

### HUME HIGHWAY

**Hume Highway**, which is without doubt the most traveled road in Australia, connects the cities of Sydney and Melbourne. The 875-kilometer-long road is now mainly a four-lane highway; it is only between Yass and Albury-Woodonga that the trip is sometimes made more difficult by a few two-lane stretches (passing lanes in some parts). The arterial road South West Motorway towards Liverpool is a toll road.

**Liverpool, Campbelltown,** and **Camden** are the first towns you come to on Hume Highway, and most travelers generally take the bypass around them as it is hardly worth stopping along this section of the road.

In **Mittagong ❶** (109 kilometers), the Gateway to the Southern Highlands, it might be worth taking a rest at the Butterfly House (Bessemer Street) among green plants and colorful butterflies. In February, there is a Dahlia Festival at nearby Lake Alexandra.

*Previous pages: Road Trains are the method of transportation in the Outback. Left: Blowhole of Kiama – a rugged play of nature.*

**\*Berrima ❷** is usually overlooked by travelers. Founded in 1831, it has many historic buildings. At the Surveyor-General Inn alcohol has been served without a break since 1835 – a record for Australia!

Although there is as yet no bypass at **Goulburn ❸**, visitors come to see the October *Lilac Festival*. At the *Big Merino,* right beside the Hume Highway, souvenirs of everything to do with sheep and agriculture are sold all year round. There is an agricultural show every day at 10 a.m. at the *Australian Agrodrome*, also part of the Merino complex. About 12 kilometers beyond Goulburn, it is worth leaving Hume Highway by taking the Canberra turning. 94 kilometers along the **Federal Highway**, you will arrive at Australia's capital, Canberra. Stop for a while at one of the pleasant picnic areas beside Lake George before entering the **Australian Capital Territory** (ACT).

### \*CANBERRA

If you are hoping for a spectacular panoramic view of the Australian capital as you approach, you will be in for a disappointment, but **\*Canberra ❹** has been nicknamed the Green City, and her assets will be very apparent as you draw near, no matter from which direction. In autumn

monwealth of Australia had not been formed on 1 January 1901. At the same time, the authorities began looking for a suitable capital. This was an honor which the two arch rivals, Sydney and Melbourne, had long insisted was theirs.

In order to avoid conflict, the decision was made to find a location in the territory of New South Wales, not more than 100 miles away from Sydney, no smaller than 100 square miles, and which could be placed at the disposal of the Commonwealth without any kind of payment.

After whittling down the choice to one of 40 districts, the area around Yass and Canberra was picked in 1908, and in 1911 an international architects' competition was announced for the planning of the new capital.

Landscape architect Walter Burley Griffin from Chicago was the winner from among 137 applicants. He saw the area around the town as a natural amphitheatre and planned on incorporating and preserving as many natural features as possible, even in the town center. He also came up with Canberra's nickname, Bush Capital.

On 12 March 1913, on Capital Hill, the foundation stone was laid for the project. However, its designer felt that he could not wait to see it finished and in 1920 Griffin departed, extremely disappointed with the length of time the work seemed to be taking.

Both the pace of the work and the love of the Aussies for their capital did, indeed, appear somewhat limited for many decades.

Members of Parliament met in Canberra for the first time only in 1927, and even then it was another nine years before the British High Commission became the first diplomatic mission to put up its brass plate in the capital.

The final break-through for Canberra probably came about on the occasion of Australia's bicentennial celebrations, when the New Parliament Building was

and spring, particularly, Canberra forms a colorful oasis in an otherwise bare hilly countryside where the winters are icy cold, the summers unbearably hot and bushfires common.

The name Canberra did not appear on maps before the beginning of this century. In 1820, explorers Joseph Wild, James Vaughan, and Charles Thorsby Smith came here on one of their expeditions from Moss Vale. They were the first white Australians to visit the area where present-day Canberra stands.

In 1824, a certain Joshua Moore staked his claim to a piece of land on the same site, which he called Canberry, a name derived from the Aboriginal word *kamberra*, meaning meeting place, and used by the original inhabitants of this limestone plain.

The place-name would have gathered dust in the historical records if the Com-

*Above: Big Merino in Goulburn. Right: On January 26 the entire country celebrates Australia Day.*

opened and the Head of State, Queen Elizabeth II, made a special trip down under for this event.

Canberra itself is a place worth visiting for its landscaping and architecture alone. Apart from that, the tourist highlights of the town are associated mainly with the history and government of Australia.

Most of the people who live here are enthusiastic about their capital city, and they have every reason to be proud, as Canberra probably includes more green spaces than does any other city in Australia. Traffic jams and air pollution are virtually unheard of in this pleasant, relaxed capital. Tourists from abroad seem less enthusiastic about a visit, but if you are on Hume Highway it is definitely worth making a short detour to the capital.

On the other hand, anyone thinking of making a special journey or a long detour to get there should consider carefully whether they really need to visit Canberra, the only Australian city, by the way, which is not situated beside the ocean.

No Australian city is as controversial as this one. You either love Canberra or you hate it! There is no in-between – not even for tourists.

### Sites of Interest

Griffin had planned for a city of 25,000 inhabitants, which could eventually expand to 75,000, but these projected figures have long since been overtaken by reality.

Today Canberra and the surrounding Australian Capital Territory number approximately 260,000 inhabitants, of whom a large proportion are civil servants and administrative employees of Australian federal departments.

More or less in the center of the city is **Lake Burley Griffin**, about 11 kilometers long, which was constructed in 1963 by damming the Molonglo River. Most of the sites worth visiting are outside the center of the city. As Canberra is spread out over a very large area, the best policy is to travel by bus. The Explorer Bus takes

a set route for 18 A$, and you can get on or off wherever you want to, as often as you want; if you use the Action bus system you will pay only 2.00 A$ per trip.

One of the first goals will most probably be to **Capital Hill,** where the *★New Parliament House* ❶ is the obvious attraction. This building, which cost one billion dollars to construct, was opened in 1988 and has since been visited by well over a million people.

In fact, Griffin had planned that the Parliament Building should be on a different site. Where Capital Hill is today he wanted a People's Hill – a place that should be accessible to anyone at any time of day.

It all turned out differently, yet some of Griffin's basic ideas were preserved, so that the Parliament Building is, for the most part, hidden by Capital Hill. With the exception of an 8-meter-high mast

*Above: New Parliament House on Capital Hill.*
*Right: View from Mount Ainslie of the ANZAC Parade and Parliament.*

bearing the Australian flag, no parts of the building rise any higher than 1 meter above the hill.

Another feature is that there are no restricted areas, so that everyone (after a general security check) may take a seat in the spectators' galleries of the House of Representatives Chamber or in the Senate Chamber. If you arrive by car, you will find a public car park located right underneath the Parliament House!

In the foyer stand 48 marble columns which are supposed to evoke a eucalyptus forest, and the Great Hall is decorated with one of the world's largest wall-hangings, by the Australian artist Arthur Boyd.

Adjacent to this is the Members' Hall, the informal meeting place for Members of Parliament. Here, too, the walls are decorated with works by Australian artists. With more than 3000 works of art, Parliament must be one of the largest art galleries in the country.

Question Time in Parliament (when the opposition gets a hearing) starts at 2 p.m. The ensuing verbal duels are very popular with Australian visitors.

If you wish to be there, you should book a free entrance ticket early enough at the information desk by the entrance. There are no guided tours during parliamentary sessions.

At other times, from 9:20 a.m. daily, there are guided tours every 20 minutes, which last about 50 minutes. The general opening time for visitors is between 9:00 a.m. and 5:00 p.m.

If the whole thing seems a bit too dry for your taste, then why not quench your thirst in true political style in the Parliament canteen.

Nowhere else in Australia will you find a Speaker's Ale or a President's Lager. It's best to drink it while enjoying a beautiful view of Canberra from the terrace.

There are frequent demonstrations in front of the Parliament Building, some lasting for days on end. A leaflet or two

will probably be thrust into your hand, informing you about the problems of farmers, or the Aborigines' struggle, as you make the short walk over to King George Terrace and the **Old Parliament House** ❷, which was the seat of government from 1927 to 1988 and is where much of Australia's history was made.

Many Australians still cherish the memory of Prime Minister Gough Whitlam, who was one of the most radical reformers the country has known.

Although Whitlam experienced defeat in a vote in the Senate in 1975, and his government had fewer parliamentary seats than the Conservatives under Malcolm Fraser, he refused to quit.

It was on the steps of Parliament House that he finally heard he had been sacked as Head of Government by the Governor General.

This was one of Australia's greatest political scandals, and all over the country there were heated discussions about his removal, but Gough Whitlam's political career had come to an end.

Not far from here, on the shore of Lake Burley Griffin, stands the *National Gallery of Australia* ❸, nowadays the home of the famous Ned Kelly series by the artist Sydney Nolan. There are many works by foreign artists (among others, Jackson Pollock's Blue Poles), as well as a large and intriguing collection of Aboriginal works of art. A total of some 70,000 works are on exhibition in eleven different galleries. If you arrive at midday, you will find the museum restaurant a wonderful place in which to eat and relax. Well fortified, you may continue your trip around the city along the lake shore. Quite close to the National Gallery is the **High Court of Australia** ❹ with three court rooms (guided tours are available), and the **National Science and Technology Centre, Questacon** ❺ (150 exhibits, and some experiments that you can conduct yourself), as well as the **Australian National Library** ❻ to the west (3.5 million books and one jewel of great price: Captain Cook's ship's log covering the years 1768-71).

Taking the Commonwealth Avenue Bridge, you can cross Lake Burley Griffin. In the middle of the lake you will see the **Captain Cook Memorial Jet 7**, one of the largest fountains in the world, which projects a 140-meter-high spray each day from 10:00 a.m. to noon and from 2:00 p.m. to 4:00 p.m., but only when there is no strong wind.

At nearby **Regatta Point 8**, a globe recalls the discovery of eastern Australia 200 years ago. The history of Canberra is made real every day from 10:00 a.m. to 4:00 p.m. in **Blundell's Farmhouse 9**, built in 1860.

The **Carillon 10**, consisting of a tower with 53 bells, is situated on **Aspen Island**, and is one of the largest of its kind. It was a gift from the British government on the occasion of the 50th anniversary of Canberra's founding.

The wide ANZAC Parade will lead you to the **Australian War Memorial 11**, where everything to do with warfare is on display.

Of course, most attention is given to the wars in which Australian soldiers took part, and if the statistics are to be believed, this war memorial is the most visited attraction in Australia after Sydney Opera House.

Towering over the War Memorial is **Mount Ainslie 12** (842 meters, from where there is a wonderful view over Canberra and its surroundings.

On its northern shore is the city center (City Walk, Alinga Street, Bunda Street), but do not expect too much of this.

However, the **Canberra Centre 13** is worth mentioning. Having 150 shops under one roof, it is the ideal base for any kind of shopping.

Apart from that, there is a kind of pride in Canberra in not having a proper center in which commerce dominates (one of Griffin's basic concepts).

The **National Film and Sound Archive 14** (McCoy Circuit / Acton), exhibits all that is best in Australian film-

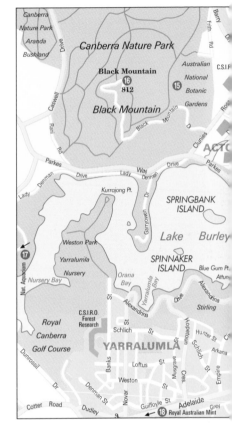

making and is of interest to everyone, not only to film buffs. Excerpts from various weekly newsreels offer a very lively glimpse back through the history of Australia.

In the **Australian National Botanical Gardens 15** (entrance in Clunie-Ross Street), over 6000 species of native plants flourish. From the revolving restaurant on **Black Mountain 16** (812 meters) there is a splendid view of the city and surrounding areas.

It is planned to open the **National Museum of Australia** on Acton Peninsula in the year 2000. The museum will house various interesting exhibitions of Australian history and culture. Numerous fish from native rivers and lakes swim merrily

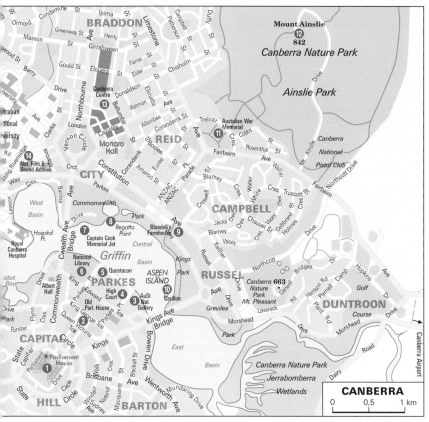

in the basins of the **National Aquarium** which is located in **Yarraluma** on the western side of lake Burley Griffin. Typical Australian wild life such as kangaroos and emus roam the enclosed grounds of the National Wildlife Sanctuary, which is part of the Aquarium.

It is well worth making a detour to Deakin in the south to visit **The Royal Australian Mint**, where, in addition to Australian coins, currencies of several foreign countries are struck.

If you wish to become involved in sporting activities, there are facilities for rowing on Lake Burley Griffin in the center of the town, and you can also cycle around the shore. In the vicinity of Canberra there are pleasant bush walks to go

on, especially in the **Tidbinbilla** nature reserve (some 40 kilometers southwest).

It is a characteristic of Canberra that several embassies have been declared sites of special interest in the city. Among others, the ambassadors of India, Thailand, and Papua New Guinea live in the Yarralumla quarter and their residences are considered to be especially attractive. There are more than 60 diplomatic missions in Canberra.

Finally, if saying goodbye to Canberra should prove difficult, this may not be entirely due to the more obvious beauties of the city. There can hardly be as many hostess agencies in any other Australian city as there are in the city of Canberra. Perhaps this is one of the reasons why

such a large proportion of the vast army of government bureaucrats keeps finding reasons to visit the Australian capital.

Northbourne Avenue leads out of the city, and, after a few kilometers, the road divides. To get to Melbourne, take the Barton Highway in the direction of Yass. The Federal Highway will take you in the direction of Sydney via Goulburn.

**Yass** ❺ is the center of wool production. In 1821, Hamilton Hume discovered the area, and his home can be viewed near Barton Highway.

About 8 kilometers before Gundugai, you will pass the Dog on the Tucker Box, a monument to the pioneer days. Like the community itself, it is well known to many Aussies through ballads and country music.

If you are traveling in winter, you really should include a trip into the mountains. A left-hand turn a few kilometers

*Above: The Australian War Memorial is a must, at least for Australian tourists. Right: Cross-country skiing in the High Country.*

beyond Gundagai connects to the Snowy Mountains Highway in **Tumut** ❻ (population 7000), which leads straight up into the mountains. (For a description, cf page 62).

If, however, you decide instead to continue along Hume Highway, you will leave the State of New South Wales beyond the town of **Albury** (which is located on the banks of the Murray River). Before arriving at **Wodonga** in Victoria, you will pass a fruit and plant check point. Because of the risks of allowing fruit flies to spread, taking fresh fruit and plants across the border into Victoria is prohibited.

## HIGH COUNTRY

From Wodonga, Kiewa Highway will take you straight up into the High Country, the highest points of which are Mount Bogong (at a height of 1986 meters), Feathertop (at a height of 1922 meters) and Hotham (at a height of 1862 meters).

There is hardly anything left to remind one of the Koorie, the Aborigines who lived here many thousands of years ago. The period when this mountainous area was opened up by white people has, however, left traces in many places. Exploration began in 1824, when Europeans Hume and Hovell discovered Mount Buller.

If you do not intend to stay overnight in the High Country, preferring to make a day trip out of it, then the well-maintained former gold digger village of ★**Beechworth** ❼ is the best place to start (24 kilometers south of the Hume Freeway).

The main tourist interest of this area centers on a personality who is long dead and gone: Ned Kelly. Because he was something like Australia's answer to that most honorable of robbers, Robin Hood, he has long been considered a hero, and has thus been raised to the status of a tourist attraction.

Kelly and his henchmen were the scourge of the countryside in the late 1870s. Ambush and murder were everyday activities for the band, and Kelly's grotesque metal armor became his trademark.

About halfway to Benalla is the little community of **Glenrowan ❽**, where you can visit **Katie's Cottage** and the **Ned Kelly Outdoor Museum.**

This is where fate eventually caught up with Ned Kelly. During a final shoot-out with the police, he was able to escape with his life, but was later captured and imprisoned. But even he was unable to evade death by hanging in Melbourne in 1880, and so the legend was born. At least the people of Glenrowan are grateful to Ned Kelly these days: the souvenir trade is positively flourishing!

The highway passes **Benalla ❾**, with its **Kelly Museum** and annual Festival of Roses celebrated each October. It also runs past **Seymour** on the Goulburn River. Those wishing to make a short stop here will have to leave the highway.

Probably the best known section of the High Country is the very accessible **★Mount Buffalo National Park ❿** ("Island in the Sky") with its attractive, precipitous granite rocks and beautiful Lake Catani.

Another tourist center, **★Mount Hotham** with neighboring **★Dinner Plain ⓫**, is an ideal place for riding and fishing in summer.

**★Mount Buller ⓬** is one of the best skiing areas in the country. Here the ski-lifts give access to 75 kilometers of ski slopes, and Bourke Street offers the best après-ski in the whole of Australia. Skiing is also possible in Falls Creek (good facilities), Mount Buffalo, Mount Stirling, and Mount Hotham (ideal powder-snow slopes).

In the summer, the greatest sporting challenge is the **Alpine Walking Track**. This 400-kilometer-long trail begins in **Walhalla** in the south, takes you through the mountains and valleys of the High Country and ends in **Cowombat Flat** in the northern part of Victoria. The total distance can be walked in about 30 days, but water is scarce along the track. Another factor you should take into consideration is the possible rapid changes in weather conditions.

For those planning to travel through the High Country to the coast, please remember that most roads through the mountain range are unsurfaced. In bad weather they should be attempted only in vehicles with four-wheel drive.

### – ALONG THE COAST – PRINCES HIGHWAY

In the very center of Sydney the main roads diverge so that Hume Highway leads inland and Princes Highway stays close to the coast and heads south. Leaving behind the hectic city atmosphere, this route, once again bearing the name Highway No. 1, will take you past historical **Botany Bay** with **Captain Cook's Landing Place** and *★The Royal National Park** to the south (cf page 43). There are a number of beautiful surf beaches stretching from the kite-flyers' paradise of **Stanwell Park** all the way to **Shellharbour**.

The rather industrialized town of **Woolongong** is hardly worth a diversion, though, and you can substitute with a sweeping view from Mount Keira Lookout (exit signs to the right on the highway.) When the sea is stormy and the tide high, the main attraction of **Kiama ⓭** comes alive in a cloud of spray and foam. At such times a column of water reaching a height of up to 60 meters will shoot up out of the Blowhole on Blowhole Road in the center of the town.

For most tourists, this natural wonder surpasses even the nearby lighthouse with its fine view of the coast. Just below the Blowhole, Park Pool, a salt water pool carved out of the rock, offers an ideal place for dipping more than just a toe in the ocean. Another memorable sight in Kiama is its famous pink post office.

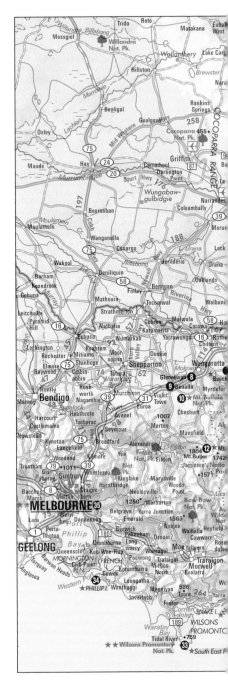

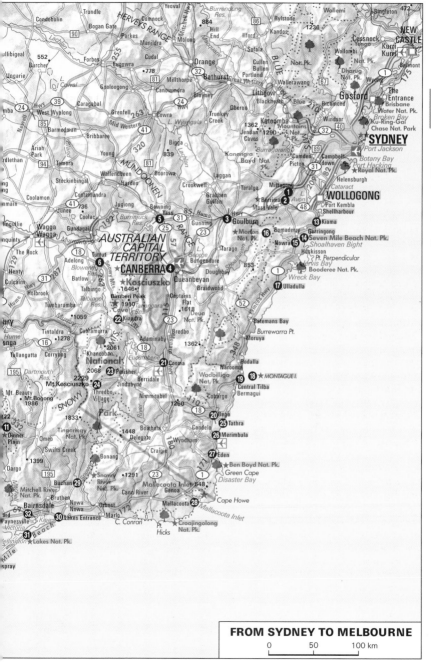

**FROM SYDNEY TO MELBOURNE**

0     50     100 km

If you leave Princes Highway at **Gerringong** and drive along the coast in the direction of Shoalhaven, at the half-way point you will find **Seven Mile Beach National Park ⑭**, a particularly beautiful stretch of beach with very fine sand. You can rejoin Highway 1 at **Nowra ⑮**, which has an interesting Historical Museum worthy of a visit.

Beyond Nowra, State Highway 79, flanked by giant ferns, veers off towards **Kangaroo Valley**. The town of the same name is surrounded by green farming country, fertile meadows, and oak and willow trees, and seems to come alive only during the Annual Show in February, when the farmers from the surrounding area meet for a sort of combined horse fair and fairground. **At Hampden Bridge** there is a perfect picnic spot. This big suspension bridge across the Kangaroo River was opened on May 19, 1898.

*Above: Morton National Park fascinates with its luxuriant vegetation; the coast beckons with water sports. Right: Hampden Bridge.*

The attractive river beach is a favorite with the locals, and Pioneer Farm Village, the Coffee Shop and the camping site make this a pleasurable stopover for travelers too.

If you should plan to go walking in nearby Morton National Park, this is a good place to stock up with provisions.

### *Morton National Park

**\*Morton National Park ⑯** (encompassing 150,000 hectares) has many impressive waterfalls, spectacular rocky escarpments, and splendid views.

A walking trail follows each side of the escarpment; each is 3 kilometers long and can be walked in an hour and a half.

The third walk, down to Yarrunga Creek, is steep and requires some care (approximately one hour).

**\*Fitzroy Falls** are best viewed from Jersey Lookout on the western side. At Fitzroy Falls there is a National Parks information center, as well as a picnic area and a camping site.

### Beaches and Bays

Beyond Nowra, the highway returns to the coast. Huskisson is situated on peaceful **Jervis Bay**, where once enormous quantities of timber were shipped out, but where tourism has now taken over. **Booderee National Park** has some good trails for bush walking, and Cave Beach is a relaxing spot.

**Ulladulla**  has long been a significant tourist resort. This town of approximately 6000 inhabitants – a figure which is multiplied several times over during the summer months – is also an important fishing port, and is another starting point for trips into Morton National Park.

Bathing at Ulladulla is not restricted to the sea, as there are seven lakes, all situated to the south, from Burrill Lake to Durras Lake, which also offer excellent water sports facilities. The same goes for Bateman's Bay on the shores of the Clyde River. The best way to explore the area is by traveling along the 3-kilometer-stretch to Culendulla Creek.

If you are planning a detour to the Australian capital, the best way is to exit Princes Highway at **Bateman's Bay** and drive the 140 kilometers to Canberra via the old gold-rush town of **Braidwood** (cf page 50).

Continuing down the coast, you will pass through **Moruya**, which provided the foundation pillars for Sydney Harbour Bridge, **Bodalla** (the parish church of All Saints, dating from 1880, is worth a visit), as is **Narooma**, well known for the fine big-game fishing off *Montague Island. All have two things in common: numerous beaches and good surfing.

Nature enthusiasts should definitely plan on visiting the **Montague Island** nature reserve near Narooma. There are countless water fowl here, and every evening, fairy penguins waddle from the water back to their nests – this event is not yet quite as touristy as the penguin parade on Philip Island in Victoria.

*From Sydney to Melbourne*

At **Tilba Tilba** (where many artists exhibit their work in the town center), you can leave the highway and carry on along a side road in the direction of Tathra.

This route takes you through Mimosa Rocks National Park (south of Bermagui), which is an excellent place to stop for lunch.

### SNOWY MOUNTAINS

Coastal landscapes are not all there is to see in this region. **Bega** is a good place to turn off into the Snowy Mountains. Very soon, the highway, flanked by thick forest and beautiful ferns, begins to climb in the direction of **Nimmitabel** which soars to a height of 1070 meters.

**Cooma** is then another 111 kilometers away. This town is a perfect starting point for trips into the surrounding region, for walking in summer and skiing in winter (100 kilometers to Thredbo), as it is situated at the crossroads of the Snowy Mountains and Monaro Highways (114 kilometers to Canberra).

Locals in the Snowy Mountains like to amaze newcomers with the surprising statistic that in winter a greater area of New South Wales and Victoria is snow-covered than all of Switzerland! People who visit in the summer shake their heads in disbelief.

In winter, on the other hand, they are soon convinced: there is snow as far as the eye can see, and many good skiing areas, something you don't really expect in Australia!

Depending on the snow conditions, the skiing season can last from June to mid-October.

It all began in 1862, when Norwegian gold prospectors unpacked their skis in **Kiandra ㉒**, and thus started a new sport in Australia. Now it's a favorite sport.

Above the town, **Mount Selvyn** is a good area for a day's skiing (eight lifts; ideal for cross country).

*Above: The fifth continent abounds with kangaroos. Right: Merimbula is the Sapphire Coast's tourist center.*

The top ski resorts, however, are **Perisher ㉓** (100 kilometers of pistes; but the hotels are rather far apart) and **Thredbo Village ㉔**, at an altitude of 1420 meters.

Here you will find the best skiing in the country, with 15 lifts that carry you up to slopes that suit all capabilities, from beginner to experienced.

The village of 1200 inhabitants offers accommodation in all price categories and the most ambience at the après-ski facilities.

Both resorts are situated on the slopes of **Mount Kosciusko**, which, at 2229 meters, is the highest mountain on the Australian continent, and is also the center of the **\*Kosciusko National Park**. Climbing this peak in the summer is one of the most popular mountaineering expeditions.

In the eastern parts of the national park there are two artificial lakes, **Lake Jindabyne** and **Lake Eucumbene**, which offer excellent water sports and angling during the summer.

## SAPPHIRE COAST

**Tathra** ㉕ (population 1100 ) is situated on the mouth of the Bega River. Here you can see the last harbor installation for servicing steamships on the entire Australian east coast.

About 10 kilometers to the south, on a side road that is more enjoyable to drive along than Highway 1, is the yachting center of **Wallagoot Lake**.

This is the beginning of the **Sapphire Coast**, stretching all the way to Eden, with Merimbula as its tourist center.

\***Merimbula** ㉖ is not only one of the best known bathing resorts in New South Wales, but also one of the most beautiful.

In the mornings you can sit down to a second breakfast of cappuccino and a croissant in the waterfront cafe, while gazing at a view of Merimbula Lake, and afterwards there's the agonizing choice among several superb beaches.

**Surf Beach** lives up to its name, with excellent breakers. Much quieter is little **Bar Beach** on the other side of the bay, where penguins dive in the clear water. Beyond the hill is **Middle Beach**, which is just as beautiful as the others. In the evenings anglers and sightseers gather at Fishing Point, next to the Aquarium, to watch the spectacular sunset.

Before reaching **Eden** ㉗, it is worth making a detour to **Pambula Beach** (camping site right on the beach), as well as to \***Ben Boyd National Park**, which stretches around both sides of the former whaling harbor.

The most beautiful spots in the northern section are The Pinnacles, and Haycock Point, and, to the south, Boyd's Tower and the trip out to Green Cape.

The harbor at Eden is still full of activity, although tuna fish instead of whales are landed here today.

The **Eden Killer Whale Museum** has an extensive and very interesting collection of whaling memorabilia.

Included in this collection are the skeleton of a notorious whale named Old Tom, and several interesting documents pertaining to the heydays of Eden.

From here it is only the distance of another 44 kilometers until the border to Victoria is reached.

## VICTORIA – ON THE WAY TO MELBOURNE

**Genoa** likes to advertise itself as the first town in Victoria, but most tourists are unimpressed by this superlative and generally turn off to **Mallacoota ㉘** (24 kilometers) in the direction of the coast.

This town on the Mallacoota River inlet, surrounded by ★**Croajingolong National Park**, is one of the most beautiful tourist centers on the Victoria coast, and the national park offers some very peaceful and pleasant bush walks along the coast.

The stretch to **Orbost** is flanked by numerous state forest parks. **Buchan ㉙** (55

*Above: Stalactite caves near Buchan. Right: One of Australia's lovliest churches – St. Mary's Church in Bairnsdale.*

kilometers) is interesting, not only for the caves of stalactites and stalagmites in **Buchan Cave Reserve**, but also as the best starting point for trips into the ★**Snowy River National Park**, which can best be explored via the 15-kilometer-long **Silver Mine Walking Track**. There are camping facilities at MacKillops Bridge on the Deddick River.

Long before arriving at **Lakes Entrance ㉚**, there are signs praising the virtues of its specialty, fresh crayfish.

This seafood delicacy is probably best bought straight from a fishing boat down at the harbor, where it is guaranteed freshly caught every day.

The lovely beaches throughout the entire vicinity tempt many visitors to stay a while longer.

This is especially true of ★**Ninety Mile Beach**, a narrow strip of dunes, unique in Australia. This solitary stretch of sand can only be reached by a detour to **Longford** in the south.

From there, a side road leads to **Seaspray** (with good camping facilities) and further on to beautiful **Golden Beach**, **Letts Beach** and **Loch Sport** (with beautiful Woodside Beach).

★**Lakes National Park ㉛** is best explored by houseboat, starting from **Metung**.

The shores of this labyrinth of lakes are a gold mine for birdwatchers, with more than 140 species of birds, not to mention kangaroos.

Stop to have a look at **St. Mary's Church** at **Bairnsdale ㉜**, one of the most beautiful churches in the whole of Australia.

After your visit, you will encounter another parting of the ways some 53 kilometers further on, at Sale.

Melbourne is located some 212 kilometers further along the Princes Highway. If you wish to catch the ferry to Tasmania from Port Welshpool, then you should follow the South Gippsland Highway towards the south.

## **\*\*Wilsons Promontory National Park**

Leave the highway at **Foster**, a former gold-mining town in the foothills of the Strzelecki Range. Beyond Yanakie is **\*\*Wilsons Promontory National Park** ❸, *The Prom*; the entrance fee will be deducted if one stays overnight.

This area of about 47,000 hectares is best explored from **Tidal River**, where shops, an information center and camping are available.

The Prom is the most popular area for walking in Victoria. There are about 100 walks to choose from, with a total length of 80 kilometers, most of which offer wonderful views of the coast and lead to quiet coves and white sandy beaches.

Depending on one's mood, the walks can last from one hour to four days. The most beautiful walks lead to the lighthouse on **\*South East Point** (it is best to plan on staying overnight), to **\*Five Mile Beach,** and, for visitors in a hurry, to **\*Mount Oberon** (two hours), from where you will have the best views.

However, during vacation time, you will have to reckon with crowds, so booking ahead for a camping space at Tidal River is advisable.

Those planning to spend the night anywhere else in the National Park will require a permit from the *Information Centre*, tel. 03 568 09 555.

## **\*Phillip Island**

There are many side roads running close to the coast and which are surfaced only in parts. Fish Creek, Buffalo, and Pound Creek access Bass Highway, which leads to Newhaven and then to **\*Phillip Island** ❸. During the day, the island is quite silent.

Every evening at sundown, however, there is a peaceful invasion. Crowds of tiny silver and black fairy penguins, also known as little penguins, (some only 33-centimeters-long, troop out of the sea

*From Sydney to Melbourne*

each evening heading home to their burrows for the night, especially in summer when they are feeding their chicks. Their trek is eagerly awaited by the thousands of visitors in the viewing stands.

Do make note of the fact the the use of a flash is strictly forbidden! Most visitors to Melbourne include Phillip Island in their program, but usually only allow themselves a day trip. However, this cosy island does indeed merit a longer stay.

Phillip Island offers diverse experiences for everyone, from families to bushwalkers, rock climbers to anglers, natural historians to surfers, as well as for those just wanting to experience an island of nature.

If you can manage it timewise, spend the night in Cowes. In the harbor area you will find some charming old pubs, and The Anchor at Cowes is a restaurant in a class of its own.

A perfect ending to your enjoyable stay, before tranquilly wending your way the next morning towards **\*\*Melbourne** ❸, some 130 kilometers away.

## CANBERRA (☎ 02)

 **Canberra Visitors' Centre**, Northbourne Ave, Dickson, Tel. 62050044 and 1800-026166, daily 9:00 a.m.-5:00 p.m.

City guides and information can be obtained at **Traveller Maps and Guides**, Jolimont Centre, Northbourne Ave, City, Tel. 62496066. **NRMA** (Automobile Club), 92 Northbourne Ave, Dickson, Tel. 131111.

🛏 ☺☺☺ **Capital Parkroyal**, 1 Binara St, Tel. 62478999 and 1800-020055. **Hyatt Hotel Canberra**, Commonwealth Ave, Yarralumla, Tel. 62701234 and 1800-131234. **Country Comfort Inn**, Federal Hwy, 102 Northbourne Ave, Braddon, Tel. 62491411 and 1800-065064.

☺☺ **Acacia Motor Lodge**, 65 Ainslie Ave, Braddon, Tel. 62496955. **Blue and White Lodge**, 524 Northbourne Ave, Downer, Tel. 62480498. **Canberra Motel Deakin**, 70 Kent St, Deakin, Tel. 62811011. **Canberra Motor Village**, Kunzea St, Tel. 62475466. **Macquarie Hotel**,18 National Circuit, Barton, Tel. 62732325. **Miranda Lodge**, 534 Northbourne Ave, Downer. Tel. 62498038.

☺ **Canberra YHA**, corner of Dryandra und O'Connor Streets, Tel. 62489155. **Victor Lodge**, 29 Dawes St, Kingston, Tel. 62757777.

🏛 **National Aquarium & Australian Wildlife Sanctuary**, Lady Denman Drive, Scrivener Dam, Tel. 62871211, daily 9:00 a.m.-5:30 p.m. **National Gallery of Australia**, Parkes Place, Parkes, Tel. 62406502, daily10:00 a.m.-5:00 p.m. **Australian War Memorial**, ANZAC Parade, Tel. 62434211, daily10:00 a.m.-5:00 p.m. **National Film and Sound Archive**, McCoy Circuit, Acton, Tel. 62093111, daily 9:00 a.m.-5:00 p.m. **Questacon – National Science and Technology Centre**, King Edward Terrace, Tel. 62702800, daily10:00 a.m.-5:00 p.m. **Royal Australian Mint**, Denison St, Deakin, Tel. 62026999, Mon-Fri 9:00 a.m.-4:00 p.m., Sat-Sun 10:00 a.m.-3:00 p.m. Information and tickets for **Parliament** sessions at Tel. 62775399.

🍴 **Glebe Park Food Court and Tavern**, 15 Corranderk St, Reid. Snack bars and pub food. **Boffins at University House**, Balmain Crescent, Acton, Tel. 62495285. Daily breakfast and dinner, Mon-Fri lunch as well. New Australian cuisine. **Hill Station**, 51 Sheppard St, Hume, Tel. 62601393. Mon-Sat dinner in front of an open fireplace, in a homestead built in 1909. **The Tower Restaurant**, Telstra Tower, Black Mountain, Tel. 62486162. Dinner with magnificent panoramic view over the city. In addition, many Australian **clubs** offer good meals (usually) ,with entertainment, such as the Canberra Labor Club, The Canberra Club, Canberra Southern Cross Club, Canberra Tradesmen's Union Club. For those seeking a night-club atmosphere and a cold beer: **Pandora's**, corner of Mort and Alinga Streets, Tel. 62487405, and **Bobby McGee's** in Rydges Hotel, London Circuit, Tel. 62577999, offer both.

Men travelling alone to Canberra needn't remain alone for long: numerous **escort services** cater to the needs of male visitors.

📅 From mid-December to mid-January, the various cultural influences in Canberra are the focal point of the **National Multicultural Festival**.

In March is the 10-day **Canberra Festival**, with cultural and sporting events, fireworks and a Mardi Gras parade.

In September / October Canberra blossoms, especially around Commonwealth Park – celebrating the **Floriade Spring Festival**.

## HIGH COUNTRY (☎ 03)

 For tours to the mountainous terrain of the High Country, contact **Ecotrek & Bogong Jack**, PO Box 4, Kangrilla, SA 5157, Tel. 08-83837198.

**National parks and nature reserves in Victoria**: Information can be obtained from the telephone information service of *Parks Victoria*, Tel. 131963, as well as the local *Tourist Information Centres*.

🛏 Choice of accommodation in **Falls Creek**, **Mt Hotham** and **Dinner Plain**, Tel. 1800-344555; for Mt Hotham, reservations also via Skicom Mt Hotham, Tel. 1800-032061.

☺☺☺ **MOUNT BUFFALO**: **Mount Buffalo Chalet**, Tel. 57551500 and 1800-037038

☺☺ **FALLS CREEK**: **Viking Alpine Lodge**, 13 Parallel St, Tel. 51583247.

**MOUNT BEAUTY**: **Mt Beauty Holiday Centre**, Kiewa Valley Highway, Tawonga South, Tel. 57544396. **MOUNT BUFFALO**: **Mt Buffalo Lodge**, Mount Buffalo National Park, Tel. 57551988 and 1800-037038. **MOUNT BULLER**: **Abom**, 18 Goal Post Rd, Tel. 57776091. **Arlberg**, 189 Summit Rd, Tel. 57776260.

☺ **MOUNT BULLER**: **Mount Buller YHA**, 2 The Avenue, Tel. 57776691 (only open June-October).

## PRINCES HIGHWAY

🚗 **FRENCH ISLAND**: Two thirds of the flat island is a national park. Reachable by ferry from Stony Point on the Mornington Peninsula (train-bus connection from Melbourne via Frankston) and as a day excursion: *Bay Connections* from Cowes (Phillip Island; twice weekly, not in winter), Tel. 03-56785642.

🚗 **MOUNT KOSCIUSZKO**: *Alpine River Adventures*,

Tel. 02-64561199, organizes canoe trips; *Paddy Pallin*, Tel. 02-64562922, offers rafting, mountain biking, skiing and riding around the Top of Australia. Both promoters are located in Jindabyne.

### BATEMANS BAY (☎ 02)
**Information Centre**, Princes Hwy, Tel. 44726900.

❸❸❸ **Coachhouse Marina Resort**, 49 Beach Rd, Tel. 1800-670715.

❸❸ **Mariners Lodge on the Waterfront**, Orient St, Tel. 44726222. **Sunseeker**, Old Princes Hwy, Tel. 44725888.

❸ **Batemans Bay Tourist Park & YHA**, Old Princes Hwy, Tel. 44724972.

### BAIRNSDALE (☎ 03)
**Information Centre**, 240 Main St, Tel. 51523444 oder 1800-637060.

❸❸ **Mitchell Motor Inn**, 295 Main St, Tel. 51525012.

❸ **Mitchell Gardens Caravan Park**, Main St, Tel. 51524654.

### BOODEREE NATIONAL PARK (☎ 02)
**Bristol Point und Cave Beach Camping Area**, bookings at the *Visitor Centre*, Tel. 44430977.

### PHILLIP ISLAND / COWES (☎ 03)
**Information Centre**, Newhaven, Tel. 59567447 oder 1300-366422.

❸❸ **Castle Inn by the Sea**, 7 Steele St, Tel. 5952 1228. **Rothsaye B&B**, 2 Roy Court, Tel. 59522057. **The Continental Phillip Island**, Esplanade, Tel. 59522357.

❸ **Amaraoo Caravan Park & YHA**, 57 Church St, Tel. 59522548.

All located on the Esplanade: **Jetty Restaurant**, Tel. 59522060. **Harry's Restaurant** and **Sails Family Restaurant**, both in the Continental Hotel, Tel. 59522316.

**Penguin Parade** on **Summerland Beach** every evening, best observed in December and January. Information at the *Visitor Centre*, Tel. 59568300, daily from 10:00 a.m. A detour to Seal Rocks and the Nobbies is also wll worth it.

### EDEN (☎ 02)
**Information Centre**, Princes Hwy, Tel. 64961953.

❸❸ **Twofold Bay Motor Inn**, 166 Imlay St, Tel. 64963111.

❸ **Eden Tourist Park**, Aslings Beach Rd, Tel. 64961139

### LAKES ENTRANCE (☎ 03)
**Information Centre**, The Esplanade, Tel. 51551966 oder 1800-637060.

❸❸ **Abel Tasman Motor Lodge**, 643 Esplanade, Tel. 51551655. **Deja Vu B&B**, 17 Clara St, Tel. 5155 4330.

❸ **Koonwarra Caravan Park**, 687 Esplanade, Tel. 51551222. **Silver Sands Caravan Park**, 33 Myer St, Tel. 51552343.**Riviera Backpackers YHA**, 5 Clarkes St, Tel. 51552444.

**Nautilus Floating Dockside Restaurant**, Cunningham Arm, Tel. 51551400, seafood.

### LOCH SPORT (☎ 03)
❸ **Loch Sport Holiday Park**, Charles St, Tel. 51460264.

### MALLACOOTA (☎ 03)
❸❸ **Adobe Holiday Flats**, 17 Karbeethong Ave, Tel. 51580329. **Gypsy Point Lodge**, Gypsy Point, Tel. 1800-063556.

❸ **Mallacoota Lodge YHA**, 51 Maurice Ave, Tel. 51580455. **Shady Gully Caravan Park**, Lot 5, Genoa Rd, Tel. 51580362.

### MERIMBULA (☎ 02)
**Information Centre**, Beach St, Tel. 64951129.

❸❸ **Black Dolphin Resort Motel**, Arthur Kaine Drive, Tel. 64951500. **Sapphire Waters Motel Inn**, 32 Merimbula Drive, Tel. 64951999.

❸ **Merimbula Caravan Park**, Cliff St, Tel. 64951269. **Wandarra Lodge YHA**, 8 Marine Parade, Tel. 64953503.

**Lakeview Hotel**, Market St; Pub-Essen. **Pedros Mexican Restaurant**, 13 Princes Hwy, Tel. 64951546, Mexican cuisine. **Waterfront Café**, corner of Beach und Market Streets, good breakfast.

### MORTON NATIONAL PARK (☎ 02)
**Visitor Centre**, close to Fitzroy Falls, 16 km southeast of Moss Vale, Tel. 48877270.

### NAROMA (☎ 02)
❸ **Pub Hill Farm B&B**, Scenic Drive, Tel. 44763177. **Whale Motor Inn**, 141 Wagonga St, Tel. 44762411.

❸ **Bluewater Lodge YHA**, 11-13 Riverside Drive, Tel. 44764440. **Island View Beach Resort**, Princes Hwy, Tel. 44764600.

### NOWRA (☎ 02)
❸❸ **George Bass Motor Inn**, 65 Bridge Rd, Tel. 44216388.

### SHOALHAVEN HEADS (☎ 02)
❸❸ **Coolangatta Estate Resort**, 1335 Bolong Rd, Tel. 44487131.

### ULLADULLA (☎ 02)
❸❸ **Harbour Royal**, 29 Burrill St, Tel. 44555444. **Ulladulla Guesthouse**, 39 Burill St, Tel. 44551796.

❸ **Beach Haven Holiday Resort**, Princes Hwy, Tel. 44552110.

### WILSONS PROMONTORY (☎ 03)
❸❸ **Tidal River Area**, Tidal River, Tel. 6809555. Cabins or camping grounds.

# MELBOURNE – COSMOPOLITAN METROPOLIS

**HISTORY**
**CITY TOUR**
**SHOPPING**
**EXCURSIONS TO THE**
**SURROUNDING AREAS**

*Melbourne*

All the tables in the street cafes are full. A delicious aroma of pizza and freshly roasted coffee hangs in the air. Cars are queuing, hooting impatiently, in front of crowded ice-cream parlors. The traffic is completely snarled up. From every side you can hear fragments of Italian, and fashionable, elegantly dressed women are making their way through the crowds to some select rendezvous.

The scene in front of the Pasta Veloce restaurant is reminiscent of a hot summer evening in Italy, and yet Europe is over 10,000 kilometers away. This is an example of one of Australia's better sides; even in Italy itself you could hardly find a more cheerful and typically Italian atmosphere than Lygon Street in **\*\*Melbourne.** This scene in the Carlton quarter of the city emphasizes just one of the great attractions of Melbourne. The state capital of Victoria is remarkable for its ethnic and cultural variety. More than 140 different nationalities are represented, and all live peaceably together in this city of three million inhabitants.

Most of these nationalities have donated their own special atmosphere to one particular street or even a whole district.

After Athens and Thessaloniki, Melbourne is said to be the third largest Greek city in the world. No wonder then, that you feel as though you really are in Greece when you walk along Swan Street in the Richmond section of town. Or you think you are in Vietnam in Bridge Road and Victoria Road (nicknamed Little Saigon), both in Richmond. Or in Turkey in Sydney Road (Brunswick), or China in Little Bourke Street. However, Melbourne merits a visit for other reasons too, as some of the very best museums, art galleries, and theaters in Australia can be found here. The parks and gardens are also really quite exceptionally beautiful.

Shopping in Melbourne can hardly be matched anywhere else in Australia, and some of the sporting events in the city can bring the whole continent to a standstill for a few hours. Over all this there still hangs a strong sense of British tradition, though not everyone would admit to it.

## HISTORY
### A Boost From The Gold Rush

The founding of the city did not look at all promising to begin with. In 1803, the first disappointed settlers abandoned the area around Port Phillip Bay to try their luck in Tasmania. In 1835, John Batman returned from the island, tried a second

*Previous pages: Melbourne on the Yarra River.
Left: Italian delicacies on Lygon Street.*

*City map page 74, Guidepost pages 79-81*

time, and was soon convinced he had found the right location for a new settlement on the Yarra River. Proceeding in true settler tradition, Batman bought land, by means of an illegal contract, from the Woeworung and Kurnai Aborigines, who had lived in this area for hundreds of years.

Despite this injustice, Melbourne was founded in 1837. The city was named in honor of Lord Melbourne, the British prime minister at the time. It was the gold rush, however, which gave a really dramatic boost to Melbourne's development. In 1851, gold was found in nearby Ballarat, and Melbourne's harbor soon became a most important crossroads for everything and everyone who had any connection with gold. The University of Melbourne was founded in 1853. In 1854, the first railway line in Australia (Melbourne to Sandridge) was laid. In the

*Above: View of Melbourne's skyline. Right: Flinders Street Station isn't just a meeting place for Melburnians at night.*

1860s and 1870s many new industrial installations were built, and in 1880 Melbourne finally achieved global recognition thanks to the World Exhibition, which took place here.

For more than one hundred years, Melbourne was considered the cosmopolitan financial center of Australia. The city is still cosmopolitan, but, where business is concerned, Sydney has long taken over the number one rank. Critics of Melbourne like to tell you that over half the city's skyline was built on borrowed money and no one knows how it will ever be paid back. There is a good deal of truth in this. No other Australian state suffered quite as badly as Victoria from the economic crisis and high unemployment of the early 1990s and the capital, Melbourne, suffered most.

The Conservatives who recently came into power grabbed the political economy rudder firmly in both hands, changing the face of the city with a series of ambitious building plans. Now strollers can saunter from Southgate Centre – Melbourne's an-

swer to Sydney's Darling Harbour – on the new promenades on the southern banks of the Yarra River to the Crown Casino Complex, an equally popular and controversial amusement temple, in which everything revolves around Mammon.

Further large projects are currently being constructed: Federation Square across from Flinders Street Station, a new museum in Carlton and Docklands, a new city precinct west of the city.

Memories of the good old days can still be found in Melbourne, for example, at Como House in the suburb of South Yarra, built in 1847, and Rippon Lea (192 Hotham Street, Elsternwick). This fine 33-room residence, built in 1887, and surrounded by a beautiful garden, is well worth visiting.

### A TOUR OF THE TOWN

**Flinders Street Railway Station ❶** is considered the most attractive railway station in Australia – the remarkable clocks at its main entrance are a traditional meeting place for Melburnians and tourists alike.

**Federation Square**, across from the station, is to be embellished with a new art gallery showing works by Australian artists, a movie theater and a medical center, as well as cafes and restaurants, once work on this construction site is completed in the year 2001.

The story of immigration to Victoria is told in the **Immigration Museum ❷** located in the former Customs House on Flinders St., one of the few museums on this topic in Australia (daily 10:00 a.m. to 5:00 p.m.) On fair days, aim your steps towards the **★★Rialto Tower Observation Deck ❸** on the western end of Collins St; there is an excellent view of the city's expanse from the 55th floor of the skyscraper. Now turn your back to the city and cross **Yarra River** via Princes Bridge. In the summer, the residents of Melbourne enjoy the evening as they picnic along the river banks east of the bridge. Afterwards, a visit to one of the

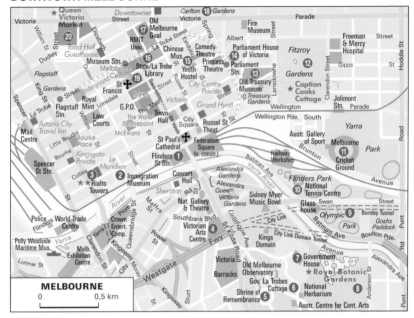

Melbourne
0          0,5 km

shows at the **Victorian Arts Centre** ❹, which comprises the concert hall and the Theatres Building (booking for all shows and concerts at ticketmaster Tel. 136166).

The **Performing Arts Museum** in the Theatres Building exhibits everything to do with the theater and what goes on there. Towards the south is the **National Gallery of Victoria**, (closed for renovations; upon reopening at the end of 2001 it will display a collection of art works from overseas).

On the other side of St. Kilda Road, you may observe Melbourne from another, equally important angle. **Alexandra Gardens** and **Queen Victoria Gardens** are as peaceful and relaxing to walk in as the nearby **King's Domain**, where the **Sidney Myer Music Bowl** provides a first-class, open-air entertainment venue. On no account should you miss the opportunity of spending a mellow

*Right: The Yarra River is both a popular picnic area and sports grounds.*

summer evening listening to a classical concert in this delightful and very popular setting!

At the southern end of the Kings Domain stands the **Shrine of Remembrance** ❺. This was built in memory of the Australian soldiers who fought and died in the First and Second World Wars, as well as in the conflicts in Korea, Malaysia, Borneo, and Vietnam. In spite of the somber memories associated with this shrine itself, there is a truly fantastic view of Melbourne's skyline from the small hill.

Hidden away near the old government building is **Governor La Trobe's Cottage** ❻, near Dallas Brooks Drive, the residence of the first Governor of Victoria. Another reminder of England is the much more imposing **Government House** ❼ to the north, which is a copy of Queen Victoria's residence, Osborne House, on the Isle of Wight.

A walk through the **\*Royal Botanical Gardens** ❽ which extend over 36 hectares, is best begun with a visit to the Visi-

tors' Centre at **Observatory Gate** on Birdwood Avenue. Not far from there is the **National Herbarium**, whose collection was founded by the first director of the Botanical Gardens, Baron Ferdinand von Müller, who was of German descent. The park is bordered to the north by the Yarra River, and you may return to the town center along its banks. Or you can choose to rent a bicycle (near Princes Bridge), at which point you will have a choice of 20 kilometers of idyllic cycling paths (13 kilometers up-river, and 7 kilometers down-river).

Sport dominates the scene once you cross Swan Street Bridge. **Olympic Park** ⑨ was the site of the 1956 Olympic Games. To the north, in the **National Tennis Centre** ⑩ in Melbourne Park, the world's best players compete in the Australian Open Tennis Championships every January, and at **Melbourne Cricket Ground** ⑪ (MCG) over 100,000 spectators gather for the Grand Final of Australian Rules Football in September. Whenever the world's top cricket teams hold their championship matches here, you will find that the spectator stands are almost as full.

The **Fitzroy Gardens** ⑫ are much quieter. The attraction for Anglophile visitors is **Captain Cook's Cottage**, open daily from 9:00 a.m. to 5:00 p.m. Captain James Cook's house came from Yorkshire, England. In 1934 it was packed into more than 300 crates, sent to Australia and rebuilt there.

Afterwards, go through **Treasury Gardens** to the **Old Treasury Museum** ⑬, where the exposition on the gold rush and the development of Melbourne deserves a visit. On the hill at the western end of Bourke Street is the imposing **Victoria Parliament House** ⑭ and the no less impressive **Princess Theatre**, opposite. This is a reminder of the gold rush of 1854, and is one of the most prestigious venues in the city's cultural night-life.

Bourke Street leads down the pedestrian zone Bourke Street Mall. Along the narrow parallel Little Bourke Street is Melbourne's **Chinatown**, where Chinese

gold prospectors settled in the mid 19th century. Those times are remembered in the **Chinese Museum** ⑮ (22-24 Cohen Place, Sun to Fri 10:00 a.m. to 5:00 p.m., Sat from noon). A visit here will put you in the right frame of mind for a walk around Chinatown, which will take you past historic buildings, to Chinese shops, bookstores, and markets, and would not be complete without a taste of Chinese cuisine.

While the restaurants along Little Bourke Street are mostly in the higher price category, Asian students eat their fill in the cheap eateries located in the side streets (Tattersalls Lane, Heffernan Lane). Economical and authentic is **Ong Food Court** (basement of the Welcome Hotel, Little Bourke Street between Swanson and Elizabeth Streets), at which one can compose one's own menu at little

*Above: Chinatown of Melbourne. Right: Queen Victoria Market is one of the lovliest markets in Australia.*

counters. However, if your taste leans more towards European food, then the **Hyatt Food Court** (at the corner of Russell and Collins Streets) will also provide a rich choice of self-service restaurants in more modern surroundings. Wherever you go, you should avoid the hour between noon and 1:00 p.m., when Melbourne's office workers take their lunch break, and seating becomes a problem.

After lunch, you can follow Russell Street in a northerly direction and after a few minutes you will arrive at the **State Library** and **La Trobe Library** ⑯. The oldest public library in Australia, it was established in 1856 and has more than one million books. A visit is really something for those with more specialized interests. Until the National Gallery of Victoria reopens, part of its collection will be kept in rooms in the former Museum of Victoria behind the State Library (entrance on Russell Street). A peek behind the old walls of **Old Melbourne Gaol** ⑰ is recommended, (built in 1845; Russell Street). This is the prison in which the no-

torious Ned Kelly, who had been hunted all over the state, was executed in 1880. This famous highwayman was just one of 104 criminals whose lives were cut short here by the rope. Today, a museum keeps alive the memory of those cruel times when justice was fierce and punishment severe (daily 9:30 a.m. to 4:30 p.m; night tours Sun and Wed at 7:30 p.m.). Afterwards, you might wish to make a little detour to **Carlton Gardens** ⑱. Next to the **Royal Exhibition Building**, a supreme achievement of Victorian architecture, the **IMAX movie theater** beckons with its curved giant screen. An additional attraction will be opening here at the end of 2001, when the Museum of Victoria, which is currently closed, moves in to its new rooms, under the name *Melbourne **Museum**.

Now stroll quietly down Swanston Street, and plunge right into the bustling city life of Melbourne. After passing **Town Hall**, **City Square**, and **St. Paul's Cathedral**, you will arrive back at Flinders Street Station, and if a glance at

the station clock does not remind you to rush off somewhere, why not go and have a beer in Young and Jackson's, a pub full of tradition and very popular with local Australian office workers after office hours. It is conveniently situated directly opposite Flinders Station.

### Shopping

Melbourne is notorious for its changeable weather. It is quite usual to experience all four seasons in a single day. If you are unlucky, you will soon learn this yourself; but never fear, Melbourne has plenty of attractions to offer visitors even in bad weather, and the most beautiful shopping arcades and alleys in the country are to be found right here, with numerous elegant shops and architecture.

Starting at **Bourke Street Mall**, you can stroll comfortably under a continuous roof through the **London Arcade** and the **Royal Arcade** or through the **Causeway** to Little Collins Street and on to **Block Place** and prestigious *Block Arcade** to

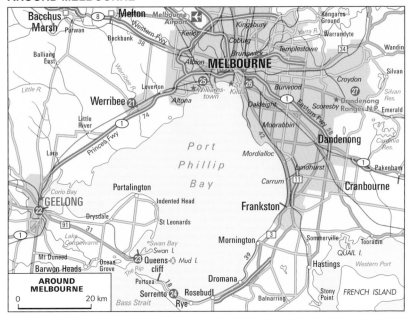

Collins Street, through **Centreway** and **Centre Place** to Flinders Lane and back through **Campbell Arcade** and **Degraves St.** to Flinders St. North of Bourke Street Mall the **Melbourne Central ⓳** (Lonsdale and La Trobe Streets) shopping center stretches over two city blocks with numerous shops, a Japanese shopping centre, restaurants and a food court. The eye-catcher of the shopping centre is a gigantic 19th-century bastion. In Toorak Road and Chapel Street (both are in South Yarra) many fashion designers display their work, some of which is extremely exclusive. On Saturday mornings there is only one place for a Melburnian to go shopping – *Queen Victoria Market ⓴* (corner of Victoria and Peel Streets). There are fruit, vegetables, meat, and fresh fish, as well as bric-a-brac, among the goods offered for sale at more than 1,000 stalls. The color and variety of the bustling market activities and the veritable Babel of different languages that are spoken by Melbourne's multiplicity of nationalities, make the visit to

Queen Victoria Market an unforgettable experience. (Opening times, Tues and Thurs 6:00 a.m. to 2:00 p.m.; Fri. 6:00 a.m. to 4:00 p.m.; Sat 6:00 a.m. to 1:00 p.m.; Sun 9:00 a.m. to 4:00 p.m.; Sun no food is sold).

**Excursions in the Surrounding Areas**

Queen Victoria Market is also the best place to stock up on provisions for a good picnic. The surroundings of Melbourne are in fact ideal for this sort of relaxing activity. The trip by car or bus to Geelong is very pleasant. Stop on the way in **Werribee ㉑** at the **Mansion at Werribee**, built from 1874 to 1877, and neighboring **Open Range Zoo**. The *National Wool Museum ㉒* in **Geelong** is one of Australia's loveliest museums, – it is one of the ironies of fate that this sector of the economy, along with the former flourishing car industry, is also in the midst of a deep depression. The museum gives a detailed glimpse into the lives of sheep farmers. On three floors, you will find

78        *City map page 74*

displayed everything to do with wool, from sheep to pullovers. Many of the exhibits may be handled, and you will come across some astounding objects and statistics. From Geelong, the Bellarine Highway leads to the lovely old town of **Queensclff** ㉔ at the entrance to Port Phillip Bay. It dates back to the days of the last century when the area flourished during the boom and gold rush years. Every other hour a ferry sails across to Sorrento, an attractive resort town on Mornington Peninsula, and from here you can return to Victoria's capital. Or drive to **★Williamstown** ㉕, which has some good pubs and restaurants right on the shores of Port Phillip Bay, with a fine view of Melbourne's skyline. At least one excursion on the tramway is almost a duty during a stay in Melbourne (perhaps in one of the over 60-year-old trams) out to the suburb of **★St. Kilda** ㉖. When the weather is fine, half of Melbourne promenades through the **★Arts and Crafts Market** along the Esplanade. Street musicians and artists offer all sorts of entertainments. Follow this up with a visit to a kiosk on the St. Kilda Pier, or a coffee on **★Acland Street**. Until the 1980s, this street's character owed much to its postwar Jewish immigrants. Relics of this era are the cake shops such as the Monarch (Number 13), where sweet, tempting cakes and confectioner's goods are piled high in the shop window, or the Scheherazade Restaurant. The far-out decor of a hairdresser famed throughout the city and numerous café-bars attract the younger crowd. Kilda is Melbourne's shrill beach side, where you can find anything – except boredom. An alternative would be an expedition into the **★Dandenong Ranges** ㉗, covered with eucalyptus and tree-ferns. The National Park and the magnificent **National Rhododendron Gardens** offer lovely walks. Children will enjoy a trip on the steam train Puffing Billy from Belgrave to Emerald Lake Park.

## MELBOURNE (☎ 03)

**ℹ** **Victoria Tourism Information Service**, Tel. 1800-132842. **Victoria Visitor Information Centre**, Melbourne Town Hall, Swanston St, corner of Little Collins St, Tel. 96589955, for booking accommodation: Tel. 69501522, Mon-Fri 9:00 a.m.-5:30 p.m., Sat and Sun until 5:00 p.m.

Right next door: **City Experience Centre & Melbourne Greeter Service**, Tel. 96589955, provides tourist information on computer screens in foreign languages, and arranges contact with locals sharing similar interests and foreign-language knowledge, who then offer a free tour; registration at least three days in advance. Mon-Fri 10:00 a.m.-7:00 p.m., Sat and Sun 10:00 a.m.-5:00 p.m.

**Information booths** in the pedestrian zone Bourke Street Mall (Mon-Thurs 9:00 a.m.-5:00 p.m., Fri 9:00-7:00 p.m., Sat 10:00-4:00 p.m., Sun and holidays 11:00 a.m.-4:00 p.m.) and in Flinders Street Station (opening hours as for Bourke St Mall, Fri only until 6:00 p.m.).

**RACV** (automobile association), 360 Bourke St, Tel. 131955. **National parks and nature reserves**: central telephone information service of **Parks Victoria**, Tel. 131963. Information brochures concerning individual areas in the Visitor Information Centre (see above) as well as at the NRE Information Centre, 8 Nicholson St, East Melbourne, Mon-Fri 9:00 a.m.-5:00 p.m.

The daily newspaper The Age (especially the Friday supplement EG = Entertainment Guide) as well as the broschure Melbourne Events (available at the Visitor Information Centre) provide information about current events of all types.

**🛬** **Melbourne Airport (Tullamarine)** lies approximately 22 km northwest of the city's center. The Skybus travels between the airport and downtown (Skybus / Greyhound Pioneer Terminal, 58 Franklin St) every 30 minutes and costs $A 10. A taxi will set you back between $A 25-30.

**🏨** **⊙⊙⊙ Downtowner on Lygon**, 66 Lygon St, Carlton, Tel. 96635555. **Eden on the Park**, 6 Queens Rd, Tel. 92502222. **Grand Hyatt Melbourne**, 123 Collins St, Tel. 96571234 and 1800-339494. **Le Meridien at Rialto**, 495 Collins St, Tel. 96209111. **Novotel Bayside Melbourne**, 16 The Esplanade, St. Kilda, Tel. 95255522. **The Chiefley on Flemington Melbourne**, 5 Flemington Rd, North Melbourne, Tel. 93299344. **Rydges Riverwalk Melbourne**, corner of Bridge Rd and River St, Richmond, Tel. 92461200.

**⊙⊙ Astoria City Travel Inn**, 288 Spencer St, Tel.

96706801. **Cosmopolitan Motor Inn**, 6 Carlisle St, St. Kilda, Tel. 95340781. **Lygon Lodge**, 220 Lygon St, Carlton, Tel. 96636633. **Magnolia Court Boutique Hotel**, 101 Powlett St, East Melbourne, Tel. 94194222. **Marco Polo Inn**, corner of Harker St and Flemington Rd, North Melbourne, Tel. 93291788. **Park Avenue**, 461 Royal Parade, Tel. 93806761. **Ramada Inn**, 539 Royal Parade, both Parkville, Tel. 93808131. **Richmond Hill Hotel**, 353 Church St, Richmond, Tel. 94286501 (less expensive rooms as well). **The Victoria Hotel**, 215 Little Collins St, Tel. 96530441. **Tolarno Boutique Hotel**, 42 Fitzroy St, St. Kilda, Tel. 905370200.

⑤ **Chapman St YHA**, 76 Chapman St, North Melbourne, Tel. 93283595. **City Centre Private Hotel**, 22 Little Collins St, Tel. 96545401. **Kingsgate Private Hotel**, 131 King St, Tel. 96294171. **Miami Motor Inn**, 13 Hawke St, West Melbourne, Tel. 93298499. **Olembia Private Hotel**, 96 Barkly St, Tel. 95371412. **Queensberry Hill YHA**, 78 Howard St. **Toad Hall Guesthouse**, 441 Elizabeth St, Tel. 96009010.

❌ There is a plethora of choice in Melbourne. It used to be possible to clearly classify the various national cuisines to certain streets and neighborhoods, today things are not quite so clearly defined.

**Chinatown** is of course the center for Asian restaurants (mostly Malaysian, Thai, Cantonese and Shanghai cuisine). Victoria St, Richmonds „Little Saigon", is the **Vietnamese center.**

**Turkish** and **Libyan** food is mostly served along Sydney Road in Brunswick. **Italian** cuisne can be found everywhere, especially, however, along Lygon St in Carlton and peripheral streets.

One of the livliest streets for a stroll and delightful snacks is Brunswick St in Fitzroy. Cafe-bars and restaurants abound here – the decor is very hip, the cuisine eclectic.

*CHINESE:* **Empress of China**, 120 Little Bourke St, Tel. 96631883. **Shark Fin Inn**, 50 Little Bourke St, Tel. 96622681, and **Shark Fin House**, 131 Little Bourke St, Tel. 96631555.

*GREEK:* **Greek Deli & Taverna**, 583 Chapel St, South Yarra, Tel. 98273724.

*INDIAN:* **Guru da Dhaba**, 240 Johnston St, Fitzroy, Tel. 94869155.

*ITALIAN* **Papa Gino's Pizza Restaurant**, 221 Lygon St, Tel. 93475758. **Zia Teresa Restaurant**, 90 Lygon St, Tel. 93801218. Both in Carlton.

*JAPANESE* **Akita**, corner of Courtney / Blackwood Streets, North Melbourne, Tel. 93265766.

*MALAYSIAN* **Chinta Ria Restaurant**, 182 Brunswick St, Fitzroy, Tel. 93492599. Three successful branches in Prahran and St. Kilda.

*TURKISH:* **Alasya**, 555 Sydney Rd, Brunswick, Tel. 93872679.

🎵 *NIGHT-LIFE:* Melbourne is famed for having the most varied cultural life in Australia. For musicals,the **Princess Theatre**, 163 Spring St, is the place to be. The extravagant productions, famous throughout all Australia, are often sold out months in advance. The theaters of the **Victorian Arts Centre**, 100 St. Kilda Rd, also have something interesting to offer, as does the nearby **Playbox Theatre** in the CUB Malthouse on Sturt Street; bookings through *Ticketmaster*, Tel. 136166 and 136100.

*DISCOS:* You can dance the night away in a variety of discos: **Chasers Nightclub**, 386 Chapel St, South Yarra. **Metro Nightclub**, 20-30 Bourke St, Tel. 96634288, only Wed-Sat 9:00 p.m.-5:00 a.m. **The Night Cat**, 141 Johnston St, Fitzroy.

*PUBS:* Not quite so much dancing, but rather more drinking is done is some cosy pubs: **College Lawn**, 36 Greville St, Prahran. **Gowings Grace Darling**, corner of Smith and Peel Streets, Collingwood.

**Pumphouse Brewery**, 128 Nicholson St, Fitzroy. **Rainbow Hotel**, 27 David St (not far from Brunswick St), Fitzroy.

**Redback Brewery**, 75 Flemington Rd, North Melbourne.

**The Stork Hotel**, 504 Elizabeth St, City.

**Young and Jackson's**, 1 Swanston St.

🏛 **Australian Centre for Contemporary Art**, since 2000 in the new Malthouse Plaza next to the CUB Malthouse, Sturt Street (south of the Victorian Arts Centre).

**Chinese Museum**, 22 Cohen Place, Tel. 96622888, Sun-Fri 10:00 a.m.-4:.30 p.m. Sat from noon.

**Jewish Museum of Australia**, 26 Alma Rd, St. Kilda, Tel. 95340083. Sun 11:00 a.m.-5:00 p.m., Tues-Thurs 10:00-4:00 p.m.

**National Gallery of Victoria**, closed for renovations until approximately the end of 2001. A part of the collection is currently on display in the National Gallery on Russell (behind the State Library; entrance on Russell St).

**Performing Arts Museum** und **George Adams Gallery**, both in the Theatre Building of the Victorian Arts Centre, 100 St. Kilda Rd, Tel. 92818300. Mon-Sat 9:00 a.m.-11:00 p.m., Sun 10:00 a.m.-5:00 p.m..

**Polly Woodside Melbourne Maritime Museum**, Lorimer St East, Southbank (close to the new Exhibition Centre), Tel. 96999760. *Yarra River* sailboat was built in Ireland in 1885 and houses today many exhibits on seafaring. Daily, 10:00 a.m.-4:00 p.m.

**Scienceworks Museum & Planetarium**, 2 Booker St, Spotswood (train from Flinders St towards Williamstown or Werribee, get off in Spotswood), Tel. 93924800, open daily 10:00 a.m.-4:30 p.m. Technological museum with many exhibits which can be touched. The planeterium, which opened in 1999, hosts interesting events.

**January**: From mid-January to its end, the best tennis players of the world meet for the *Australian Open*. In summer (December-end of February) there are numerous open-air events in the Botanical Gardens and in the Sidney Myer Music Bowl; many of these performances are free.

**February**: In mid-February, the Chinese population clebrates the *Chinese New Year Festival* – an absolute must, not just for the Chinese.

**March**: The *Moomba Festival* has been celebrated here for over 30 years under the motto *Let's get together and have fun* , with theater, art, cabaret and a Mardi Gras parade.

**September**: As winter comes to a close, the *A.F.L. Grand Final* in Australian Rules Football takes place on the Melbourne Cricket Ground in front of some 100 000 spectators.

**October / November**: The absolute highlight of the year is the *Melbourne International Festival* in October, a great festival of theater, music and art, with many international stars and numerous free open-air events; the *Fringe Festival* runs at the same time, a festival of alternate life-style choices, featuring many international artistes now living in various Australian cities. The *Melbourne Cup, the* Australian horse race, takes place on the first Tuesday in November, and for a short time the entire country grinds to a halt. (Holiday in Victoria).

*SIGHTSEEING:* The wine-red, free **City Circle Tram** runs daily from 10:00 a.m. to 6:00 p.m. (in summer sometimes somewhat longer) every 10 minutes around the city. Route: Flinders, Spencer, La Trobe and Spring St; in both directions.

The **City Explorer** covers all important sights in the inner city area and adjacent districts, one may get off and on as often as one likes. 16 bus stops. daily on the hour, from 10:00 a.m. to 5:00 p.m. from the Town Hall, Swanston St. Day ticket $A 23, Two-day tickets $A 35. Information and bookings at Tel. 96539788.

*OBSERVATION DECK:* **Rialto Tower Observation Deck**, Collins Street, Mon-Thurs 11:00 a.m.-10:00 p.m., Fri and Sat 10:00 a.m.-10:00 p.m.

*MARKETS:* **Arts Centre Sunday Market**, along St. Kilda Rd from the Victorian Arts Centre to Princes Bridge, and further beneath the bridge to Southgate Centre. Arts and crafts. Sun 9:30 a.m.-5:30 p.m.

**Queen Victoria Market**, "Vic Markets", corner of Elizabeth and Victoria Sts. Over 1000 booths with food, delicatessen and much more. Tues and Thurs 6:00 a.m.-2:00 p.m., Fri 6:00 a.m.-6:00 p.m., Sat 6:00 a.m.-1:00 p.m. and Sun 9:00 a.m.-4:00 p.m. (no food on Sundays!)

**Esplanade Art and Craft Market**, Upper Esplanade, St. Kilda. Arts and crafts, Sun 10:00 a.m.-4:00 p.m.

**Greville Street Market**, Grattan Gardens, Greville St, Prahran. Arts and crafts and bric-a-brac. Sun noon-5:00 p.m.

**Lygon Court Piazza & Craft Market**, Lygon Court Shopping Centre, 380 Lygon St, Carlton. Ceramics, jewelry, decorations. Every second Sunday 10:00 a.m.-5:00 p.m.

**Prahan Market**, 163-185 Commercial Rd, South Yarra. Food and delicatessen are sold in a market hall built in 1864. Tues and Thurs 8:00 a.m.-5:00 p.m., Fri 7:00 a.m.-6:00 p.m., Sat 7:00 a.m.-1:00 p.m.

*PARKS AND GARDENS:* hardly any other Australian city offers more green areas in the city center. The following are the most attractive parks: **Royal Botanic Gardens**, **Kings Domain**, **Fitzroy and Treasury Gardens**, **Exhibition Gardens**, **Carlton Gardens** and **Shrine Reserve**.

*DAY TRIPS:* The best **wine estates** are in the area around Yarra Glen in the Yarra Valley, northeast of Melbourne by the Maroondah Highway. A recommended detour is the **Healesville Sanctuary**, a reserve for Australian animals in their natural bush environement with excellent tours by the rangers. Badger Creek Rd, Tel. 03-59572800, daily 9:00 a.m.-5:00 p.m.

Across from the sanctuary is the **Galeena Beek Living Cultural Centre**. It was built on the site of the former Corranderk Mission Station for Aborigines. An exhibition tells about Corranderk and the fate of the local inhabitants. Daily 9:00 a.m.-6:00 p.m.

**The Mansion at Werribee Park**, 34 km southwest of Melbourne. A grandiose mansion built in 1877, surrounded by a lovely park, open daily from 10:00 a.m.

The **Open Range Zoo at Werribee** right next to it house some typical grassland inhabitants such as giraffes, zebras and antilopes, daily 9:00 a.m.-6:00 p.m. check this hour.

The **Dandenong Ranges**, some 32 km east of Melbourne offer some attractive landscape. Take the train to Belgrave, and then continue with the nostalgic stem engine *Puffing Billy*. Particularly thrilling for children!

**Yarra River**: *Melbourne River Cruises* offer daily cruises on the river. They begin at the moorings on Princes Bridge across from Flinders Street Station. A trip upriver or downriver takes about 90 minutes and costs $A 15, round-trip costs $A 28. Advance booking Tel. 96141215.

*Melbourne*

# AUSTRALIA'S GREEN ISLAND

**TASMANIA**
**HOBART**
**PORT ARTHUR**
**EAST COAST**
**LAUNCESTON**
**CRADLE MOUNTAIN-LAKE**
**ST. CLAIR NATIONAL PARK**

*Tasmania*

## TASMANIA

Before traveling to **\*\*Tasmania**, it is probably best to forget everything you have ever associated with Australia, because Tasmania is quite different from the mainland. The people living here refer to themselves as "Tassies", and really do not like being called Aussies. Indeed, quite a few differences will soon become apparent when traveling in Tasmania (which measures roughly 319 kilometers long by 296 kilometers wide ) compared with the mainland which lies 240 kilometers away across the often stormy **Bass Strait**. Life here is more peaceful, the soil is more fertile, and the landscape, set between white sandy beaches and snow-covered mountains, is quite unspoilt. The very air seems clearer, and even on hot summer days there is a fresh, cooling breeze.

Tasmania lies far away from the main stream of tourism. It is the state with the most national parks, so that in many places the natural environment appears completely untouched by people. Wherever industry does threaten to disrupt the balance of nature, Tassies will raise their voices in protest, and even use force if

*Previous pages: Hobart Harbour is extremely popular – and not only with sailing enthusiasts! Left: At the sea near Bicheno.*

necessary (with considerable success, in fact), as in the case of a huge dam planned for a reservoir on the Gordon and Franklin Rivers. Tassies appear to live in harmony with nature, which is why so many nature lovers find the island such a fascinating place to visit.

## HISTORY

The Aborigines probably settled in the area of present-day Tasmania about 50,000 years ago. Later, rising sea levels following the last ice age separated the area from the mainland and turned it into an island.

In 1642 the Dutch explorer Abel Tasman discovered the island for the European world, and named it Van Diemen's Land after Anthony Van Diemen, the governor of the Dutch East Indies at the time. After that came the rather more famous captains James Cook and William Bligh, then the British navigator Matthew Flinders. However, all of them initially sailed past Tasmania, showing no great interest in the island. It was not until 7 September 1803 that Lieutenant John Bowen landed on the island, in order to establish a British presence there before the French had a chance to do so. After that, things began to develop rapidly. Hobart was founded in 1804, and in 1842

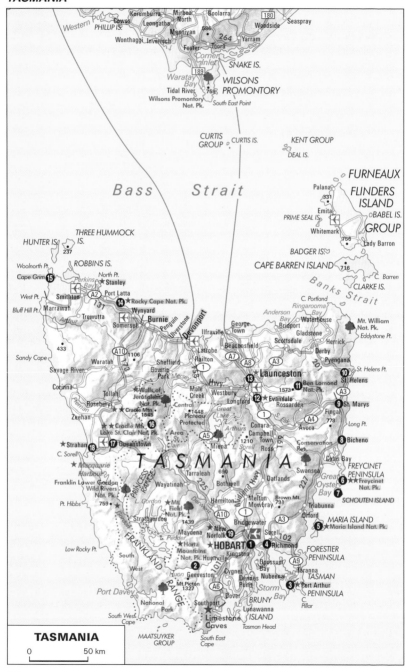

TASMANIA

0        50 km

was given its borough charter. In 1825 Van Diemen's Land became a separate colony, and in 1855 was finally renamed Tasmania.

History was overshadowed by the authorities' brutal treatment of white convicts. A total of 60,000 were transported to Tasmania, where all that awaited many of them was the certainty of an early death.

For most convicts, the end of the road was Port Arthur, today a much visited tourist attraction.

But the Aborigines suffered a fate much worse than that endured by the white convicts. In no other Australian colony were they exterminated more deliberately or ruthlessly than in Tasmania. As recently as ten years ago, the very existence of their descendants was officially denied. These were, in particular, the great-grandchildren of American and British whalers and Tasmanian Aborigine women, who had been sequestered to the Furneaux Islands and kept there as slaves.

## *HOBART

*Hobart ❶, the capital, with a population of around 180,000, is situated in the south of the island. If you fly in from one of Australia's mainland cities, this is where you will land, and it makes an ideal starting point. Many yachting enthusiasts consider Hobart to be one of the most beautiful harbors in the world, and most tourists would agree.

Much of the city's activity still takes place around **Sullivan's Cove**, where Lieutenant-Governor David Collins founded Hobart on 20 February, 1804. Every year, at the end of December, when the yachts taking part in the Sydney to Hobart Race are moored in **Constitution Dock,** is the time for one of the hottest parties in Australia's social calendar, although for most of the rest of the year the atmosphere can best be described as relaxed and peaceful. Round off the day

with a dinner at Mures Fish Centre (Constitution Dock). You have a choice of The Upper Deck (a la carte), the Lower Deck (the finest fish 'n chips), or the Japanese Sushi Bar, Orizuzu. Afterwards, you can go for your obligatory beer (the local Cascade brew, of course) at the Drunken Admiral on **Victoria Dock**, which actually looks as though many a ship's captain once dropped anchor here after a stormy passage across the Bass Strait.

If you have an urge to end the evening with a little "flutter," you could always try your luck in **Wrest Point Casino** (410 Sandy Bay Road, open daily until 3 am; Fri. and Sat until 4 am).

On Saturday mornings there is really only one place to be in Hobart – *Salamanca Place**. The whole town seems to foregather here when the busy flea market opens among the ancient warehouses (built between 1835 and 1860). The only quiet place is in the **Battery Point** district, situated just above the market, so named because of the canons installed there in 1818.

The best policy is to follow the signposted **Tourist Trail** (information at the tourist office in Elizabeth Street), which will lead you to numerous historical buildings and some good restaurants.

Australia's oldest military barracks, built in 1811 and still in use, are the **Anglesea Barracks** in Davey Street. Also worth a visit are the **Town Hall** (Macquarie Street) depicting Captain Cook's ship Endeavour on its facade, the **Theatre Royal** (Australia's oldest theater, located in Campbell Street), and **Parliament House** (on Salamanca Place).

While the old part of Hobart is always fascinating, modern Hobart, stretching from Murray Street (with the Centrepoint Shopping Centre) to Elizabeth Street (with a pedestrian precinct) to Argyle Street, does not offer quite as much excitement. There are interesting cycling routes along the **Derwent River**, and

*Tasmania*

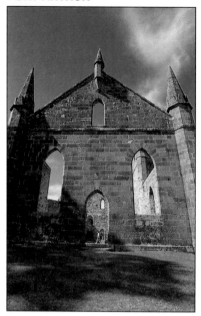

**\*PORT ARTHUR**

from **\*Mount Wellington** (1271 meters), with walking trails, (20 kilometers) north of Hobart, you will have the best view of both the city and the river.

**Mount Nelson**, to the south, is a much closer alternative, though only 340 meters high. On the summit, the Signal Station Teahouse invites you to take a pleasant break for tea, in the afternoon or at any other time of the day.

Further south, Huon Highway (A6) will take you via **Kingston**, a 2-kilometer detour to Kingston Beach, and the fruit-growing area around Huonville to **Southport**.

Before this, though, a side road turns off at Geeveston and heads westward towards the **\*Hartz Mountains National Park ❷**. From **Hartz Peak**, with a height of some 1255 , the visitor can admire the rather spectacular view over the large moorland area beneath.

*Above: Memories of the past – left, in Port Arthur, and right, beside the bridge at Richmond. Right: The harbor at Bicheno.*

A favorite day trip from Hobart is to **\*Port Arthur ❸** (102 kilometers east). Between 1830 and 1877, some 12,500 convicts were transported to the Port Arthur area on the **Tasman Peninsula**, where conditions were so harsh that they usually died fairly soon after arriving. This, the most notorious penal colony in the entire British Empire, was not closed until 1877, when the influx of convicts from Britain ceased, and the remaining convicts were housed in Hobart Gaol. Disastrous bushfires in 1884, 1895, and 1897 reduced many buildings in Port Arthur to rubble and ashes. Today, the ruins of Port Arthur, surrounded by a delightful bush and coastal landscape (the turn-off at **Eaglehawk Neck** leads to sites of interest at **\*Tasman Arch** and **\*Devils Kitchen**), are the most visited tourist attraction of Tasmania. The centerpiece of the site is the four-story ruins of the **Penitentiary**, built between 1842 and 1857. Behind it, on a slight rise, are further ruins of former homes and warehouses, and of the hospital (1842). From here, there is a superb view of the bay at **Manson's Cove**, where a ferry sails four times a day to the **Isle of the Dead**. A great many convicts and prison guards found their last resting place here.

Another site worth visiting is the **church** situated to the east (built 1836-7), where over 1000 convicts were obliged to sit in chains on narrow wooden benches and listen to the word of God. The **Asylum** (1867), a former lunatic asylum, today houses a museum and Visitor Centre which provides excellent information about Port Arthur. If none of this is gruesome enough for you, during the summer you may go on evening ghost hunts (no extra charge if you see one). Ideally, the return journey to Hobart should take in the communities of **Nubeena, Premaydena** and **Koonya** across the beautiful Tasman Peninsula, before rejoining the Arthur Highway at Eaglehawk Neck.

## THE EAST COAST

A detour to **\*Richmond ❹** in the interior is a good way to begin a drive along the east coast. A charming colonial atmosphere reminiscent of "the old country" (Britain) has been preserved all along Bridge Road. At the gates of this town of 2200 inhabitants, Australia's oldest bridge (built 1823 to 1825 by convicts) crosses a small river, on the banks of which stands **St. John's Church**, Australia's oldest Catholic church. Here, there are ideal places for a picnic. Before carrying on towards the east coast, take a look at **Richmond Gaol** (1825). You will reach the coast at Orford, where, from nearby **Triabunna**, a ferry makes the trip over to **\*Maria Island National Park ❺**, a rewarding visit for its interesting wildlife and historic ruins dating from the colonial period. If you decide to stay on the main island, the coast offers some wild and romantic panoramas and beautiful

beaches. Among these are Spiky Beach (before Swansea, founded in 1821), and **Nine Mile Beach**, on Great Oyster Bay, on the way to Coles Bay, and reached by a gravel track. **\*\*Freycinet National Park ❻**, with its wonderful beaches, lonely walks (**\*Wineglass Bay Track**) and good climbing, offers some of the most beautiful landscapes in Tasmania. From Freycinet there are good connections by boat to **Schouten Island ❼**. This and the nearby Maria Island are both absolute "musts" for visitors with plenty of time. However, do make sure you buy provisions at Swansea or Hobart, as the walks can take several days. In **Bicheno ❽** there is hardly anything left to remind one of the long-gone days of whaling. Instead, there are several inviting sandy beaches right in the center of town. **Dennison Beach** extends for more than 10 kilometers northward, where long stretches of the Tasman Highway meander beside the coast. At **St. Mary's ❾**, a decision has to be made: the Tasman Highway runs along to the popular bathing and angling town

*Tasmania*

of **St. Helen's** ⑩, on **George's Bay**. At the old tin mining town of **Pyengana**, the 11-kilometer detour to **\*St. Columba Falls** (90 meters high) is recommended, before going on to **Derby** and **Scottsdale**. Both communities owe their modest prosperity to the fertile soil of the surrounding area. In winter it is worth making a detour at Targa, to get to **Ben Lomond National Park** ⑪ where good winter sports facilities are available on the slopes of Legges Tor (1573 meters). The **Esk Main Road** leads through flat grazing land into the interior, where you will reach the **Midland Highway** at Conara. From here, turning south, it is a distance of only 143 kilometers back to Hobart. Launceston is some 54 kilometers to the north. Do not forget to stop at historic **\*Evandale** ⑫, especially in mid-February when the great Penny Farthing Race takes place. Whichever direction

*Above: The old school at Launceston is a reminder of the early period. Right: A trip on the Tamar River with the Lady Stelfox.*

you choose to take, your journey should in any case end in the north of Tasmania, at Launceston.

### \*LAUNCESTON

**\*Launceston** ⑬, with 67,000 inhabitants, is the second largest town in Tasmania. Its foundation in 1804 also makes it the third oldest town in Australia, and that is why this town located on the **Tamar River** is so fascinating. Wherever you look, there is history: **Franklin House** (built in 1838, 6 kilometers to the south), **Entally House** (1820, Hadspen), and **Macquarie House** (1830, Wellington Street). In between these are numerous parks and gardens. The miniature landscape of **Penny Royal World** offers various attractions, a gun powder factory, a windmill, an old railway and a paddle wheel steamer. Just outside the town is the impressive, deep **\*Cataract Gorge**, which can be negotiated by paddle steamer or which you can stroll around on **Cataract Walk. Queen Victoria Mu-**

seum (Wellington Street; a complete survey of Tasmanian history) and the old-fashioned bar of the **Batman Fawkner Inn**, founded in 1822 (35-39 Cameron Street) call for a visit. Launceston is an excellent place to begin a trip along the north coast. The best plan is to follow the west bank of the Tamar River for the first few kilometers until you get to **Exeter**, and then turn off westward in the direction of **Devonport** on the Mersey River which, for many tourists, is where their Tasmania trip begins. Three times a week, the car ferry from Melbourne docks here after a 15-hour crossing of the Bass Strait.

The Bass Highway goes via Burnie and Wynyard beside **\*Rocky Cape National Park ⑭** (beautiful beaches, good bushwalks) to **\*Stanley**, founded in 1835, dominated by a 143 meters high rock, **The Nut**. Stanley has hardly changed in 150 years. After that, if you want to travel further west, beyond **Smithton**, a road that is for the most part unsurfaced leads to **Cape Grim ⑮**, where you can breathe the cleanest air in the world, or at least that is what scientific readings at the cape are supposed to have proved and what locals will tell you.

## \*\*CRADLE MOUNTAIN-LAKE ST. CLAIR NATIONAL PARK

One of the most beautiful roads in Tasmania takes you from Launceston to **\*\*Cradle Mountain-Lake St. Clair National Park ⑯**, which enjoys the special protection of inclusion on UNESCO's World Heritage List because of its natural and cultural importance.

After passing through Westbury, Deloraine and Mole Creek (the **\*King Solomon Caves** are nearby), you will see the ranges of the **Great Western Tiers** and the **\*Walls of Jerusalem National Park**, which offer good bushwalks, beginning to rise up to the south. An unsurfaced road turns off Highway C132 towards **\*\*Cradle Mountain** and takes you right into the mountainous heart of Tasmania. Spend the night either in the

luxurious Cradle Mountain Lodge, or in the adjoining campsite (with its pleasant stonework and open fireplace), in the Cradle Mountain Highlander Cabins, or in simple huts in Waldheim, operated by the Visitors' Centre. It is some 2 kilometers from here to the Visitors' Centre, and a further 5.5 kilometers to **Lake Dove**, with spectacular views of Cradle Mountain (1545 meters). Halfway along this route, the road forks towards **Waldheim**, to the former residence of Gustav Weindorfer, instrumental in the creation of this national park. His home has been turned into a museum. There are several possible day tours to go on in **Cradle Valley** and around **Lake Dove**, but the most popular one is the **Overland Track**, 80 kilometers long and lasting six to eight days, (registration at the Visitors' Centre is required) which ends at Lake St. Clair. Provisions, weatherproof clothing (the weather is changeable and temperatures

*Above: Lake Lilla and Lake Dove in Cradle Mountain-Lake St. Clair National Park.*

can be low, even in summer!) and a tent (between November and March, most huts will have already been booked) should be taken along on this beautiful, albeit rather demanding, bushwalk. The Overland Track ends near **Derwent Bridge**, which can be reached by car along the west coast road. This route passes **Queenstown** ⓱, rather a sorry sight as giant copper mines have turned the area into an eerie, barren moonscape. *Strahan ⓲, the only port on the west coast, and a good starting point for trips to *Macquarie Harbour** and the 193-kilometer-long *Gordon River**, is a charming sight by comparison. Further west, rafting trips are popular on the **Franklin River**, reached on Lyell Highway before meeting with the **King William Range**. *Mount Field National Park**, with good skiing facilities in the winter, and *Gordon River Road**, leading to **Lake Gordon** and **Lake Pedder**, are possible choices for a detour, before returning to Hobart via historic *New Norfolk ⓳ on the **Derwent River**.

## TASMANIA (☎ 03)

**CRADLE MOUNTAIN: Visitor Centre**, Tel. 64921133.

**DEVONPORT: Visitor Information Centre**, 5 Best St, Tel. 64244466.

**HOBART: Tasmanian Travel and Information Centre**, corner of Elizabeth and Davey Sts, Tel. 62308233. **Tasmanian Travel and Information Centre**, corner of Paterson and St. John Sts, Tel. 63363122.

**STRAHAN: Visitor Information Centre**, The Esplanade, Tel. 64717622.

**National Parks Pass**: is required for a visit to the National Park. It can be obtained at all *Visitor Information Centres* in Tasmania, on the ferries as well as at the *Land Information Services*, 134 Macquarie St, Hobart. A day ticket costs $A 9; less expensive is the the Holiday Pass for $A 30, valid for two months and a car.

**The car ferry** *Spirit of Tasmania* plies between Melbourne and Devonport. Departure in Port Melbourne Mon, Wed, Fri 6:00 p.m., return Sat, Tues, Thurs 6:00 p.m. The journey takes 14.5 hours.

From December to April the *Devil Cat* catamaran also plies between Port Melbourne and Georgetown (north of Launceston), in Januar daily, otherwise 3-4 times a week, the journey takes 6 hours. Book as early as possible in summer; Reservations for both ferries and catamaran TT Line, Tel. 132010.

**HOBART: ⊜⊜⊜ Hotel Lenna of Hobart**, 20 Runnymede Street, Battery Point, Tel. 62323900. **Quest Waterfront Hobart**, 3 Brooke Street, Tel. 62248630.

⊜⊜ **Barton Cottage**, Hampden Road, Battery Point, Tel. 62241606. **Country Comfort Hadleys Hotel**, 34 Murray Street, Tel. 62234355. **Cromwell Cottage**, 6 Cromwell Street, Battery Point, Tel. 62236734.

⊜ **Sandy Bay Caravan Park**, Peel Street, Tel. 62251264. **Adelphi Court YHA**, 17 Stoke Street, Newtown, Tel. 62284829.

**BICHENO: ⊜⊜ Bicheno Holiday Village**, Esplanade, Tel. 63751171.

**CRADLE MOUNTAIN: ⊜⊜⊜ Cradle Mountain Lodge**, Tel. 64921303. ⊜⊜ **Cradle Mountain Highlanders Cabins**, Tel. 64921116. ⊜ **Cradle Mountain Campgrounds**, Tel. 64921395.

**DEVONPORT: ⊜⊜ Edgewater Motor Inn**, 2 Thomas Street, East Devonport, Tel. 64278441. **MacFie Manor**, 44 Macfie Street, Tel. 64241719. ⊜ **Abel Tasman Caravan Park**, 6 Wright Street, East Devonport, Tel. 64278794. **MacWright House YHA**, 115 Middle Road, Tel. 64245696.

**FREYCINET NATIONAL PARK: ⊜⊜⊜ Freycinet Lodge**, in the National Park, Tel. 62570101.

⊜ **Iluka Backpackers YHA Coles Bay**, Esplanade, 1 km from the enttrance to the National Park, Tel. 62570115.

**LAUNCESTON: ⊜⊜⊜ Novotel Launceston**, 29 Cameron Street, Tel. 63343434.

⊜⊜ **Hillview House**, 193 George Street, Tel. 63317388.

⊜ **Treasure Island Caravan Park**, Glen Dhu Street, Tel. 63442600.

**PORT ARTHUR: ⊜⊜ Port Arthur Motor Inn**, Arthur Highway, Historic Site Port Arthur, Tel. 62502101.

⊜ **Roseview YHA**, Champ Street, Tel. 62502311.

**QUEENSTOWN: ⊜ Mount View Holiday Lodge**, 1 Penghana Road, Highway to Strahan, Tel. 64711163.

**RICHMOND: ⊜⊜ Prospect House**, Tel. 626032207.

**STANLEY: ⊜⊜ Captains Cottage**, 30 Alexander Terrace, Tel. 64581109.

⊜ **Stanley Caravan Park & YHA**, Wharf Road, Tel. 64581266.

**STRAHAN: ⊜ Gordon Gateway Chalet**, Grining Street, Tel. 64717165.

**ULVERSTONE: ⊜⊜ The Lighthouse Hotel**, 33 Victoria Street, Tel. 64251197.

**HOBART: Mures Fish Centre**, Victoria Dock, Tel. 62312121. **Salamanca's Food Fair & Cafe**, 55 Salamanca Place, Tel. 62243667.

**LAUNCESTON: Quigleys**, 96 Balfour Street, Tel. 63316971. **Fee & Me**, corner of Charles and Frederick Streets, Tel. 63313195. Both grand, with fresh Tasmanian ingredients.

**SCOTTSDALE: Anabel's of Scottsdale**, 46 King Street, Tel. 66352 3277.

**HOBART: Tasmanian Museum and Art Gallery**, 40 Macquarie Street, daily 10:00 a.m.-5:00 p.m. Tours through the **Cascade Brewery**, Cascade Road, Australia's oldest brewery, are Mondays through Fridays at 9:30 a.m. and 1:00 p.m., $A 8. Reservations required, Tel. 62241144.

A visit to the **Cadbury Schweppes chocolate factory** in Claremont is always popular, tours at 9:00 a.m., 9:30 a.m., 10:30 a.m., 11:15 and 1:00 p.m., reservations required, Tel. 62490333.

Beautiful nature and a magnificent view of the Derwent River can be enjoyed from the **Queens Domain**, where the Botanic Gardens and Government House are located, close to the Tasman Bridge.

**LAUNCESTON: Queen Victoria Museum & Art Gallery**, Wellington Street, Mon-Sat 10:00 a.m.-5:00 p.m., Sun from 2:00 p.m.

**Active tours**: *Tasmanian Expeditions*, 110 George Street, Launceston, Tel. 63343477 and 1800-0030230, offers bike tours (Tasmania is a bikers paradise) and extensive hikes, and also has rafting trips.

*Tasmania*

# FROM MELBOURNE TO ADELAIDE

### INLAND DRIVE:
### GOLD RUSH TOWNS / GRAMPIANS
### RIVER DRIVE
### COASTAL DRIVE:
### GREAT OCEAN ROAD / FLEURIEU PENINSULA / KANGAROO ISLAND

There are three different routes from Melbourne to Adelaide, the metropolis of South Australia. The fastest route between the two cities is the Inland Drive along the Western and Dukes Highways (741 kilometers), although it is still worth taking the time to stop at one of the old gold rush towns and Grampian National Park.

Still further to the north is River Drive (1,003 kilometers). The Calder, Murray Valley, and Sturt Highways lead to the Murray River and run partially along the river to Adelaide.

If you have the time, it is worth taking the Great Ocean Road and Princes Highway along the coast (1,025 kilometers). A high point of this Coastal Drive is the Port Campbell National Park with its Twelve Apostles

### INLAND DRIVE

#### Gold Rush Towns and Grampians National Park

Ballarat, Bendigo, St. Arnaud, and Ararat have one thing in common: a past steeped in the romance of the gold rush,

*Previous pages: Sunset on the Twelve Apostles. Left: Solitary beaches along Great Ocean Road.*

which was triggered off in Clunes in July 1851 by one James Esmond who is said to have been the first man to strike gold there. However, 25 per cent of all the gold found in the area came from **\*Ballarat ❶** alone.

Today, tourists are able to follow in the footsteps of the gold prospectors and try their luck at panning for gold in the river at **\*Sovereign Hill**, a museum reconstruction of a gold rush town of the mid-19th century. Highly recommended is a visit to the **Gold Museum** near Sovereign Hill, the **Art Gallery**, and the **Botanical Gardens**.

If you continue driving along the Western Highway for another 91 kilometers you will reach the old gold rush town of **Ararat ❷**. Between 1854 and 1857 it seemed that everyone here was looking for gold.

Today, most of the inhabitants earn their living from agriculture. From **One Tree Hill**, 6 kilometers to the west, there is a good view towards the Grampians (Gariwerd), from which Ararat is an excellent point of departure.

The **\*Grampians (Gariwerd) National Park ❸**, the largest national park in Victoria, extending for 167,000 hectares, lies west of Ararat. The park is famous for the weird sandstone formations found there, which are over 400 million years old. It is also noted for numerous rock paintings and etchings in the caves cliff overhangs, which bear testimony to the centuries-long connection of the Aborigines with the Grampians, which they called Gariwerd.

The **Brambuk Aboriginal Living Cultural Centre** in **Halls Gap**, run by the Koories provide information about their culture; it is also possible to book tours to some of the sites with rock paintings. The National Park Visitors' Centre near by offers an excellent exhibition on the region's geology, flora and fauna. From Boroka Lookout, Lake View Lookout and Sundial Peak, there is a splendid view of Halls Gap and Lake Bellfield, from Reid Lookout (lovely view to the West into Victoria Valley) there is a short walk to the rock formation known as The Balconies (Jaws of Death). Some 50 different walks link the mountains, waterfalls and lakes. From **Mount William** (Mount Duwil), the highest mountain in the park at 1,167 meters, you may watch a spectacular sunrise.

**⋆Bendigo ❹** (population 65,000) is situated much further north on Calder Highway (167 kilometers from Melbourne) and is notable for its Victorian architecture. The **Chinese Joss House** on Finn Street, and the **Golden Dragon Museum** on Bridge Street are reminders of the Chinese gold prospectors.

### RIVER DRIVE

The source of this 2500-kilometer-long river is south of Corryong / Victoria in the Australian Alps. For most of its course, it forms the border between the states of Victoria and New South Wales, and on the final stretch between Victoria and South Australia. The **Murray River** was important even in the dreamtime of the Koorie Aborigines. Its European discoverer, Captain Sturt, named it after an English river in 1830. Many species thrive along its banks. The river itself can

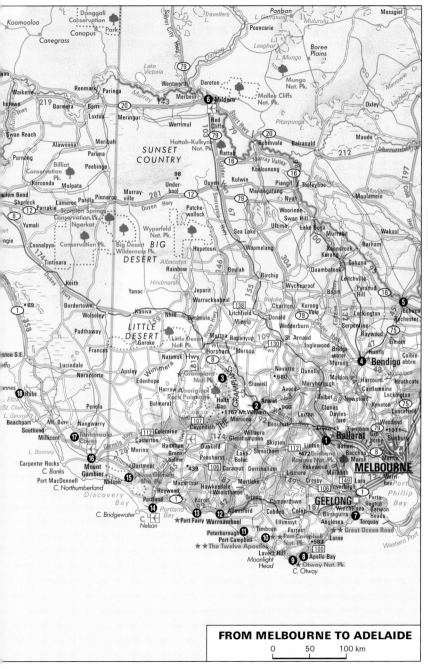

## FROM MELBOURNE TO ADELAIDE

0    50    100 km

be navigated by paddle steamer or explored in a cruiser from **Echuca ❺** (205 kilometers north of Melbourne) or **Mildura ❻** (555 kilometers northwest of Melbourne).

## COASTAL DRIVE
### **Great Ocean Road

The multiple carriageway of Princes Highway brings you to **Geelong**. The *National Wool Museum*, one of Australia's most attractive museums (cf page 78) is located here. One the way to Adelaide, one leaves the Princes Highway behind Geelong to reach the coast again at **Torquay ❼**.

Belts Beach, Jan Juc, Torquay Surf Beach and Point Impossible don't just offer good wind and surfing conditions, there are also good bathing beaches and hiking facilities.

*Above: In the Outback the postmann doesn't ring – mail boxes near Ararat. Right: Remains of the mighty London Bridge.*

Torquay is the gateway to the ★★**Great Ocean Road** (State Route B100). For the next 230 kilometers you will be driving along one of the most spectacular stretches of Australia's coastline. In **Lorne**, a favorite bathing spot for Melburnians, summer activities center on Loutitt Bay and Mountjoy Parade.

**Apollo Bay ❽** is a much quieter place, where green hills reach right down to the coast. This is the place to buy everything you need for an evening picnic. You are now gradually getting closer to one of the most beautiful picnic areas in Australia. About 20 kilometers west of here, it is worth making a detour into ★**Otway National Park ❾** where rain forest, eucalyptus woods and ferns over 1 meter-high line the road to spray-washed **Cape Otway** (15 kilometers). Here, a lighthouse built in 1848 still guards the coast.

In the nearby forests of the **Otway Range**, grow some of the highest trees in all the world. This is also one of the wettest regions of Victoria. Do take time to visit the two magnificent waterfalls of

*From Melbourne to Adelaide*

Hopetoun Falls and of Beauchamp Falls.

**★★Port Campbell National Park ❿** impresses with its breath-taking nature. Suddenly you are confronted with a coastline that has become petrified in the form of stone pillars standing upright in a churning tide. For centuries the wind and waves have beaten back the coast, but left these rocky pinnacles, standing up to 60 meters (197 feet) high.

**★★Gibsons Steps** is one of the few places where it is possible to climb down to the beach. It is only from this worm's-eye view that you can really appreciate the great height of the towering rock pillars.

The beach, which is approximately 2 kilometers long, is the place for that atmospheric evening picnic mentioned earlier. However, for a good view of the sunset, you should move on to the nearby lookout point at the **★★Twelve Apostles**, and wait there for a wonderful view of the glowing red coastline.

**Port Campbell** is the place for an overnight stay, offering a camping site,

motels, and an information center. Next morning, you can make an unhurried start to the interesting rock formations of the deeply fissured coastal cliffs. First, the trail backtracks a few kilometers to **Loch Ard Gorge**, where the *Loch Ard* foundered nearby in 1878 and 52 souls perished. From there, paths lead towards **Blowhole** and **Thunder Cave**.

The never-ceasing pounding of the surf against the cliffs does not just destroy ships. **London Bridge**, a natural arch of rock located just before **Peterborough ⓫** (with a lovely golf course on the cliffs), collapsed without warning into the wild seas in January, 1990. The new island thus created is an impressive example of the way the sea washes away more and more bits of coastline every year. For this reason alone, you should hurry to visit Port Campbell National Park.

### Along the Coast to Adelaide

At Peterborough (with a fine golf course on the cliffs), the Great Ocean

Road terminates and with it the most spectacular stretch of Victoria's west coast. Here, State Route 100 joins Princes Highway again. **Warrnambool ⑫**, with 24,000 inhabitants, is the center of the Shipwreck Coast, on which more than 700 ships were wrecked in the 19th century. Many of the wrecks can be visited or offer excellent sport for divers. Another piece of seafaring history is Flagstaff Hill Maritime Village (Merri Street) with reconstructions of harbors and ships from the period around the turn of the century.

Although **\*Port Fairy ⑬**, founded by whalers in 1835, once was home to the largest fishing fleet in Victoria, it has now yielded to tourism of a contemplative kind. Numerous buildings have preservation orders on them, and can be discovered by taking the **History Walk**.

The tranquil harbor extends along the banks of the **Moyne River**, but for those who prefer something a bit rougher, the best beaches along the open sea are South Beach and East Beach, which can be reached via a pedestrian bridge from the center of the town. Thousands of mutton-birds nest on **Griffiths Island** from September to April.

The next few kilometers of Princes Highway take you along the edge of Portland Bay. Although there are a few good beaches in the surrounding area, the port of **Portland ⑭** itself (the oldest settlement in Victoria) with its enormous grain storage facilities, does not offer much to visitors beyond a few historic buildings in the center.

It is probably best to leave the highway now and drive on one of the coastal side roads to **Lower Glenelg National Park ⑮**, where there are some fine walking tracks along 60 kilometers of the Glenelg River. There is some good angling here, and the beautiful **Princess Margaret Rose Caves** can also be viewed. After-

wards, carry on to **Nelson**, which is a good place to hire a houseboat, and where you can cross the border into South Australia (please note that there is a time-zone change of half an hour).

About 32 kilometers on this detour will finally end in Port MacDonnell, the perfect place for a lunch stop as its harbor is the base for Australia's largest lobster fleet. You can sample the day's fresh catch in several small restaurants and take-outs along the promenade (try the Breakwater Cafe,).

The town of **Mount Gambier ⑯** is not named after a mountain, but after a volcano which became extinct about 5000 years ago, and whose crater now forms four lakes. One of them, **Blue Lake**, provides a natural spectacle of a very unusual kind. Twice a year, in November and April, the color of its water changes. In the summer the water is bright blue; as winter approaches the water suddenly turns gray overnight. Until now, scientists have found no convincing explanation for this phenomenon. If you would like to try to get to the bottom of the mystery yourself, the lakes are situated along the road to MacDonnell and you can drive around them on the scenic route. Another interesting feature of the town is the labyrinthine system of caves extending beneath Mount Gambier. Guided tours and fascinating cave trips are available. Some of the entrances to the system are right in the center of town, where the **Cave Garden Reserve** is also worth a visit.

It is thanks to the timber industry that the area enjoys some economic importance. On the way to **Millicent**, the highway is lined with forests of stone pine and Scots pine, the timber of which is processed for its cellulose in numerous factories in the area. A large proportion of this output is later shipped to Japan. En route, you will pass **Tantanoola Caves ⑰**, an extensive system of limestone caves with stalagmites and stalactites, which can be visited daily.

*Right: Seals in Seal Bay Conservation Park.*

Beyond Millicent, it is suggested that you leave the highway again to drive along the coast. **South End** and **Beachport**, where fresh fish can be bought straight off the boats, and good beer is served in the nearby restaurant, Bompa's, are favorite beach resorts in the summer.

**Robe** ⓲ is worth a stop at any time of year. In the middle of the last century, thousands of Chinese gold prospectors landed here illegally in order to avoid paying the exorbitant immigration tax at other ports. Today, numerous artists have opened studios and shops along Smillie Street. Romantic Robe is perfect for an overnight stay or just a lunch stop, which is probably best enjoyed in the very pleasant, old world atmosphere of Wilson's At Robe (a combined restaurant and gallery). However, the same problem applies to all three resorts; you cannot avoid crowds during the summer months.

At **Kingston S. E.**, whose trademark is a gigantic lobster, you will pick up Princes Highway again after 43 kilometers. From there, the highway follows **Coorong National Park** ⓳ all along the coast. This 150-kilometer-long strip of sand and dunes (Younghusband Peninsula) is bordered by salt lakes, and numerous species of birds can be found nesting on their shores. The multiple carriageway of the Western Highway begins at **Tailem Bend**. About 17 kilometers further west, you cross the river at **Murray Bridge**.

### *Fleurieu Peninsula

Just south of Adelaide, lonely beaches and peaceful hill country stretch across the *Fleurieu Peninsula ⓴. On land, countless kangaroos and wallabies, and penguins in the offshore waters dominate the scene. A horse-drawn tram runs over a dam to Granite Island, where the **Penguin Interpretive Centre** provides information about the Fairy Penguins and where rangers offer observation tours at night. The tourist center of this island is situated at Encounter Coast in the southeast with **Victoria Harbour** (population

*From Melbourne to Adelaide*

7,000). The Fleurieu Peninsula encompasses the wine-growing area around **McLaren Vale,** where some 50 vineyards cultivate excellent grapes for winemaking. Goolwa is the starting point for a paddle-steamer trip on the Murray River.

### *Kangaroo Island

Most tourists, however, choose to cross the peninsula in the direction of **Cape Jervis**, where a ferry connects with Penneshaw on **\*Kangaroo Island ㉑**. On Australia's third largest island (4450 square kilometers) there are several national and recreational conservation parks. The best known is **\*Seal Bay Conservation Park**. On the beach, you might even get within a few meters of some of the many sea-lions and seals. The following places are also worth a visit: **\*Remarkable Rocks**, with their strange rock formations, **\*Admirals Arch** (both

*Above: Hahndorf retains many reminders of its first German settlers.*

of these places are south of the South Coast Road in Flinders Chase National Park), **\*Cape Borda**, with steep cliffs and a lighthouse built in 1858, the sand dunes of **Little Sahara**, and the **Kelly Hill Caves** (limestone caves). Along the coast there are many lonely beaches, most of which are only accessible at the end of fine bushwalks. Kangaroo Island is known for its wild life. In addition to the many camping sites, overnight accommodation is available in all price categories at **Penneshaw, American River**, and **Kingscote** (where a third of the island's 4500 inhabitants live, and which is the best place to enjoy a cool beer). Back on the mainland, most roads lead in the direction of Adelaide. **Hahndorf ㉒**, on the South Eastern Freeway, is the last stop before the city, and has a lively crowd and numerous street stands.

From nearby **Mount Lofty** (727 meters) you can enjoy your first glimpse of **\*Adelaide ㉓**. From this vantage point, the city can be seen stretching across the landscape below, 7 kilometers away.

## FROM MELBOURNE TO ADELAIDE

### APOLLO BAY (☎ 03)

📧 😊😊 **Seafarers**, Great Ocean Rd, Tel. 52376507.
😊 **Waratah Caravan Park**, 7 Noel St, Tel. 52376562.
**Surfside Backpackers YHA**, corner of Gambier St and Great Ocean Rd, Tel. 52377263.

### ARARAT (☎ 03)

📋 **Tourist Office**, Barkly St, Tel. 53522096 o. 1800-657158.
📧 😊😊 **Statesman Motor Inn**, Western Hwy, Tel. 53524111.

### BALLARAT(☎ 03)

📋 Information Centre, corner of Sturt und Albert Sts, Tel. 53322694 oder 1800-648450.
📧 😊😊 **The Ansonia**, 32 Lydiard St South, Tel. 53324678. 😊 **Sovereign Hill Lodge YHA**, Magpie St, Tel. 53333409.
🏛 **Fine Art Gallery**, 40 Lydiard St, Tel. 53315622, tägl. 10.30-5:00 p.m. The open-air museum **Sovereign Hill** takes visitors back to the times of the goldrush around 1860, daily 9:30 a.m.-5:00 p.m., Tel. 53311944.

### ECHUCA (☎ 03)

📋 Info Centre, 2 Heygarth St, Tel. 1800-804446.
📧 😊😊 **Caledomian Hotel Motel**, 110 Hare St, Tel. 54822100.

### GEELONG

🏛 National Wool Museum, Moorabool St, Tel. 1800-620888, daily10:00 a.m.-5:00 p.m.

### GRAMPIANS (☎ 03)

📋 National Park Visitors Centre, Halls Gap-Dunkeld Rd, Tel. 53582314.
📋 The National Park west of Ararat is one of the lovliest in Victoria. Many hiking possibilities (sometimes for several days).

### HAHNDORF (☎ 08)

📋 Information Centre, 41 Main St, Tel. 83881185.
📧 😊😊 **Hahndorf Inn**, 35 Main St, Tel. 83881000.
😊 **Hochstens Hahndorf Caravan Park**, 145a Main St, Tel. 83887921.

### KANGAROO ISLAND (☎ 08)

📋 KI Gateway Visitor Information Centre, Penneshaw, Tel. 85531185
📧 **AMERICAN RIVER**: 😊😊 **Linnetts Island Club Hotel**, The Esplanade, Tel. 85537053. 😊 **Linnetts Island Club Caravan Park**, The Esplanade, Tel. 85537053. **KINGSCOTE**: 😊😊 **Wisteria Lodge**, Cygnet Rd, Tel. 85532707. 😊 **Nepean Bay Tourist Park**, Brownlow Beach, Tel. 88532394. **PENNESHAW**: 😊😊 **Sorrento Resort Motel**, North Terrace, Tel. 85531028. 😊 **Penneshaw Caravan Park**, Talinga Terrace, Tel. 88531075.

### LORNE (☎ 03)

📧 😊😊 **Coachman Inn Motel**, 1 Deans Marsh Rd, Tel. 52892244. 😊 **Lorne Foreshore Reserve**, Great Ocean Rd, Tel. 52891382. **Great Ocean Rd Backpackers YHA**, 10 Erskine Ave, Tel. 52892508.

### MILDURA (☎ 03)

📋 Alfred Deakin Visitor Information Centre, 180 Deakin Ave, Tel. 1800-039043.
📧 😊😊 **Mildura Inlander Sun Resort**, 373 Deakin Ave, Tel. 50233823. 😊 **Rosemount Guesthouse**, 154 Madden Ave, Tel. 50231535.

### MOUNT GAMBIER (☎ O8)

📧 😊😊 **Silver Birch Motor Inn**, Jubilee Hwy, Tel. 87255122. 😊 **Blue Lake City Caravan Park**, Bay Rd, Tel. 87259856.

### MURRAY RIVER

📋 *HOUSEBOATS: Rivermen Houseboats*, Tel. 1800-809152, in Mildura / Wentworth, or in South Australia *Houseboat Hirers Association*, Tel. 08-83950999. Several days trips on the *Murray Princess* paddle steamer (from Mannum) with *Captain Cook Cruises*, Tel. 1800-804843, and on the *Coonawarra* (from Mildura), Tel. 1800-034424.

### PORT CAMPBELL (☎ 03)

📋 National Park Information Centre, Tregea St, Tel. 55986382.
📧 😊😊 **Great Ocean Road Motor Inn**, 10 Great Ocean Rd, Tel. 55986522. 😊 **Port Campbell Caravan Park**, corner of Tregea and Morris Sts, Tel. 55986492.

### PORT FAIRY (☎ 03)

📋 Information Centre, Bank St, Tel. 55682682.
📧 😊😊 **Caledonian Inn**, corner of Bank and James Sts, Tel. 55681044. **Seacombe House Motor Inn**, 22 Sackville St, Tel. 55681082. 😊 **Port Fairy Gardens Caravan Park**, 111 Griffith St, Tel. 55681060.

### PORTLAND (☎ 03)

📧 😊😊 **Hotel Bentinck**, corner of Bentinck and Gawler Sts, Tel. 55232188. 😊 **Portland Haven Caravan Park**, 76 Garden St, Tel. 55231768.

### ROBE (☎ 08)

📧 😊😊 **Robetown Motor Inn**, Main St, Tel. 87682185. 😊 **Robe Long Beach Tourist Park**, Esplanade Long Beach, Tel. 87682237.

### SWAN HILL (☎ 03)

📋 Information Centre, 306 Campbell St, Tel. 1800-625373.
📧 😊😊 **Swan Hill's Resort Motor Inn**, 405 Campbell St, Tel. 50322726.

### WARRNAMBOOL (☎ 03)

📋 Info Centre, 600 Raglan Parade, Tel. 56647847.
📧 😊😊 **Colonial Village**, 31 Mortlake Rd, Tel. 55621455. 😊 **Warrnambool Surf-Side Parks**, Pertobe Rd, Tel. 55612611.

# ADELAIDE
# SOUTH AUSTRALIA'S
# TRANQUIL CAPITAL

**HISTORY**
**CITY TOUR**
**SHOPPING AND NIGHT-LIFE**
**BEACHES**

At first glance, **★Adelaide** seems to offer none of the right ingredients for a city which aspires to charm and excite its visitors to any degree.

As it has more than a million inhabitants and is known as "the capital and economic centre of the state of South Australia," visitors tend to come here expecting the typical fast pace and bustling life of a big city with its bustle and noise, traffic jams and rushing people. However, a pleasant surprise greets the visitor immediately upon arrival.

There is a relaxed atmosphere throughout the parks and gardens; you can go for a peaceful stroll in the pedestrian precinct of Rundle Mall; there is culture wherever you look, and water everywhere within easy reach, whether in the center of the city on the Torrens River or in the western suburbs on the beaches of the Gulf of St. Vincent.

In this city you will look in vain for the great tourist highlights that can be found in Sydney or Melbourne.

Only those who truly appreciate a kind of contemplative peace, with just a touch of big-city flair, will really get the best out of Adelaide and will heartily enjoy their stay here.

*Left: Rundle Mall – the lively pedestrian zone in the heart of Adelaide.*

## HISTORY - MARCHING TO THE BEAT OF ANOTHER DRUM

The remarkably peaceful atmosphere Adelaide enjoys today is due to very careful planning in the past. Kaurna Aborigines had been living in this area for many centuries before Dutchman Peter Nuyts's ship appeared off the coast in 1627. It was not until 28 December 1836, that the British captain John Hindmarsh proclaimed the foundation of the new settlement while standing, so the story goes, under a gum tree in McFarlane Street that is still in existence today! Even in those early days, the authorities seem to have had a rather more open-minded attitude than in other Australian colonies. This was probably due to the influence of the Quaker minister, Edward Gibbon Wakefield, who led the earlier colonists.

For example, in South Australia the intention was to build up the colony without the help of convicts from far-off Britain. In the mid-19th century, increased immigration of Lutheran refugees from Prussia was actively encouraged, and their descendants shape the character of the Barossa Valley to this day. In 1857, Parliament opted for a constitution that was unusually advanced and democratic for its time. Extensive social reforms and free school education were introduced, as

*Adelaide*

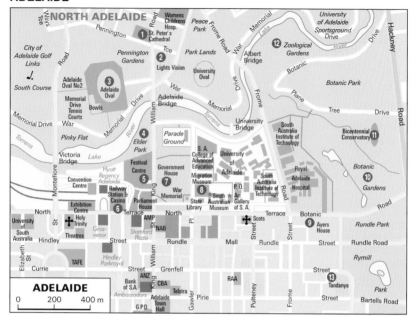

well as votes for women (the second country in the world to grant the vote!)

Not only in the political field, but in matters of urban development too, the authorities showed considerable skill. Colonel William Light, South Australia's first surveyor-general, chose the site for the capital. His design for Adelaide, which admittedly created a great deal of controversy at the time, included a street grid extending for approximately one square mile. Even though the city has long since outgrown its original boundaries, boasting 1.1 million inhabitants today, the logic of the inner city structure, and with it the ease of finding one's way around as a tourist, has survived to the present day.

## CITY TOUR

The best place to begin a tour of Adelaide is down by the **Torrens River**,

*Right: An artistic representation showing Adelaide's inner city from an unusual perspective.*

which separates the busy commercial center from the residential areas of **North Adelaide**. Incidentally, the latter include not only many beautiful houses with mature gardens, but also **St. Peter's Cathedral ❶**, built in 1876 (King William Street) and definitely worth a visit.

Close by is **Montefiore Hill**, with **Light's Vision Lookout ❷**. By standing at the foot of the statue of Colonel William Light, you will be able to enjoy a good view of the **Adelaide Oval ❸**, the oldest sports stadium in Australia.

Built in 1870, it is the venue for cricket matches in summer and Australian rules football games in winter. Beyond it stretches the skyline of Adelaide, a wonderful sight at any time of the year.

Back at the Torrens River, you may visit a beautiful Victorian pavilion majestically sited in **Elder Park ❹**. You have a choice of going out in a pedal boat on Lake Torrens, taking a bicycle tour around the lake shore, or else walking over to the **Festival Centre ❺** (King William Street), to which Adelaide owes

*Adelaide*

its nickname, City of Festivals. The most prestigious of these, and renowned worldwide, is the Adelaide Festival, which has been held here in March on every even-numbered year since 1960. Top names in the international world of art and theater (music, theater, film and dance are represented in more than 100 events) come to Adelaide especially for this festival. The Festival Centre building, which regularly stages exhibitions in its foyer, is surrounded by the corridors of political power.

Immediately to the south is **Parliament House,** where the South Australia Parliament meets. Spectators are allowed to sit in on sessions from 2 pm onwards. Right next door is **Old Parliament House** (1855), which is not only one of the oldest buildings in town, but also home to a large exhibition of the state's history (**Constitutional Museum**) under the slogan, "South Australia starts here."

Next to the lovely **Railway Station** is *the* night-life attraction, the **Adelaide Casino ⑥** (cf page 111). It is well worth trying to return here later on at night. On the eastern side of King William Street is **Government House ⑦**, built between 1838 and 1840, and set in the beautiful Prince Henry Gardens. Another reminder of the history of the city is the **Migration Museum ⑧** (82 Kintore Avenue, behind the State Library), which is housed in the restored premises of the Destitute Asylum, and which gives a fascinating insight into the life of the first immigrants.

Close to the Migration Museum are two other interesting exhibits: the ★**South Australian Museum** is easily recognizable by a giant whale skeleton enclosed behind a glass frontage next to the entrance; behind it are five floors of exhibits of the fauna and flora of South Australia, as well as a large and informative section dealing with the culture of the Aborigines and the greater Pacific area.

Next door is the ★**Art Gallery of South Australia**, with its collection of contemporary Australian and international works of art. In the Mitchell Build-

ing (first floor), set back a little on the campus of the University of Adelaide, is the **Museum of Classical Archaeology**, which holds around 500 exhibits.

On the opposite side of the road is **Ayers House** ⑨, the construction of which was begun in 1846, but which was not completed for another 30 years. This building, housing two restaurants, owes its name to the 19th century politician Sir Henry Ayers, who lived here during his seven periods of office as prime minister of South Australia.

After being subjected to such a concentrated dose of culture, you can recover your breath in the **Botanical Gardens** ⑩, founded in 1855. Here you will find many subtropical and Mediterranean plants and a hothouse dating from 1871.

The centerpiece is the **Bicentennial Conservatory** ⑪. This giant glass pyramid, 27 meters high and 100 meters long, was opened in November 1989 as the big-

gest greenhouse in the southern hemisphere, and recreates a tropical rain forest in the middle of the city. Here, among palms, orchids, and ferns, you can really imagine for a moment that you are far away from civilization. An artificial sprinkler system provides the necessary humidity, which causes authentic perspiration among the visitors! North of the Botanical Gardens lies **Adelaide Zoo** ⑫, which you can also reach by boat along the Torrens River.

If you want to combine culture with some unusual cuisine, the place to go is **Tandanya** ⑬. You can reach the Aboriginal Cultural Institute in a few minutes from the Botanical Gardens via East Terrace. Fortunately, Tandanya has nothing to do with the trendy Aborigine art boom, which is represented everywhere by dreamtime T-shirts and kitschy boomerangs. Instead, the institute and gallery give visitors a good impression of the daily life of Australia's original inhabitants. Contemporary scenes, painted with a primitive but charming artlessness, are the main theme of the gallery.

A changing program of exhibitions and workshops, as well as a book shop, is managed by the Aborigines themselves, and the profits are ploughed back into the project.

In the language of the indigenous Kaurna Aborigines, Tandanya means kangaroo place, and is a reminder of their past. Here in ancient times, on the site of present-day Adelaide, there was a sacred site of the Kaurna, in which the Red Kangaroo Ceremony and Red Kangaroo Dreaming took place. The **Tandanya cafe** gives visitors a chance to sample the flavor of Aborigine cooking. The menu includes kangaroo steaks and bushtucker. Be warned, the witchety grubs may not be to everyone's taste!

Take extra care if you are eating here in early November. Adelaide's motor racing circuit is right next door, and when the Formula 1 Grand Prix is taking place, the

*Above: The nostalgic Adelaide tram on a journey to Glenelg.*

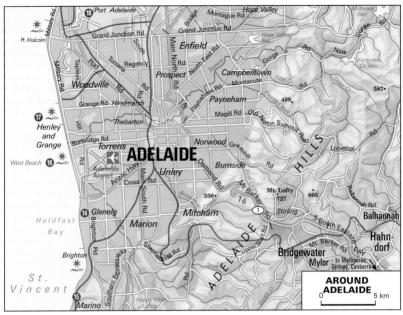

ear-splitting howl of high-revving engines practically makes you choke on your food. Incidentally, this event sends the whole city mad as it is the end-of-season final of the Formula 1 world championships. It also means that for four days one of Australia's greatest carnivals takes place. Hundreds of thousands of visitors come to Adelaide from all over the country. For most of them the actual races are of secondary importance: beer runs in the fountains, you meet friends, there are live concerts everywhere (in 1991 Paul Simon appeared here), and many other entertainments. For a few hours at least, country visitors can forget the rigors of their life in the dusty Outback. 1995 marked the last time in Adelaide. For the ensuing 10 years the Grand Prix will take place in Melbourne.

## SHOPPING AND NIGHT-LIFE

Adelaide's shopping area is centered round **Rundle Mall**. You will find branches of the large department stores here, such as David Jones, Myer, and John Martin's. If you are preparing for a lengthy journey into the Outback, this is the best place to stock up with provisions and to make sure all your equipment is up to scratch.

If you disregard the beautiful Regent, Rundle and Adelaide Arcades, then the pedestrian precinct is hardly distinguishable from the malls in other Australian cities, despite two very photogenic sculptures of glinting metal. At midday, you may have great difficulty finding a seat in any of the small street cafes.

In the evening, the activity shifts to **Hindley Street**, further to the west. This is where you will find the city's best known night-clubs, pubs with live music, theaters, and numerous international restaurants. In the end, however, you should head back to the North Terrace, where, behind the handsome Railway Station, you will see the crowning glory of the city's night-life, **Adelaide Casino** (**6**).

Be warned before you go in: this gaming hell has very little in common with

the up-market atmosphere of other casinos around the world. Here, things are done the South Australian way, yet proper attire is requested: no shorts, no sneakers, no hiking clothes. Sydney bankers meet opal prospectors from Coober Pedy, civil servants from Canberra rub shoulders with sheep farmers from the Outback, and everyone has a great time. Things really warm up during the typically Australian game of chance called two-up. The object of the game is to predict which sides of two coins will be face up when they are tossed and land on the floor.

### BEACHES

Whether or not you are still recovering from a hangover after a long night at the casino, there is an enjoyable and nostalgic day trip to be made out to **Glenelg ⑭**. It is a good idea to stock up beforehand with the ingredients for a picnic at the

*Above: The Adelaide Casino ist the center of the city's night-life.*

nearby Central Market (Grote Street, behind the Hilton Hotel; open Tues, Thurs, Fri, and Sa.). Then go to **Victoria Square** and pick up the old-fashioned tram which will get you to Glenelg in 20 minutes. From there it is only a few meters to **Glenelg Jetty** (a favorite spot for anglers). In 1836, the first settlers landed in Glenelg under the command of Captain John Hindmarsh, and founded the city of Adelaide

Most visitors today come for the beautiful beaches on the Gulf of St. Vincent. To the south, beyond the busy City Beach, are the beaches of **Somerton, Seacliff, Kingston Park,** and **Marino ⑮**.

**West Beach ⑯**, with two golf courses nearby, and the very long **Grange** and **Henley Beaches ⑰** (in the summer there are open-air concerts on Henley Square), lead northward to **Port Adelaide ⑱**, where the **South Australian Maritime Museum** (117 Lipson Street; open Sat. thru Wed. from 10 a.m. to 5 p.m.) has many fascinating exhibits which recount South Australia's seafaring history.

## ADELAIDE (☎ 08)

**ℹ South Australian Travel Centre**, 1 King William St, Tel. 83032033 and 1300-655276.

**Royal Automobile Association of South Australia** (RAA), 41 Hindmarsh Square, Tel. 82024600.

🛏 ⊖⊖⊖ **Hilton International Adelaide**, 233 Victoria Square, Tel. 82172000. **Hindley Parkroyal**, 65 Hindley St, Tel. 82315552.

**Hyatt Regency Adelaide**, North Terrace, Tel. 82311234. **Stamford Plaza Adelaide**, 150 North Terrace, Tel. 84611111. **Adelaide South Park Motel**, corner of South and West Terrace, Tel. 82121277.

⊖⊖ **Ambassadors**, 107 King William Street, Tel. 82314331. **Central Adelaide**, Tower Wing, 208 South Terrace, Tel. 82232744.

**Grosvenor Vista Hotel**, 125 North Terrace, Tel. 84078888, **Holiday Inn**, 255 Hindley St, Tel. 82172500. **Motel Adjacent Casino**, 25 Bank St, Tel. 82318881.

**Plaza Hotel**, 85 Hindley St, Tel. 82316371. **Prince Of Wales Hotel**, 215 Port Road, Tel. 84471252. **Princes Arcade Motel**, 262 Hindley St, Tel. 82319524.

⊖ **Adelaide Backpackers Inn**, 112 Carrington St, Tel. 82236635. **Adelaide YHA**, 290 Gilles St, Tel. 82236007.

**Albert Hall Backpackers**, 16 South Esplanade, Glenelg, Tel. 83760488. **East Park Lodge**, 341 Angas St, Tel. 82231228. **Adelaide Caravan Park**, Bruton St, Hackney, Tel. 83631566.

❌ **Amadora**, 18 Leigh St, Tel. 82317611. international cuisine, with a touch of French. **Beijing Restaurant**, 73 Angas St, Tel. 82321388. Chinese cuisine.

**The Bull and Bear Ale House**, 91 King William St, in the basement of the State Bank Centre. Import beer and tasty food.

**Eccolo Restaurant & Bar**, 22 Grote St, Tel. 84100102. Innovative Italian cuisine.

**Gaucho's**, 91 Gourger St, Tel. 82312299. Argentinian cuinse, specilizing in meat dishes.

**Irodori Japanese Brasserie**, 291 Rundle St. **Red Ochre Grill**, Ebenezer Place (close to Rundle St), Tel. 82237566, typical Australian *bush tucker* (such as kangraoo and emu meat) deliciously prepared.

**Red Rock Noodle Bar**, 187 Rundle St, Tel. 82236855. Asian, several branches throughout the city.

**Universal Wine Bar**, 285 Rundle St, Tel. 82325000. Impressive wine list, expensive, but very good.

🍸 *NIGHT-LIFE:* The **Casino** of Adelaide, North Terrace, Tel. 2122811, has a slight Outback character, one mostly plays *Two-up* or simply enjoys the (difficult to comapre with other casinos) atmosphere. Sun-Thurs 10:00 a.m.-4:00 a.m., Fri and Sat until 6:00 a.m.

🏛 **Art Gallery of South Australia**, North Terrace, Tel. 82077000, daily 10:00 a.m.-5:00 p.m., Australian and international art, also a collection of 22 Rodin sculptures.

**Ayers House**, 288 North Terrace, Tues-Fri 10:00 a.m.-4:00 p.m., Sat / Sun 1:00 p.m.-4:00 p.m.

**Migration Museum**, 82 Kintore Ave, Tel. 82077580, Mon-Fri 10:00 a.m.-5:00 p.m., Sat, Sun and holidays 1:00 p.m.-5:00 p.m.,The history of the settlement of South Austrlia.

**South Australian Maritime Museum**, 126 Lipson St, Port Adelaide, Tel. 82076255, Sat-Wed 10:00 a.m.-5:00 p.m., numerous interesting objects about the sea and seafaring.

**South Australian Museum**, North Terrace, Tel. 82077500, daily 10:00 a.m.-5:00 p.m., extensive collection of Aboriginal art.

**Tandanya – National Aboriginal Cultural Centre**, 253 Grenfell St, Tel. 82243200, daily 10:00 a.m.-5:00 p.m., Aboriginal art collection with adjacent cafe and bookshop.

🎭 **Adelaide Festival**: Every two years (even numbers) beginning of March with extensive world-class cultural program.

**Africa Week**: African Festival, in October, with many events.

**Carnevale**: Italian Festival, in Februar, Rymill Park.

**Feast Festival**: Gay Festival, October / November, numerous events.

**Fringe**: Alternative Festival with many international artists, February / March, http://www.adelaidefringe.com.au

**Glenelg Jazz Festival**, in October, http://www.jazz.adelaide.net.au

**Schützenfest**: German Festival, in January, Bonython Park.

🌳 **Botanical Gardens**: Since 1855 Adelaide's green lung, which reached new heights since 1989 with the **Bicentennial Conservatory** (tropical rain forest under glass). Garden Mon-Fri 8:00 a.m.-6:30 p.m., Sat / Sun 9:00 a.m.-6:30 p.m., Conservatory daily 10:00 a.m.-4:00 p.m.

🌳 **Central Market**: Between Grote and Gouger St, Tues 7:00 a.m-5:30 p.m, Thurs 11:00 a.m-5:30 p.m, Fri 7:00 a.m.-9:00 p.m., Sat 7:00 a.m.-5:00 p.m., food and arts and crafts.

🌳 **Glenelg**: A detour to the nostalgic suburb is a must. Take the ancient tramway from Victoria Square.

🌳 **O-Train-Busway**: A bus ride of a different type. Lovely views of the Adelaide Hills when you take this system for some 12 km of cement track (stations at Grenfell St / Klemzig Station and Paradise Interchange).

*Adelaide*

# FROM ADELAIDE TO PERTH

**BAROSSA VALLEY
YORKE PENINSULA ·
EYRE PENINSULA
NULLARBOR PLAIN
TO PERTH VIA KALGOORLIE /TO
PERTH ALONG THE COAST**

After taking a last look at the Torrens River and the skyline of Adelaide, follow King William Road as it rises gradually through the northern part of town and meets Highway 1 a few kilometers further on. If you would like to discover the wine-growing area of the Barossa Valley, turn off at Gepps Cross in the direction of Elizabeth and Gawler. Alternatively, you can choose to head for Port Wakefield (97 kilometers) without any lengthy stops en route. Along the harbor front are some old buildings that recall the long-forgotten wool-trade boom.

## BAROSSA VALLEY

More than 50 per cent of Australian grapes for wine-making are produced in South Australia. At an annual consumption of some 30 liters per head of the population, most of the wine is drunk here too. A trip into the **Barossa Valley** is one of the most popular excursions from Adelaide (an additional 50 kilometers northeast).

The route takes you through Gawler, Lyndoch, Rowland Flat, Bethany, Angaston, Nuriootpa, Greenock, Seppeltsfield,

*Left: These gigantic trees in Southwestern Australia are among the oldest on the continent.*

and Tanunda, where you can meander peacefully among the endless vineyards. This trip is especially interesting during the autumn grape-picking season. Many of the 36 or so vineyards in the Barossa Valley offer wine tastings. The best known tours are organized by the Chateau Yaldara Estate (Gomerstal Road, Lyndoch), and Seppeltsfield Winery (Seppeltsfield).

Both wine and tradition are offered in equal measure at two of the best known festivals in the Barossa Valley: in January, **Tanunda** ❶ celebrates its annual **Oompah Festival**, a rather bucolic mixture of the Munich Oktoberfest and a competition for the best oompah bands in the country. Here every year about 20,000 visitors raise their wineglasses in toast after toast. On alternate (odd numbered) years, there is the **Barossa Valley Vintage Festival**, celebrated in April. The center of all this activity is once again the community of Tanunda, with its four Lutheran church spires soaring to the heavens, and its German bowling club. During the **Barossa International Music Festival** every October, concerts and performances by well-known artistes take place in the churches and wine cellars. The **Kev-Rohrlach Museum,** which exhibits items from all over the world, is a special treat. Rohrbach was a bridge engi-

*From Adelaide to Perth*

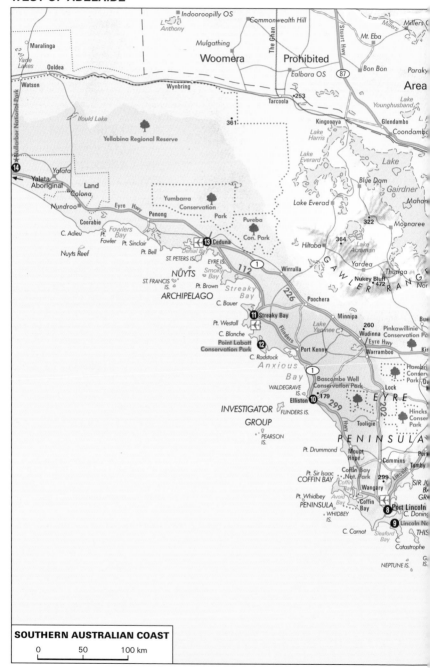

SOUTHERN AUSTRALIAN COAST

0    50    100 km

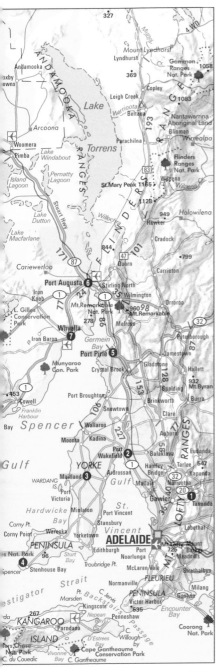

neer and inventor. Other sites worth visiting are St. George's Anglican Church and Gawler Mill in Gawler, the Gnadenfrei Church in Marananga, the town of Angaston with its Lindsay Park, and finally Nuriootpa. If you cannot face the return journey to Adelaide, many vineyards offer not only wine-tasting, but accommodation for an overnight stay.

## YORKE PENINSULA

In **Port Wakefield ❷**, a few old buildings along the harbor bear witness to the bygone wool boom. Nearby Yorke Peninsula is notable for its striking scenic contrasts. Beyond the gently rolling wheat fields stretching to the horizon, the coast plunges suddenly and spectacularly downwards into the Gulf of St. Vincent in a series of steep, rugged cliffs. At the center of the peninsula is **Maitland ❸**, but those who are looking for solitude would be advised to continue on to **Innes National Park ❹** where there is good surfing and angling. In **Kadina**, **Wallaroo** and **Moonta**, museums and heritage trails are a reminder of the copper boom which provided wealth and employment during the mid-19th century.

For a long time **Port Pirie ❺** was an important harbor, as most of the ore mined in Broken Hill was shipped out from here. The Old Railway Station is home to an exhibition by the National Trust, reminding one of the days when sailing ships set sail from Port Pirie down the Spencer Gulf to the ocean.

**Port Augusta ❻**, a thrusting industrial town with a checkered history, is set in the midst of a landscape of large sheep farms, which provide a sharp contrast to the open-cast coal mines around Leigh Creek. Definitely on the list of places to visit is the **\*Wadlata Outback Centre** with its excellent and informative exhibition of the dreamtime and way of life of the Aboriginals of Flinders Range as well as the geology of the region and of the

*From Adelaide to Perth*

history of the pioneers of this Outback region. The **Homestead Park Pioneer Museum** is dedicated to this last topic; it is a reconstructed sheep farm with a historical homestead and old tools.

From Hancock's Lookout, south of the town, there is a wonderful view of Port Augusta and the steel manufacturing center of Whyalla. At Port Augusta there is a station for the famous **Ghan Train** line, which runs from Adelaide to Alice Springs.

You can board the train at Port Augusta for a trip through one of the most magnificent regions of Australia, the Nullarbor Plain, where you will pass through such remote Outback stations as Tarcoola, Deakin, and Avoca Downs. The train will then continue its journey into Western Australia's goldfields.

Names like Kalgoorlie, Coolgardie and Boulder will bring back memories of

*Above: Barossa Valley – wine estates and idyllic villages. Right: West Australian gold prospectors.*

the fever that gripped the gold prospectors who streamed into this area during the gold rush of early 1892.

## EYRE PENINSULA AND NULLARBOR PLAIN

If you are traveling from Port Augusta to Perth by car, you should take the old Highway 1 to **Whyalla** ❼, the gateway to the **Eyre Peninsula**. Whyalla is an industrial town and the home of the giant BHP Iron and Steel Works. From here follow the coastal road in a southwesterly direction and you will arrive at **Tumby Bay**, an attractive coastal resort. Another town on this very beautiful stretch of coastline is **Port Lincoln** ❽, the home of Australia's largest tuna fishing fleet. On *Australia Day* weekend (26 January) the whole town is out celebrating the **Tunarama Festival**, which marks the beginning of the tuna fishing season. Around Port Lincoln there are many small secluded bays, towering cliffs, and lovely surfing beaches, all worth a visit. The area is famous as a center for wool and grain, and is also known for its seafood, including lobsters, prawns and abalone. The scenic drive ★**Whalers Way** encompasses the magnificent coastal landscape of the area – secluded coves, high cliffs and surf beaches. On the way, stop in at the Constantia Designer Craftsmen (Mon-Fri 9:00 a.m. to 5:00 p.m.). The cabinet-makers, who have been awarded international accolades, have made tables for the Canberra Parliament, among others. This stretch of coast offers numerous water sports; swimming, water skiing and surfing, to name a few. Just 10 kilometers to the south is **Lincoln National Park** ❾, richly stocked with wildlife. The many offshore islands are also worth a trip: peaceful **Thistle Island** has good paths for walking, **Boston Island** is a paradise for birds, and **Wedge Island** just offers solitude. Leaving Port Lincoln, you continue along the coast road to the resort town of **Elliston** ❿, set in the hills of Waterloo Bay. The rugged coastline offers good fishing and some safe and sheltered bathing beaches. Further down this coast you will finally reach the holiday resort and fishing port of **Streaky Bay** ⓫, which owes its to a name to a local seaweed that creates a streaked effect in the sea. Here, too, there are lovely sandy beaches, small secluded coves, and towering cliffs.

**Point Labatt** ⓬, 40 kilometers to the south, is known for its colony of sealions. From Streaky Bay the coastal road leads to **Ceduna** ⓭, situated on the edge of vast Nullarbor Plain. The fishing fleet which is based in this small town sails out to catch whiting, snapper, salmon, and crab. The Eyre Peninsula can be crossed from Port Augusta either by train or on the highway. You can continue exploring the coast of the Great Australian Bight while driving through ★**Nullarbor National Park** ⓮. From June to October, southern right wales swim past the souther coast of Australia. One of the

best places to observe this is ★**Head of Bight**, 78 kilometers west of Yalata. Five additional lookouts in Nullarbor National Park are worth the detour. The road crosses the state border into Western Australia just before you reach Eucla. Caution: Both states (South and Western Australia) prohibit the importation of fruits and vegetables.

### TO PERTH VIA KALGOORLIE
#### – In the Footsteps of the Gold Prospectors –

From there Eyre Highway does a loop, taking you through the gold-mining town of **Norseman** ⓯, which is steeped in history. Once again the road divides, so that the capital of Western Australia, Perth, can be reached either by taking the Great Eastern Highway 94, a route which evokes memories of the gold rush, or by staying on Highway 1 and following the coast. Some 168 kilometers further on, the Great Eastern Highway will take you through **Coolgardie** ⓰. Over 15,000

*From Adelaide to Perth*

*Map page 116-117 / 120-121, Guidepost page 123*          119

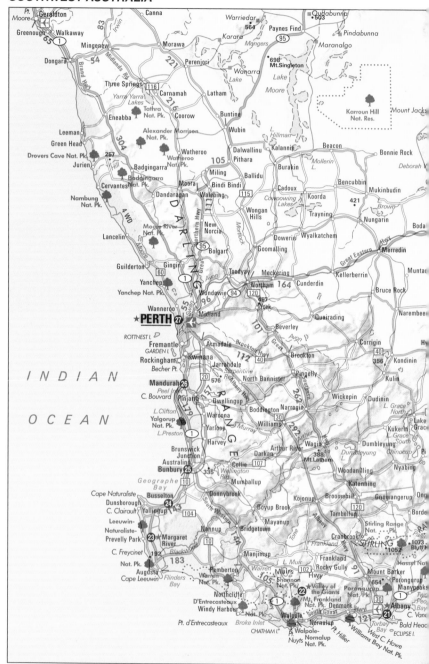

Lake Minigwal

Lake Raeside

L. Marmion

Lake Ballard

Lake Barlee
nals  L. Giles

Riverina

Menzies

237

Menangina

Edjudina

Goongarrie Nat. Pk.

Lake Rebecca

Goongarrie

Pinjin

Ponton

Broad Arrow

Carbine

Queen Victoria Spring Nat. Res.

Yindi

Kanowna (abandoned)

L. Roe

Cundeelee Community

Cundeelee Aboriginal Res.

olyenobbing

L. Deborah East

17 ★ Kalgoorlie-Boulder

Mt.Burges 553

16 Coolgardie

Lake Yindarlgooda

Avoca Downs

Coonana

Indian - Pacific

Zanthus

Creek

L. Seabrook

Boorabbin

nch

hern Cross Nat. Pk.

297

94 Yellowdine

57

39

83

Coolgardie-Esperance

444

Mount Monger

Kambalda

415

Widgiemooltha

Lake Lefroy

114

Binningie

Lake Cowan

Jilbadji Nat. Res.

94

Eyre Hwy

Fraser Range

Balladonia Motel

371

4 WD

15 Norseman

1

4 WD

Lake Johnston

586

Dundas

Balladonia

Nanambinia

Lake Dundas

Nat. Res.

ve Rock

L. Hope

4 WD

RHH

Gilmore

RUSSEL RANGE

Hanns Track Nat. Pk.

L. Sharpe

688 Peak Charles

Frank Hann Nat. Pk.

Salmon Gums

Peak Charles Nat. Pk.

4 WD

L. Tay

205

Mt.Ridley

L.Halbert

4 WD

Cape Arid 585

194

Lake King

Mends

Gras Patch

Israelite Bay

Newdegate King

40

L. Lockhart

Cascades

Scaddan

Orleans Farms

Nat. Park

Oldfield

Dalyup

19 Zeehan

198

Sandy Bight

C. Pasley

Ravensthorpe

1

187 Stokes Nat. Pk.

Munglinup

Esperance 18

Cape Le Grand Nat. Pk.

C. Arid

L. Magenta

Shoal C.

Esperance Bay

352

19 Rossiter Bay

MIDDLE I.

SALISBURY I.

Hassel

Fitzgerald

Powell Pt.

WEST GROUP

C. Le Grand

Mississippi Pt.

mungup

River

Hopetoun

MONDRAIN I.

Nat. Pk.

ARCHIPELAGO  OF  THE  RECHERCHE

Doubtful Island Bay

wood Hill

Hood Pt.

Bremer Bay

Pt. Henry

eyne Bay  C. Knob

. Riche

*Great      Australian      Bight*

*From Adelaide to Perth*

**SOUTHWEST AUSTRALIA**

0          50          100 km

people were already living here when this town was given its charter during the 1892 gold rush. There were 60 shops, 27 hotels, and 3 breweries! Today only a few historic buildings and museums remain as reminders of that golden age. Things are better in nearby ★**Kalgoorlie** ⓱, which does benefits economically from the nickel mines at Kambalda. However, tourists come to Kalgoorlie mainly because they are following the trail of the gold prospectors. The **Golden Mile** east of the town center proved to be a particularly rich vein. Today, the *Kalgoorlie Consolidated Mines* extract gold in opencast mining, digging ever deeper into the earth – the gigantic crater known as **Super Pit** is 300 meters deep (lookout daily 6:00 a.m. to 6:00 p.m.). ★**Hanna's North Tourist Mine** (daily 9:00 a.m. to 4:00 p.m.) and the **Museum of the Gold-Fields** located in Hannan St. offers an opportunity to savor the gold mining past. Through Southern Cross, Merredin and

*Above: Wave Rock is 2.7 million years old.*

Northam in the Avon valley, the highway will take you to Perth, a distance of another 556 kilometers.

### TO PERTH ALONG THE COAST

For those staying on Highway 1, the beckoning ocean will overcome the everlasting lure of gold. **Esperance** ⓲ lies 207 kilometers south of Norseman. Its beautiful sandy beaches and protected bays, especially in neighboring **Cape Le Grand National Park** ⓳, make it the perfect starting point for a journey along the coast. From Esperance or Albany you can cross the country through small towns like **Ravensthorpe**, an old gold and copper mining town, and **Katanning**, surrounded by gentle grazing land. North of these two towns, on Highway 40, is **Wave Rock** ⓴ (near Hyden), one of the most celebrated tourist attractions in the whole of Western Australia. This petrified wave, 15 meters high and 100 meters long, was created by erosion 2.7 million years ago. The coastal road runs towards ★**Albany** ㉑ via the South Coast and South Western Highway, through the remnants of the magnificent eucalyptus forests of the southwest. West of **Walpole**, a rewarding detour leads to the ★**Valley of the Giants** ㉒, famed for its towering Karri and Tingle trees. The highway runs to Perth through the orchards of **Bridgetown** and **Donnybrook**, and along the west coast. Make a detour to ★**Margaret River** ㉓, if you have the time. The area between Cape Leeuwin and Cape Naturaliste is renowned for its wine cellars, good surfing conditions, and limestone caves. Further along the coast is the unspoilt coastal town of **Busselton** ㉔ and the tourist center of **Bunbury** ㉕, which enjoys a warm climate and magnificent beaches. Have a look around the fishing village of **Mandurah** ㉖, where both the ocean and the river offer excellent conditions for water sports. From here, it is 80 kilometers to ★**Perth**.

### ALBANY (☎ 08)

🛏 😊😊 **Fredrickstown Motel**, 41 Fredericks St, Tel. 98411600. 😊 **Panorama Holiday Cottages & Caravan Park**, Frenchman Bay Rd, Tel. 98444031. **Bayview YHA**, 49 Duke St, Tel. 98423388

### AUGUSTA (☎ 08)

ℹ️ **Information Centre**, c/o Leeuwin Souvenirs, Blackwood Ave, Tel. 97581695.

🛏 😊😊 **Augusta Motel**, Blackwood Ave, Tel. 97581944. 😊 **Augusta Manor Resort YHA**, 88 Blackwood Ave, Tel. 97581290. **Doonbanks Caravan Park**, Blackwood Ave, Tel. 97581517.

### BAROSSA VALLEY (☎ 08)

ℹ️ **Barossa Wine & Visitor Centre**, 66-68 Murray St, Tanunda, Tel. 85630600 o. 1800-812662.

🛏 **ANGASTON**: 😊😊 **Vineyards**, Stockwell Rd, Tel. 85642404. 😊 **Barossa Brauhaus**, 41 Murray St, Tel. 85642014. **LYNDOCH**: 😊😊 **Chateau Yaldara Motor Inn**, Barossa Valley Hwy, Tel. 85244268. 😊 **Barossa Caravan Park**, Barossa Valley Hwy, Tel. 85244262. **TANUNDA**: 😊😊😊 **The Hermitage of Marananga**, Seppeltsfield Rd, Tel. 85622722. 😊😊 **Barossa Motor Lodge**, Murray St, Tel. 85632988. **Tanunda Caravan Park**, Barossa Valley Hwy, Tel. 85632784.

🍷 *WINE-TASTING*: **Basedows**, Murray St, Tanunda, Tel. 85630333. **Elderton**, Nuriootpa, Tel. 85621058. **Peter Lehman Wines**, Para Rd, Tanunda, Tel. 8563 2500. **Chateau Yaldara**, Lyndoch, Tel. 85244268.

🎪 **Oom-Pah-Festival**: End of January, Tanunda, Brass music and Bavarian *gemütlichkeit*. **HARVEST**: March / April. Every two years *Barossa Valley Vintage Festival*. **Wine and Music**: In October, concerts in churches and cellars of the valley (chamber music)

### BUNBURY (☎ 08)

ℹ️ **Tourist Bureau**, Carmody Pl, Tel. 97217922.

🛏 😊😊 **Chateau La Mer Motor Lodge**, 99 Ocean Drive, Tel. 97213166. 😊 **Backpackers Residency YHA**, corner of Stirling and Moore Sts, Tel. 97912621.

### CEDUNA (☎ 08)

ℹ️ **Tourist Centre**, 58 Poynton St, Tel. 86252780.

🛏 😊😊 **Ceduna Foreshore Community Motel**, O'Loughlin Terrace, Tel. 86252008. 😊 **Ceduna Caravan & Tourist Centre**, 29 McKenzie St, Tel. 86252150.

### COOLGARDIE (☎ 08)

ℹ️ **Tourist Bureau**, 62 Bayley St, Tel. 90266090.

🛏 😊 **Coolgardie Motel**, 49 Bayley St, Tel. 9026 6080. 😊 **Railway Lodge**, 75 Bayley St, Tel. 90266238.

🏛 **Old Railway Station Museum**, Woodward St, Tel. 90266388, daily 9:00 a.m.-5:00 p.m., closed Friday afternoons.

### ESPERANCE (☎ 08)

🛏 😊😊 **Bay of Isles**, 32 Esplanade, Tel. 90713999. **Esperance Beachfront Resort**, 19 Esplanade, Tel.

90712513. 😊 **Blue Waters Lodge YHA**, Goldfields Rd, Tel. 90711040.

### EUCLA (☎ 08)

🛏 😊😊 **Eucla Motor Hotel**, Eyre Highway, Tel. 90393468 (11 km east of the border)

### KADINA (☎ 08)

ℹ️ **Tourist Information**, 57 Main St, Tel. 88532477.

🛏 😊😊 **Kadina Gateway Motor Inn**, Adelaide Rd, Tel. 88212777. 😊 **Kadina Caravan Park**, Lindsay Terrace, Tel. 88212259

### KALGOORLIE (☎ 08)

ℹ️ **Tourist Centre**, 250 Hannan St, Tel. 90211966.

🛏 😊😊 **Mercure Inn Overland**, Hannan St, Tel. 90211433. **Goldfields Backpackers**, 166 Hay St, Tel. 90911482.

🏛 **Museum of the Goldfields**, 17 Hannan St, Tel. 90218533, daily 10:00 a.m.-4:30 p.m.

🚗 6 km to the south, on the Broad Arrow Rd, one of Australia's most unusual gambling places: the **Bush Two-up School**. This game has been played here since 1983 in a rustic atmosphere.

### MARGARET RIVER (☎ 08)

ℹ️ **Tourist Bureau**, corner of Tunbridge Rd / Bussell Hwy, Tel. 97572911.

🚗 The nearby **Strand** is one of the best for surfing in Australia (contests Oct. / Nov.).

🚗 The approximately 30 **wine estates** in Leeuwin Naturaliste National Park produce excellent wines.

### NORSEMAN (☎ 08)

ℹ️ **Tourist Bureau**, Robert St, Tel. 991071.

🛏 😊😊 **Great Western**, Prinsep St, Tel. 90391633.

### NULLARBOR (☎ 08)

🛏 😊😊 **Nullarbor Hotel & Caravan Park**, Eyre Hwy, Tel. 86256271.

### PORT AUGUSTA (☎ 08)

ℹ️ **Wadlata Outback Centre**, 41 Flinders Terrace, Tel. 86410793.

🛏 😊😊 **Augusta Westside**, 3 Loudon Road, Tel. 86422488. **Flinders Hotel**, 39 Commercial Road, Tel. 86422544.

🚗 It is imperative to fill your gas tank and water reserves and to purchase provisions.

### PORT LINCOLN (☎ 08)

ℹ️ **Information Centre**, 66 Tasman Terrace, Tel. 86833544 and 1800-629911.

🛏 😊😊 **Hilton Motel**, 13 King St, Tel. 86821144.

### STIRLING RANGE NAT. PARK (☎ 08)

🛏 😊 **Stirling Range Retreat**, Chester Pass Rd, Tel. 98279229. **Porongurup YHA**, approximately 40 km to the south near the Porongurup Tearooms, Tel. 98531100.

🚗 In the wildflower season (Sept.-Oct.) the state's flower (and emblem), the kangaroo paw, blooms.

*From Adelaide to Perth*

# PERTH
# THE TRANQUIL
# SOUTHWEST

## CITY TOUR
## AROUND PERTH

Water is to **\*Perth** what Central Park is to New York, or St. Peter's Square to Rome. Life is pleasant for the 1.1 million people who live in this capital city of Western Australia.

On typically sunny summer days, life and leisure are concentrated on the elegant, palm-lined shores of the broad estuary of the Swan River. Flotillas of black swans glide on the deep blue waters of the river where it meets the brine of the Indian Ocean. So it is hardly surprising to find that water sports like sailing, surfing, and water-skiing are especially popular.

The people of Perth like to refer to their city as the most isolated capital in the world, and it is a fact Perth is situated in the middle of nowhere. South Australia's capital, Adelaide, the closest city to Perth, is 2700 kilometers away. Jakarta, the capital of Indonesia, to the north across the Indian Ocean, is actually closer than Australia's own capital, Canberra, which is 4000 kilometers distant.

It was precisely this position, on Australia's geographical and political margin, which held back Perth's development for many years. This very isolation has given the people of Perth a most distinctive character. They possess a potent blend of

*Left: Perth skyline.*

independence, self-confidence, and ambition, which even today gives them a certain drive and vitality.

Of all the Australian cities, Perth, sometimes known as the City of Lights or the Gateway to the West, has the most days of sunshine per year (on average eight hours a day). This rubs off on the inhabitants and puts them in a predominantly cheerful mood. Even tourists quickly learn to share this relaxed enjoyment.

Perth appears at once clean, prosperous, and futuristic, as its glinting skyscrapers soar heavenwards above the pedestrian precinct. Rows of old houses, carefully restored in their candy floss colors and preserved as relics of the pioneer age, huddle in front of it like a stage set.

Less than 200 years ago, this area belonged only to the Nyungar Aborigines. Not until 1829 did a handful of white people arrive along the Swan River, following the old routes of Dutch seafarers.

This small group, led by the British captain Charles Fremantle, settled on the river's green fertile banks. Later, from 1850 to 1868, hundreds of convicts were transported to Perth. They laid the foundations not only for the first houses and the railway, but also for the future of the city. Towards the end of the last century, the gold rush triggered a new economic

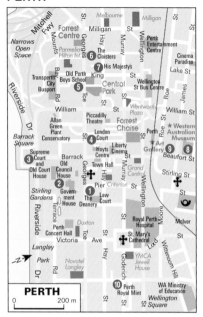

boom. However, it was only after the discovery of extensive mineral deposits over the last few decades, that Perth was able to emerge from its isolation from the rest of the world.

## CITY TOUR

A good starting point for a tour around the city is **The Deanery** ❶, the residence of the Anglican Dean of Perth, on the corner of St. George's Terrace and Pier Street. It is one of the very few buildings that have been preserved from the middle of the last century.

Opposite is the **Government House** (1864), the official seat of the Governor of Western Australia, built in a mixture of Romanesque and Gothic styles, and looking like an Australian version of the Tower of London with all its arches and turrets. In neighboring **Stirling Gardens**

*Above: The small town of Fremantle is a sailing El Dorado. Right: The old town of Perth as an attractive background for a movie set.*

❷ is the **Old Courthouse** (1836), nowadays the home of the Western Australian law offices.

From here, it is just a few minutes' walk through the park, down to Swan River, which was named by a Dutchman, Willem de Vlamingh. In 1697, he discovered the river with its many black swans, and it is this bird that was adopted as the state bird on Western Australia's heraldic coat-of-arms.

**Barrack Square** ❸, on the river bank, is the departure point for boat trips up-river to the Swan River vineyards, or downstream to Fremantle and Rottnest Island, which the inhabitants refer to as Rotto. Or take the ferry over to the other side of **Perth Water** and there visit the **zoo** in South Perth.

If you leave St. George's Terrace and carry on walking beyond Barrack Street and out towards the west, you will get to **London Court** ❹. This is a shopping arcade, with Tudor-style buildings, carved wood, wrought-iron railings and a replica of Big Ben, and all are meant to remind

one of far-off England. Further places of interest along St. George's Terrace are the **Old Perth Boys' School** ❺ (1854) and **The Cloisters** ❻ (1858), both once boys' private schools, as well as the magnificent **His Majesty's Theatre** ❼ in Hay St. (1904).

In the Northbridge district, the *★Western Australian Museum* ❽ (Francis Street) and the *★Western Australian Art Gallery* ❾ (James Street) house two of the best art collections in the state, and include numerous examples of Aborigine and pioneer history in Western Australia. Another place worth a visit is the nearby **Old Gaol** (part of the W.A. Museum), a former prison built in the Georgian style. Northbridge offers more than culture, however: Over the last few years this part of town has become famous for its night-life and its wide choice of ethnic restaurants.

**Perth Mint** ❿ is the old western Australian coin mint, in which today special coins and gold bars for collectors are struck.

## AROUND PERTH

In Perth you can get to any place you want in fifteen minutes, say the taxi-cab drivers, and they are usually right. Using busy St. George's Terrace, which slices through the center of town on four carriageways, you will arrive with great ease at the very nearest, pure white, almost empty beach in a quarter of an hour. There are a total of 19 beaches to choose from in the urban area alone.

Along the Swan River, Perthians prefer to dive in at **Como**, **Peppermint Cove**, or **Crawley**. On the Indian Ocean, cool off at **Cottesloe**, **City**, **Floreat** and **Scarborough Beach** ⓫. Further north, the **Sorrento** ⓬ aquarium **Underwater World** and **Hillary's Boat Harbour** beckon with shopping and entertainment.

Perth also has magnificently laid out parks. The largest and best known is *★King's Park* ⓭, which covers an area of 400 hectares, and brings natural bush country right into the center of town, interspersed with gardens, paths for walk-

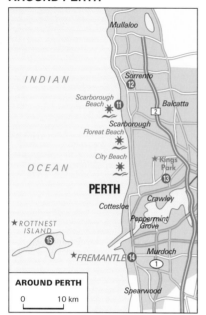

been forgotten, Fremantle attracts more and more visitors from all over the world. One reason for this is surely the appeal of its glamorous, Mediterranean-style yacht harbor. It also has its own special atmosphere, a unique blend of rugged history and a relaxed outlook on life that is typically Australian.

Along the **High Street** there are some beautiful old buildings, among them a number of pubs steeped in tradition. At the western end of the street, on Arthur Head, is the former **Round House** prison.

The nearby **Western Australian Maritime Museum** displays interesting items relating to seafaring history in the 17th century. A good lunch can be eaten in one of the fish restaurants down near the water. **Fremantle Markets** are also worth a visit (Friday and Saturday mornings).

Naturally, Fremantle has some lovely beaches, most of which are to be found along a 30-kilometer-stretch of coast running northward. On the direct route back to Perth from Fremantle you will pass through several pretty suburbs, such as **Subiaco**, which dates from around the turn of the century, or **Dalkeith**, on the river, with its exclusive luxury villas.

One of the most attractive excursions into Perth's surroundings is a boat trip or flight to **\*Rottnest Island** ⑮. It is an experience not to be missed. Rottnest Island is famous for the little marsupials called quokkas, which can only be found here, and who have grown accustomed to humans.

The Dutchman Willem de Vlamingh who landed on this island in 1696 mistook the quokkas for rats - hence the name Rottnest (Rats' Nest). On the island there are idyllic bays, fabulous spots for diving, and, best of all, no cars.

You can spend the night in a little cottage and recuperate after your hectic activity in Perth, or gather your strength for the coming ordeal of traveling along the 4205-kilometer-long route from Perth to Darwin.

ing, restaurants and a lookout tower. It is well worth a visit, especially during Western Australia's springtime (end of August to beginning of October) when wild flowers are in bloom over large areas of the park. From the high ground, at sunset, you get the most magnificent view of the city's illuminated skyline.

An appendage to modern Perth is the little port town of **\*Fremantle** ⑭ on the very mouth of the Swan River. Freo, as it is affectionately called, was for many years a sleepy little town, in which Perth's Bohemian set gradually began to establish itself. When Fremantle was chosen as the venue for the America's Cup contest in 1987, Freo received a facelift and the town was revamped at great cost.

The old houses, most of which already had preservation orders on them, were carefully restored. Today, they are used as museums, art galleries, hotels, restaurants, and pubs. Although the bustle and activity surrounding the America's Cup sailing regatta has long died down and

## PERTH (☎ 08)

**ℹ Western Australia Tourist Centre**, Forrest Place / Wellington Street, Tel. 94831111 or 1300-361351. Mon-Thurs 8:30 a.m.-6:00 p.m., Fri 8:30 a.m.-7:00 p.m., Sat 8:30 a.m.-5:00 p.m., Sun 10:00 a.m.-5:00 p.m.

**Fremantle Tourist Information Centre**, Town Hall Centre, King Square, Tel. 94317878.

**✈ The international airport is 17 km northeast of the city center, the domestic airport is 12 km northeast. The Airport Bus** provides transportation from the city to all international ($A 10) and inner-Australian flights ($A 8) respectively, Tel. 94794131. *Transperth Bus* 200 / 202 / 208 runs to the domestic airport (from St George's Terrace), fare is $A 2,40. There is no public bus to the international airport. A taxi will cost between $A 17-22.

Free **CAT-Busse** *(Central Area Transit System)* run in the city district: *Blue CAT* in north-south direction Mon-Fri from 7:00 a.m.-6:00 p.m., approximately every 10 minutes. The route changes slightly on the weekned. (*Weekend CAT*) Fri 6:00 p.m.-1:00 a.m, Sat 8:30 a.m.-1:00 p.m. and Sun 10:00 a.m.-5:00 p.m. *Red CAT* in east-west direction Mon-Fri 7:00 a.m.-6:00 p.m., every 5 minutes.

**▦ ❸❸❸ Duxton Hotel Perth**, 1 St. George's Terrace, Tel. 92618000. **Hyatt Regency Perth**, 99 Adelaide Terrace, Tel. 92251234. **Novotel Langley Perth**, corner of Adelaide Terrace and Hill St, Tel. 92211200. **Rendezvous Observation City Hotel**, The Esplanade, Scarborough, Tel. 92451000.

**Sheraton Perth**, 207 Adelaide Terrace, Tel. 93250501. **The Fremantle Esplanade**, corner of Marine Terrace and Essex St, Tel. 94324000.

**❸❸ Chateau Commodore**, 417 Hay St, Tel. 93250461. **Perth Ambassador Hotel**, 196 Adelaide Terrace, Tel. 93251455. **Wentworth Plaza**, 300 Murray St, Tel. 94811000.

**Tradewinds Fremantle**, 59 Canning Highway, Tel. 93398188

**❸ Backpackers Inn-Freo YHA**, 11 Pakenham Street, Fremantle, Tel. 94317065. **Britannia International YHA**, 253 William Street, Tel. 93286121.

**North Lodge**, 225 Beaufort Street, Northbridge, Tel. 92277588. **Northbridge YHA**, 46 Francis Street, Tel. 93287794.

**Shenton Park Hotel**, Nicholson Road, Subiaco, Tel. 92818133.

**YMCA Jewell House**, 180 Goderich Street, East Perth, Tel. 93258488.

**Fremantle Village Caravan Park**, corner of Cockburn and Rollinson Roads, Tel. 94304866.

**✗** If you need to budget, eat in Northbridge; there you will find many restaurants with reasonable prices. For tasty seafood, in abundance, Fremantle is the place to go. Aussies agree: Perth has some of the best beer gardens in Australia.

**Mamma Maria**, corner of Aberdeen and Lake Streets, Northbridge, Tel. 92279828, Italian. **Sri Melaka**, 313 William St, Northbridge, Tel. 93286406. Malayan cuisine .

**Trains, Planes & Automobiles**, 46 Lake St, Northbridge, Tel. 93282350, Steak house. **Sail & Anchor Hotel & Brasserie**, 64 South Terrace, Fremantle. has its own brewery in a historical pub, there is a restaurant on the first floor.

**Sails**, 47 Mews Road, Fishing Boat Harbour, Fremantle. **The Oyster Beds**, 26 Riverside Road, East Fremantle, Tel. 3391611. Both restaurants serve excellent seafood.

**▦ Art Gallery of Western Australia**, James St, Tel. 94926600, large collection of Australian art, daily 10:00 a.m.-5:00 p.m.

**Western Australian Museum**, Francis St, Tel. 94272700, history of the state, Sun-Fri 10:30 a.m.-5:00 p.m., Sat 1:00 a.m.-5:00 p.m..

**Western Australian Maritime Museum**, Cliff St, Fremantle, Tel. 94318444, collection pertaining to the topics of the discovery and history of seafaring in Western Australia, daily,10:30 a.m.-5:00 p.m.

**Fremantle Arts Centre**, 1 Finnery St, Tel. 93358244, daily, 10:00 a.m.-5:00 p.m. The **Fremantle Museum** is in the same building, Tel. 94307966, with numerous mementos from colonial times. Sun-Fri 10:30 a.m.-4:30 p.m., Sat 1:00 p.m.-5:00 p.m.

**▨ If you want to tempt Lady Luck in Perth, try the Burswood Casino**, Great Eastern Highway, Victoria Park, Tel. 93627777. Night-clubs with live bands and pubs are found mostly in Northbridge.

**◀ SHOPPING:** The widest selection can be found in Hay Street Mall, Murray Street, Wellington Street and Forrest Place. Claremont is upmarket (and therefore rather expensive). Subiaco presents casual chic and stylish young people shop in Northbridge.

On the weekends, (Fri 9:00 a.m.-9:00 p.m., Sat 9:00 a.m.-5:00 p.m., Sun 10:00 a.m.-5:00 p.m.) shopping and browsing are recommended at the **Fremantle Markets**, South Terrace and Henderson Street. Everything under the sun can be found there, from art to souvenir kitsch.

**▨ Festival of Perth**: Three weeks of culture and entertainment in the months of February and March.

**Western Australia Week**: Foundation Day is celebrated on the first Monday in June with a holiday. In the following weeks, numerous sports and cultural events take place.

*Perth*

# FROM PERTH TO DARWIN

## FROM PERTH TO PORT HEDLAND
## BROOME AND THE KIMBERLEY REGION
## PURNULULU (BUNGLE BUNGLE) AND MIRIMA (HIDDEN VALLEY) NATIONAL PARKS

Until recently, the route to the north was taken only by experienced bush travelers. Nowadays, the most important prerequisite for this 4205-kilometer-stretch is the ability to repair a vehicle yourself should it break down, despite the fact that the greatest distance between two service stations is now only 268 kilometers, providing you stick to the main route. From November to April, however, heavy downpours rapidly make the roads, (not just the unsurfaced stretches), practically impassable, yet during that period the climate is extremely hot and humid. As a rule, travelers taking the route from Perth to Darwin should allow about two weeks. It is advisable to travel with an all-terrain vehicle, should you wish to risk the rewarding detours to be found on the less reliable tracks.

### FROM PERTH TO PORT HEDLAND

The best plan is to leave Perth, Western Australia's capital, on the coastal road, State Route 60, which runs in the direction of Wanneroo and Guilderton. After traveling 52 kilometers you will reach

*Previous pages: Through the Outback in Western Australia. Left: Wind and erosion have shaped the Pinnacles.*

**Yanchep National Park ❶** with its famous colony of koalas. 70 kilometers further on is **Lancelin ❷**, where a quick trip to the beach is a must, as this is one of the best windsurfing beaches in the world. Another trip not to be missed is a detour (four-wheel drive only) into the snowy-white dunes that border the Indian Ocean. From Lancelin, a track leads back to Brand Highway (Highway 1).

**\*Nambung National Park ❸** stretches over 20 kilometers along the coast. Brand Highway branches off onto an access road which leads to **Cervantes** on the northern end of the park. Just after this fork, the Koonah Road leads to the wildflower farm called **Waddi Farms**. It is particularly worth visiting at the time of the wildflower harvest (end of August until beginning of October), when the flowers form endless carpets of color in the desert. In the south of the National Park rise the **Pinnacles**. These miraculous sandstone formations are more than 30,000 years old. There, in an area of desert stretching for more than 400 hectares, millions of ocher or yellow cones rise up to 5 meters in height. It is worth rising at dawn to enjoy the play of light and shadow in the early morning. There is overnight accommodation in the Nambung National Park camping ground and Cervantes Pinnacles Motel. There are

*From Perth to Darwin*

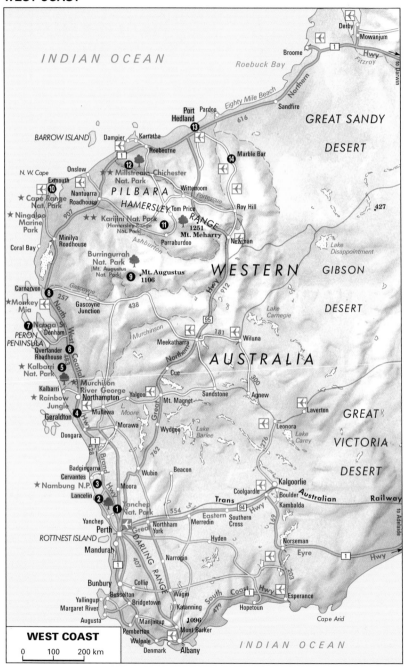

WEST COAST

0    100    200 km

many good detours to the coast, through small fishing villages like Green Head, Leeman, or Coolimba. The small town of **Geraldton** ❹ (424 kilometers) on the Indian Ocean is nicknamed Sun City, and its clean streets and houses really do gleam. If you are dining in Geraldton, ask for lobster, their culinary specialty. The town's **museum** provides a good glimpse back into the history of the whole region. Geraldton's biggest attraction, however, is the lovely beach, which is also a surfing paradise. At **Kalbarri** (an 86- kilometer-detour from the highway), surrounded by **\*Kalbarri National Park** ❺, the Murchison River flows into the Indian Ocean, and one view not to be missed is **\*Murchison River Gorge** with its huge red cliffs and rocky walls located in the National Park. This gorge, 80 meters long and up to 150 meters deep, is best explored by means of **The Loop** and **Z Bend**, **Hawk's Head** and **Ross Graham Lookout**. There is access to the river from the former. About 4 kilometers away from Kalbarri, on the road to Red Bluff, you will find **\*Rainbow Jungle**, one of Australia's finest bird sanctuaries. A further 45 kilometers to the north, you should definitely take a break at the **Overlander Roadhouse** ❻. Until a few years ago, nobody could take the risk of not stopping at the roadhouse to fill up with fuel. Even today, it is still a sensible precaution to take. At the Overlander Roadhouse the road turns off left, via a dusty, red-earth track, to the **Peron Peninsula** ❼ (783 kilometers). At **Nanga Station**, Ted and Maureen Sears have built their dream house out of seashells. You can spend the night in the adjoining caravan park, or in simple twin bedrooms in the house, and then have enough time to explore this long shell beach right in front of the station. On the other side of

the peninsula is **\*Monkey Mia** (856 kilometers). For the past 30 years, dolphins have been coming in right up to the beach in nearby Shark Bay. They have become used to people and will allow themselves to be fed. At feeding time, small buckets of fish are handed out to the tourists. But it is best to stick to the no feeding rule outside of the regular feeding hours.

In **Carnarvon** ❽ (902 kilometers), a side road turns off to Gascoyne Junction (164 kilometers) in the interior. From there, it is 230 kilometers to **Burrington (Mt. Augustus) National Park** ❾. Mount Augustus, for the most part covered in vegetation, is the largest single piece of rock in the world, twice the height and twice the length of Ayers Rock, and a veritable paradise for some 200 species of birds, as well as kangaroos, and lizards over a meter in length. The climb to the summit (1106 meters), takes some 3-4 hours (spectacular at sunrises and sunsets). Overnight accommodation can be found on some of the large sheep farms in the area, and you could

*Above: Actually, our photographer in Monkey Mia was supposed to take snapshots of the dolphins...*

*From Perth to Darwin*

hardly wish for a more typically Australian experience. The next 225 kilometers long is to **Minilya Roadhouse**, towards **Exmouth** ❿ (1260 kilometers). Those equipped with a four-wheel drive vehicle can drive from Exmouth on the west coast along the deeply fissured ★**Cape Range National Park,** with its cliffs and ravines. Otherwise, there are glimpses of the ravines from the **Shothole Canyon Road**, 16 kilometers south of Exmouth.

★**Ningaloo Marine Park** stretches along the entire west coast of the peninsula and includes a 260- kilometer-long reef with magnificent coral formations, some of which are only 200 meters from the beach. The largest fish in the world, the whale-shark, can be found here. In June and July, hump-back whales pass the park, and starting in November, turtles come to lay their eggs in the sand. **Coral Bay** is a good place for a snorkel-ing or diving trip to the reef (there is overnight accommodation available here).

Back on the North West Coastal Highway, State Road 136 beyond **Nanutarra Roadhouse** leads you in the direction of Tom Price to the ★★**Karijini (Hamersley Range) National Park** ⓫ (340 kilometers), with Australia's most spectacular deep gorges – **Dales**, **Kalamina**, **Knox**, **Hancock**, **Weano**, **Red** and **Hamersley Gorge** – and high waterfalls (Joffre Falls). You may decide not to turn off for the Hamersley Range until you get to **Roeburne**. On this route you will first come to ★★**Millstream Chichester National Park** ⓬, with picturesque oases around the waterfalls **Chunderwarriner Pool** and **Python Pool**, which also merits a visit. For all trips to the Pilbara Region, four-wheel drive vehicles are essential.

Depending on your choice of route, you will reach **Port Hedland** ⓭ (1761 kilometers), the largest industrial port in Western Australia (export of ore), either via the Great North West Coastal Highway (along the coast via Karratha), or by

*Above: The Pilbara mining region is increasingly "going to the dogs." Right: Camel trekking on Cable Beach in Broome.*

taking the Northern Highway. A little off the beaten track is **Marble Bar ⓮** (203 kilometers from Port Hedland), where the gold found in 1891 has long been forgotten, but the claim to being the hottest town in Australia is probably as true as it ever was. From October to March, temperatures of over 40 °C are quite normal. Marble Bar is the capital of East Pilbara Shire, an area which is larger than New Zealand or Italy, but with a population of less than 1000. **Eighty Mile Beach**, where camping is available at Wallal Downs, begins between **Pardoo Roadhouse** (1801 kilometers and **Sandfire** (1932 kilometers).

## *BROOME AND THE **KIMBERLEYS

*Broome ⓯** (2352 kilometers), with its 6000 inhabitants, is an attractive small town where a touch of hippy culture lingers on. The liveliness of the motley inhabitants, the old-fashioned wooden and corrugated-iron buildings and the glorious tropical scenery all add to the charm of this place. The origin of the town's existence was the discovery in the 1880s of large quantities of pearl oysters. At the height of the mother-of-pearl boom, there were more than 400 pearl fishers in the town. Many divers came here from as far away as the islands of the South Pacific, from southeast Asia, and even from Japan. Even today, pearls are the main attraction of the town. Broome is situated at the head of a peninsula and, thanks to gentle sea breezes, it enjoys a milder climate than the rest of the tropical Kimberleys. The best time to visit is the dry season, from April to October. At the end of August / beginning of September, when the colorful **Shinju Pearl Festival** takes place, more than 30,000 visitors arrive in town. **Chinatown** (Carnarvon Street) has a particularly beguiling atmosphere. Just outside Broome lies **\*Cable Beach**, only 30 kilometers long and 100

meters wide and consisting entirely of snow-white sand. A few kilometers away from the club is **Gantheaume Point** where, at low tide, you may see the fossilized footprints of dinosaurs (more than 120 million years old). The cliffs around here are particularly beautiful at sunrise and sunset. A half-hour drive leads to **Willie Creek Pearl Farm**, where you can watch the oysters being prepared for the cultivation of pearls. At the **Bird Observatory** (20 kilometers) to the east, numerous migratory birds from Siberia spend the winter in Roebuck Bay.

**Derby ⓰** (2506 kilometers), is the administrative center for the region, and is rich in memories of the 1880s when the Aborigines put up remarkably stiff resistance against the European settlers. Nowadays, the descendants of the original inhabitants of Australia have again secured a place to live on the outskirts of Derby. Thus, **Mowanjum** ("settled at last") was one of the first independent Aborigine settlements in the Kimberleys. A typical feature of the entire area is the baobab

*From Perth to Darwin*

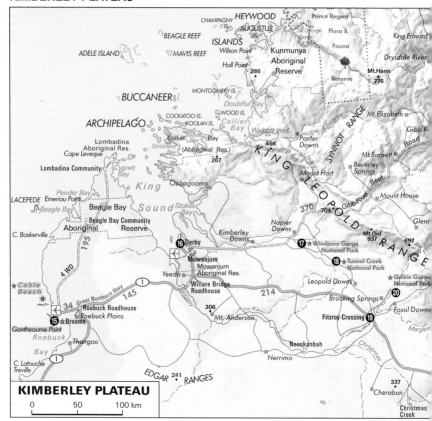

**KIMBERLEY PLATEAU**

```
0        50        100 km
```

tree, (called boab in Australia) or Monkey Puzzle Tree – looks like bottles and can measure up to 14 meters across. In the old days, a hollow tree near Derby supposedly was used, or rather misused, to imprison Aborigines. In Clarendon Street you can find one of the headquarters of the legendary the **Flying Doctor Service** and the **School of the Air**, which aims to provide children in the remote Outback with an essential education by radio.

Cruises departing from Derby are expensive but well worth it if one enjoys angling and wishes to discover the wild, as yet not opened to tourism coastal landscape of West Kimberley with its hundreds of islands and deep fjords. From Derby you can either travel through the Kimberleys to Kununurra, then along the Great Northern Highway, or drive along the legendary Gibb River Road (accessible by four-wheel drive only). The **\*\*Kimberleys** are among the last, great and almost untouched areas of wilderness in Australia. The rivers, rapid during the rainy season, have worn deep gorges into the ancient limestone formations. In the dry season the region seems less impressive, but try to come at that time (April to October) for the area can be inaccessible for weeks during the rainy season. From Gibb River Road there is a detour to **\*Windjana Gorge** ⑰ and **\*Tunnel Creek** ⑱. Windjana Gorge is about 140 kilometers east of Derby, and displays spectacular limestone escarpments which

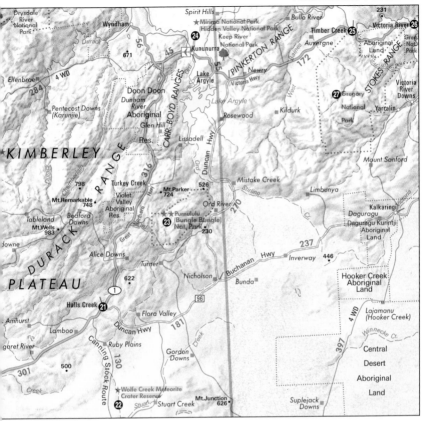

are of great interest both to anthropologists and geologists. Here are some of the best fossil deposits in the world, and Aborigine rock paintings have been preserved in numerous caves. Tunnel Creek is a completely natural tunnel cave, 12 meters high, and 75 meters long, which was tunneled out by a river in the Napier Range, and which can be explored in two hours, provided one is equipped with a flashlight. There can be very few travelers who have not followed the old tradition of stopping at **Fitzroy Crossing ⑲** (2686 kilometers) to quench their thirst, for this town is renowned for its pubs, veritable oases of beer in the dry desert. There is an inn, service stations, garage for car repairs, supermarket, hotel, motel,

caravan park, post office, hospital and police station. 20 kilometers to the west of Fitzroy, is ★**Geikie Gorge National Park ⑳**. The gorge was formed by the Fitzroy River, and is about 14 kilometers long, with spectacular cliffs reaching a height of 30 meters. The river flows all year round and river crocodiles can be found in its waters. Explore the gorge is by the boat that runs twice daily from early March through November.

### ★★PURNULULU (BUNGLE BUNGLE) NATIONAL PARK

From **Halls Creek ㉑** (2977 kilometers) there are two great natural spectacles to visit. In ★**Wolfe Creek Meteorite**

*From Perth to Darwin*

Crater Reserve ㉒ (148 kilometers), you can see the second-largest meteorite crater in the world, with a diameter of 850 meters and a depth of 49 meters, created some 50,000 years ago. The region around **★Purnululu Bungle Bungle National Park ㉓** did not enter public consciousness until the 1980s. This dramatic landscape conceals some of the oldest rock formations in the world (350 million years). The surface of the earth seems wrinkled with age and the rock rises steeply to form towers and domes, interspersed with precipitous gorges full of tropical vegetation, where waterfalls plunge into the depths. The only way through is a track (four-wheel drive only!), which begins 110 kilometers north of Halls Creek. Allow at least three-four hours to drive the 55 kilometers to the park. Camping sites have been established at two sites for tourists (with toilets and fire places). Footpaths lead to

*Above: Aerial view of the tangle of ravines in Purnululu National Park.*

Echidna Chasm to the north, and to Cathedral Gorge and Picaninny Gorge more to the south. The park is closed during the rainy season.

### ★MIRIMA (HIDDEN VALLEY) NATIONAL PARK

**★Mirima (Hidden Valley) National Park ㉔** is a miniature Bungle-Bungle landscape at the front door of Kununurra (3336 kilometers). The lively town with 4,000 inhabitants is worth a stay. Walk to Hidden Valley, see the glorious sunset at Lake Kununurra or take a drive to the Ord River, which flows into Lake Argyle.

43 kilometers beyond Kununurra you will leave Western Australia and enter the Northern Territory. From **Timber Creek ㉕** or **Victoria River ㉖**, one can explore **Gregory National Park ㉗**, or spend the night in a fishing camp (boat trips from 1 April to 31 October). At Katherine, Victoria Highway hits Stuart Highway. **★Darwin**, capital of the Northern Territory is 321 kilometers away.

## PERTH-DARWIN (☎ 08)

**National Parks entrance fees:** Day Pass $A 8 for one car with a maximum of 8 passengers, $A 3 for a motorcycle. *Holiday Pass* (valid for four weeks), $A 20 per car, or the *Annual Pass* for $A 45 per Auto; all of these can be obtained at the *WA Tourist Centre* in Perth, some other *Tourist Centres* and at the entrance to the National Parks (remote parks rely on an *honesty box* at the park entrance)

A **Roadhouse**, in addition to gas, fast food and shopping, offers simple lodgings, a bar or a restaurant. It is often the social center of the surrounding area. Inexpensive, typical Australian *counter lunches* can be obtained here (one orders at the counter and pays immediately). **Overlander**: Tel. 99425916 (24/24). **Carnarvon**: Kickstarters, Tel. 99418291 (24/24). **Cervantes**: Tel. 96527041. **Derby**: Colac Service Station, Tel. 91911 256. **Fitzroy Crossing**: Ngiyali, Tel. 919195366. **Karratha**: Fortescue River, Tel. 91845126 (6:00 a.m.-11:P00 p.m.). **Kununurra**: Elgee Automotives, Tel. 91682236. **Nanutarra**: Tel. 99430521 (24/24). **Northampton**: Tel. 99341105. **Sandfire** (300 km southwest of Broome, 6:00 a.m.-midnight), Tel. 91765944. **Pardoo** (151 km from Port Hedland, 6:00 a.m.-10:00 p.m.), Tel. 91764916. **Wooramel**: Tel. 99425910. For all, even short, trips on the Perth-Darwin stretch. it is imperative to bring along gas and (drinking) water! !

**Kimberley Flights**: Fly over the Purnululu National Park to the Mitchell Falls in the North Kimberley Region: *Alligator Airways*, Tel. 1800-632533, and *Slingair*, Tel. 1800-095500; both in Kununurra.

### BROOME

**Tourist Office**, Great Northern Hwy, Ecke Bagot St, Tel. 91922222.

**Cable Beach Inter-Continental Resort**, Cable Beach Rd, Tel. 91920400 and 1800-221335. **Ocean Lodge**, Cable Beach Rd, Tel. 91937700. **Mangrove Hotel**, Carnarvon St, Tel. 1800-094818. **Broometime Lodge**, 59 Forrest St, Tel. 1800-804322. **Broomes Last Resort YHA**, Bagot St, Tel. 19800-801918. **Palm Grove Caravan Resort**, Corner Murray / Cable Beach Rd, Tel. 91923336.

**Annelie's Swiss Restaurant**, Napier Terrace. **Palms Cafe Bar** and **Settlers Bar & Grill**, Mangrove Hotel, Carnarvon St. Lovely view of Roebuck Bay.

### CARNARVON

**Tourist Bureau**, 6 Robinson St, Tel. 99411146.

**Carnarvon Beach Holiday Resort**, Pelican Point Rd, Tel. 99412226. **Carnarvon Backpackers YHA**, 50 Olivia Terrace, Tel. 99411095. **Carnarvon Caravan Park**, Robinson St, Tel. 99418101.

### CORAL BAY

**Ningaloo Reef Resort**, Tel. 99425934. **Bayview Coral Bay**, Tel. 99425932.

### DERBY

**Tourist Bureau**, Clarendon St, Tel. 91911426.

**Derby Boab Inn**, 84 Loch St, Tel. 91911044. **Kimberley Entrance Caravan Park**, Rowan St, Tel. 91931055.

### EXMOUTH

**Tourist Bureau**, Payne St, Tel. 99491176.

**Potshot Hotel Resort**, Murat Rd, Tel. 99491200. **Petes Exmouth Backpackers YHA**, corner of Truscott Crescent & Murat St, Tel. 99491101.

### FITZRZOY CROSSING

**Fitzroy River Lodge**, Great Northern Hwy, Tel. 91915141.

### GERALDTON

**Tourist Bureau**, Bill Sewell Complex, Chapman Rd, Tel. 99213999.

**Geraldton City Resort**, 137 Cathedral Ave, Tel. 99216111. **Foreshore YHA**, 172 Marine Tce, Tel. 99213275. **Separation Point Caravan Park**, corner Portway / Separation Way, Tel. 99212763. **Geraldton Museum**, Marine Terrace, 17th / 18th century Dutch ship wrecks. Daily 10:00 a.m.-4:00 p.m.

### HALLS CREEK

**Kimberley**, Tel. 91686101. **Halls Creek Caravan Park**, Tel. 91686169, both on Roberta Ave.

### KALBARRI

**Kalbarri Palm Resort**, Porter St, Tel. 99372 333. **Kalbarri YHA**, 52 Mortimer St, Tel. 99371430.

### KUNUNURRA

**Tourist Bureau**, 559 Coolibah Dr, Tel. 91681177.

**Hotel Kununurra**, Messmate Way, Tel. 91681344. **Lake Argyle Tourist Village**, Tel. 91687360. **Desert Inn YHA**, corner Konkerberry / Tristania Sts, Tel. 91682702. **Backpackers**, 111 Nutwood Crescent, Tel. 91681711. **Hidden Valley Caravan Park**, Weaber Plains Rd, Tel. 91691790.

### MONKEY MIA / SHARK BAY

**Nanga Bay Resort & Caravan Park**, Nanga Station, 55 km south of Denham, Tel. 99483992. All others in Denham: **Tradewinds Holiday Village**, Knight Terrace, Tel. 99481222. **Bay Lodge YHA**, 95 Knight Terrace, Tel. 99481278. **Blue Dolphin Caravan Park**, Hamelin Rd, Tel. 99481385. **Shark Bay Caravan Park**, 4 Spaven Way, Tel. 99481387.

### POINT SAMSON (☎ 08)

**Caravan Park**, 56 Samson St, Tel. 91871414.

### PORT HEDLAND (☎ 08)

**Pier Hotel**, The Esplanade, Tel. 91731488. **Cooke Point Caravan & Camping Resort**, 8 km to the east, Tel. 91731271.

*From Perth to Darwin*

141

# AUSTRALIA'S WILD NORTH

DARWIN
KAKADU NATIONAL PARK
FROM DARWIN TO THE SOUTH
LITCHFIELD NATIONAL PARK
NITMILUK (KATHERINE GORGE)
NATIONAL PARK
HEADING EASTWARD TO THE
COAST

## *DARWIN

**\*Darwin ❶** is not only the capital of the Northern Territory, it is also the most important trading center for the economy of this entire region, which is familiarly known as the Top End of Australia.

The first permanent settlement was established in 1883, on the bay named after Charles Darwin. Until fairly recently, however, the outside world paid little or no attention to the town. On Christmas Day 1974, Hurricane *Tracy* almost completely destroyed Darwin. The majority of the inhabitants abandoned the town, and only 12,000 stayed.

These stalwarts started a new dating system: each succeeding year since this natural catastrophe is numbered as *after Tracy* (AT), while conversely, the years *before Tracy* are BT. Since then, what was once a sleepy tropical town has become a busy center of some 85,000 inhabitants, and though much of its former charm has been lost, there is still much to see.

Indeed, a visit is well worth it. The **Wharf Precinct** now lures tourists to the formerly neglected southeastern part of

*Previous pages: Meeting place at Mindil Beach Markets. Left: Increasing numbers of Aborigines are fighting to retain their traditions and culture.*

town. Even if one has already been to the Great Barrier Reef, there is much to be seen at the very good aquarium **\*Indo Pacific Marine ❶** on Stokes Hill Wharf.

The **Australian Pearling Exhibition** in the same building has a display on pearl fishing and cultured pearls in northern Australia. There is also an excellent seafood restaurant. From Wednesday to Sunday during the dry period (April-November), the **Deck Chair Cinema ❷** on the other side of Stokes Hill offers open-air showings that spectators can enjoy from the comfort of a deck chair.

Most of the city's historical buildings are situated along **The Esplanade**. The former **Old Courthouse ❸** is the oldest building in town, dating from 1884. **Admiralty House ❹** is on stilts. Across from it, in **Lyons Cottage**, is a small museum of the history of the Northern Territory.

In **The Mall ❺** pedestrian zone, there are small shops and cafes. Historical **Victoria Hotel** is a popular rendez-vous point here – especially on account of its cold beer.

At **Aquascene ❻** at Doctors Gully at the northwestern end of The Esplanade, tourists can feed the fish daily (times change according to the tide, for information call 08-89817837). Further to the north, on the lawns of the **MGM Grand**

Northern Territory

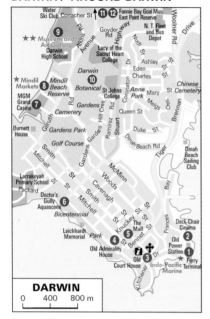

DARWIN
0    400    800 m

Casino ❼, sunset jazz concerts are often staged in the dry period (May-October).

Half of Darwin can be found picnicking or strolling along the beach at the neighboring **★Mindil Beach Sunset Markets** ❽ on Thursday and Sunday evenings.

The **★★Museum and Art Gallery of the Northern Territory** ❾, somewhat to the north, merits a visit. The collection of Australian and Aborigine art is particularly excellent. Quite interesting as well is the natural science department. Follow this up with a relaxing visit to the **Botanical Gardens** ❿.

One can find a former jail transformed into a museum in almost every large town in Australia – **Fannie Bay Goal Museum** ⓫ is one of these. The gallows, upon which the last execution was carried out, still stand here.

Further to the north, the sunsets in the **East Point Reserve** ⓬ (numerous wallabies!) and Mindil Beach are particularly

*Right: Ranger on the Arnhem Highway.*

magnificent, with the red and gold nuances for which Darwin is justly famed.

### Around Darwin

There are many commercial **crocodile farms**, such as Crocodylus Park and Crocodile Farm, in the area around Darwin where you can observe the fearsome reptiles from a safe distance.

Those wishing to relax on Darwin's beaches must exercise caution: there are *marine stingers* here in the rainy season. A mere brush with one of these poisonous jellyfish can be fatal! Therefore it is best not to swim outside the protected areas!

If you have enough time, you may wish to visit **★Bathurst** ❷ and **★Melville** ❸, islands lying offshore in the Timor Sea and accessible from Darwin by plane. These islands are inhabited by Aborigines of the Tiwi tribe who, isolated from the mainland, were able to maintain their independent culture. However, tourists may access the islands only with a tour agent.

Information and entry permits for the Aboriginal Land Trusts, including Arnhem Land, can be obtained from the Northern Land Council in Darwin (applications normally last one week).

### From Darwin to Kakadu National Park

About 34 kilometers south of Darwin, the **Arnhem Highway** branches off eastward from Stuart Highway. This 220-kilometer-long asphalted highway was originally built as a supply and access road for uranium mining operations at the Ranger Uranium Mine at Jabiru, and is now passable all year round.

After traveling for 34 kilometers, it is worth making a detour into the nearby **Fogg Dam Conservation Reserve** ❹. Here, as part of their plan for the economic development of the Top End, the Australian Federal Government had al-

lowed for a rice and cotton growing area in the 1950s. However, the project proved to be such a spectacular failure that the entire area was declared a nature conservation area.

Today, the traveler may drive along the top of the dam across the flooded countryside and observe a great variety of bird species, frogs and lizards.

Don't forget to bring binoculars! **Window on the Wetlands**, an observation platform on Beatrice Hill, offers a view over the plain, which is flooded by the Adelaide River in the rainy season. Information on this failed project is available here.

#### **★★KAKADU NATIONAL PARK**
#### **Land and Culture of the Aborigines**

With an area of almost 20,000 square kilometers, **★★Kakadu National Park** is Australia's second-largest national park. It is on UNESCO's World Heritage List, which means that the entire area is under special protection.

The entrance to the Kakadu National Park, which belongs to the Aborigines and has been leased by them to the Australian government for 100 years, is situated 150 kilometers east of Darwin and is marked with nothing more than a plain wooden board on the Arnhem Highway.

To reach the excellent information center (near Jabiru), you have to drive nearly 100 kilometers. A word of warning: 200,000 visitors per year puts this park very high on the list of tourist attractions. Another way of getting to the park is by the **Kakadu Highway**. It approaches the park from the south and is entirely surfaced.

The park shows a different face according to the changing seasons, which makes it quite difficult to recommend any one particular time. At the very height of the rainy season (between December and February) it sometimes happens that large tracts of land are flooded and negotiating some of the roads in the park becomes impossible without a four-wheel drive. At the end of the dry season (mid-

*Northern Territory*

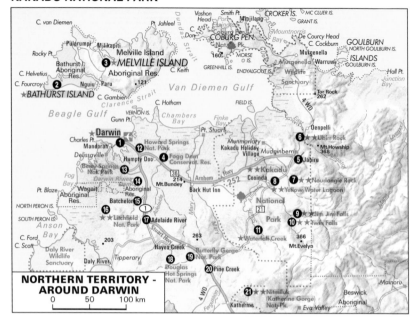

**NORTHERN TERRITORY -
AROUND DARWIN**
0        50        100 km

dle of October) the National Parks and Wildlife Service start deliberate bushfires. Because of this, a visit may be spoiled by smoke.

In **Jabiru** ❺ you may join a guided tour of the **Ranger Uranium Mine**. Buses leave from the airport terminal. The representatives of the mining company will provide a glimpse of the technology of uranium mining, and will explain the contracts, favorable to the mining companies, made between white Australians and Aborigines for the exploitation of natural mineral resources.

After the tour you may still be left with the niggling question of how long the mining companies' interests and profits will take second place to conservation and the myths of the native inhabitants, especially as there are known to be huge reserves of uranium ore beneath the nearby lake. Needless to say, mining operations are quite controversial. This is

where the Aborigines believe the Rainbow Serpent, the source of all life, lies sleeping. For most visitors, the chief attraction in Kakadu National Park must be the Aboriginal rock paintings. During the rainy season, the early inhabitants sought shelter here from the elements, and painted these scenes from their life on the overhanging rock walls.

Two locations in the Kakadu National Park are particularly important. First, the **\*Ubirr Rock** ❻, situated about 40 kilometers north of the Bowali Visitor Centre.

The oldest drawings along the 1-kilometer circular walk are estimated to be about 20,000 years old. There are excellent examples of both the simple ocher paintings and the so-called X-ray technique, which depicts the inner organs of animals and humans.

An approximately 2-kilometer walk leads from the parking area to the galleries of **\*\*Nourlangie Rock** ❼, where the paintings are approximately the same age as those near the Ubirr Rock. In the **Anbangbang Gallery** are the mythologi-

*Right: Ubirr Rock in Kakadu National Park.*

cal figures of Namarragon the Lightening Bringer and his wife Barrkinj, who are so often depicted on travel brochures. At the lookout, here is also a 12-kilometer-Barrk Walk, which is no picnic, for this path runs through the bush and should only be attempted by those in excellent physical condition and with adequate equipment.

As a general rule, all physical exertion should be undertaken in the park in the morning or evening hours. but this should not be attempted before consultation with the park rangers. Make sure you have plenty of water with you and always wear a hat. Hikes lasting more than a day must be registered with the park rangers.

After passing through Kakadu Holiday Village on the Arnhem Highway, carry on for 10 kilometers eastward to the other side of the South Alligator River.

Here, the 3-kilometer-long *Mamukala Wetlands Walk is highly recommended. In the dry season this plain is an area of hard parched earth, criss-crossed with a tracery of cracks, but only a few days after the first rains it becomes a vast, shining, silvery lake, in which tens of thousands of birds, predominantly magpie geese, dive for food.

On **Yellow Water Lagoon **8**, a few kilometers from the Cooinda Hotel, the park rangers offer boat trips that are by far the best way to observe the fauna and flora of the area. Book the tour for dawn, as there is less to see during the day. Along the shores sea eagles nest, and Jesus birds, ibis and herons hunt for food. You may be able to catch sight of salt-water crocodiles.

A single track (sometimes closed in the rainy season), suitable only for four-wheel drives, leads to **Jim Jim Falls **9** (which rush down from a height of 215 meters) and **Twin Falls **10**, 60 kilometers east of Cooinda. The waterfalls plunge down over 200 meters from the top of the Arnhem Land sandstone plateau.

From the point where the vehicle track peters out, there is a path which, after an hour's walk over rocks, brings you to the

base of the Jim Jim Falls. Twin Falls can only be reached by paddling out in a boat or on an air mattress (check beforehand whether any crocodiles have been sighted).

Access to **★Waterfall Creek ⑪** (also known as **Gunlom Falls**) is from the southern entrance of the park. The film *Crocodile Dundee* made this area famous. The camping grounds here are well furbished, there are many hikes and, naturally, the main attraction, the Pool with its photogenic waterfalls (free of crocodiles?!) surrounded by dense rain forest.

Though an excursion to this delightful part of the park should be on any list of activities, few do undertake it, especially during the rainy season. If you happen to have the time, then visit some of the abandoned mines in the area after contacting the Ranger Station located at the southern end of the park.

*Above: He opted for the hard life in the Outback. Right: A goanna in Litchfield National Park.*

After a further 59 kilometers, the Kakadu Highway ends at a sleepy little town called **Pine Creek (⑳)** on Stuart Highway. It is a distance of 231 kilometers back to Darwin. After another 90 kilometers southwards, you will arrive at Katherine and the nearby Nitmiluk (Katherine Gorge) National Park.

### FROM DARWIN TO THE SOUTH

When you finally leave Darwin behind and are heading south, you will drive by several attractive towns and parks, which are, however, very popular with the Darwinians themselves, and are hence often overcrowded. Top on the list of parks are **Howard Springs Nature Park ⑫** (24 kilometers), a rain forest oasis with attractive bathing and picnic areas, and **Berry Springs Nature Park ⑬** (47 kilometers).

Behind Berry Springs Nature Park lies the **★Territory Wildlife Park**. Native animals and animals that have been made native to the Northern Territory can be observed in their natural surroundings on an area of 4 square kilometers. Among the fauna are all types of kangaroos, wallaroos and wallabies. One large enclosure has a herd of buffaloes, and there is a lagoon with pelicans, storks and a host of other native water birds. The park has a nocturnal house in which one can observe birds which are active at night, and a gigantic volary where one can visit the "second and third stories" of a rain forest.

The **Darwin River Dam ⑭** is both a water reservoir and a grand sanctuary for countless species of birds. **Manton Dam** and **Lake Bennett** are more a sanctuary for overheated people.

**Batchelor ⑮** is an agglomeration of houses 91 kilometers south of Darwin and 13 kilometers from the Highway. The town was founded in the 1870s when copper and tin deposits were discovered in the region and a host of little mines opened. **Rum Jungle** was appropriately named back in the wild days following

World War Two when substantial reserves of uranium were discovered. Nowadays, Batchelor is principally known as the starting point for visits to Litchfield Park.

## **LITCHFIELD NATIONAL PARK

The **Litchfield National Park ⑯ was named after Frederick Henry Litchfield, a member of the Finniss Expedition, which penetrated northward from South Australia in 1864. The most recently established park in the Northern Territory, it covers 650 square kilometers and is not nearly as large as Kakadu National Park, which lies to the southeast.

Nevertheless, Litchfield Park is rapidly becoming a pleasant, uncrowded alternative to the over-popular Kakadu National Park. The center of the park is dominated by a vast sandstone plateau.

The many waterfalls, streams and cascades offer inviting spots for bathing and there are attractive walks through the rain forest. One bit of advice: depending on the selected trail, a trip into and out of the park can be up to 200 kilometers long. If you have a four-wheel drive, the distances are a lot longer, and there is no fuel in the park.

The park can be reached by two surfaced roads: one is through Batchelor, the other is the Cox Peninsula Road. Both cross the **Finniss River** by means of low bridges. In the rainy season, from November to April, the river occasionally swells to the point of making the bridges impassable. The office of the Parks and *Wildlife Commission of the Northern Territory* in Batchelor provides the necessary information.

When driving into the park from the east (through Batchelor), tarred roads lead to all the best-known places except for **The Lost City**, **Blyth Homestead**, and **Tjaynera Falls**, which can only be accessed by four-wheel drive, or not at all in the rainy season.

On the western edge of the Table Top Range, ***Wangi Falls** plunge majestically down from the plateau. At the bottom of

*Northern Territory*

the precipice a mist of spray, created by the falls, provides the moisture needed for the luxuriant tropical forest to flourish. The falls are fed by a tributary of **Reynolds River**.

All along the foot of these cascades, a magnificent natural swimming pool with gently sloping sandy banks has formed. In the dry season, it is a perfect place to bathe. During the rainy season, on the other hand, this swimming hole is closed, because the crashing waterfalls create dangerous maelstroms. Several non-swimmers have lost their lives during the past few years, because they went into the water thinking the pool was perfectly safe and were sucked under by the whirling water and drowned.

The dangerous salt-water crocodiles sometimes wander up as far as the **Wangi Falls**, even though the park administration has set up traps along their usual

*Above: Taking a rest at Buley Rockhole in Litchfield National Park. Right: Palm-ferns are relics from the Mesozoic Period.*

path. So please be careful when bathing. A picnic spot has been arranged right next to the pool, and a little further away are campgrounds.

A short drive away on asphalt roads are **★Florence Falls**, reached by a steep footpath leading to a pool surrounded by rain forest, and **Tolmer Falls**, consisting of a series of smaller waterfalls which plunge down a steep rocky cleft in a series of steps. The latter is not open to bathers because the bats living in the cave beneath the falls require their peace and quiet.

As you travel southwards, a four-wheel drive track turns off from the park's main road, leading to **Lost City**. In the rainy season the track (if it happens to be open!) meanders through a lush green forest, then through long, deep, mud gullies and finally along a stony riverbed with hair-raising bends and high rocky terraces.

After taking about an hour to cover just 10 kilometers, you will arrive at Lost City, where giant rock formations have defied erosion and remind one of buildings, monuments, or petrified giants, all surrounded by luxuriant tropical vegetation. On the rocks, frilled lizards and blue-tongued lizards sunbathe.

On the western edge of the park is the private **Petherick's Rainforest Reserve**, also well worth a visit. A well-marked path leads along the bank of a stream through dense rain forest to a series of cascades, that are excellent for bathing.

### HOT SPRINGS AND BUTTERFLY GORGE NATURE PARKS

Then it's off southwards again along the busy **Stuart Highway**. About 110 kilometers from Darwin is **Adelaide River** ❼, where the headquarters of the Australian and American armies were set up during the Second World War.

Between Adelaide River and **Hayes Creek**, driving along the old Stuart Highway seems an obvious choice, as it winds through wooded terrain west of the new road, but you will need quite a lot of time. 14.5 kilometers later, you come upon a fork to **Robin Falls**. Following an additional 600 meters by car, and a quarter-hour trek through rather dense bush, you will be rewarded with bathing beneath a splendid waterfall.

62 kilometers on the old Highway takes you to the road leading to **Douglas Hot Springs Nature Park** ❽. The springs themselves can be found in a cultivated area, about 35 kilometers from the main road (the last 20 kilometers are passable only with a normal car in the dry season).

The water in these springs is very hot and surges to the surface from deep within the earth's strata. One hot stream feeds several pools before running into the Douglas River and thence onward to the Daly River. In the actual springs, the water is far too hot for swimming, but by the time it reaches the stream, which runs along a sandy bed, it is pleasantly warm to bathe in.

Just a few kilometers away (accessible only by four-wheel drive, not at all in the rainy season) is the **Butterfly Gorge Nature Park** ❾, situated in the source area of the Douglas River. It has a shadowy rain forest criss-crossed by hiking trails.

Back on the Stuart Highway, it is worth stopping at **Pine Creek** ❿, an almost forgotten gold-mining town 132 kilometers south of Darwin. Of the 200 people living here, a few still prospect for gold in the surrounding hills.

From Pine Creek it is another 90 kilometers to Katherine and the turn-off to Katherine Gorge National Park – a fascinating place indeed.

### **NITMILUK (KATHERINE GORGE) NATIONAL PARK

**Nitmiluk (Katherine Gorge) National Park** ㉑ lies in the heart of **Never Never Land**, a wide strip of land that stretches from Joseph Bonaparte Gulf in the west to the Gulf of Carpenteria in the east. From the Stuart Highway, a side

*Northern Territory*

*Above: Boat trip along the Katherine River.*

road leads to **\*Edith Falls** in the northern part of the park. Here, the Edith River has formed a chain of waterfalls, idyllic bathing lakes and lagoons in the midst of luxuriant tropical vegetation.

In the main part of the park, which can be reached comfortably on the surfaced road from Katherine (30 kilometers, are the famous **\*ravines of the Katherine River**.

Over the course of thousands of years, the Katherine River has cut deep into the plateau. The steep gorges, with their countless tributaries, are some 30 kilometers long, and the walls of rock are 100 meters high in places.

Detailed information about the park can be obtained at the Visitors' Centre, on the edge of Katherine Gorge. Boat tours and helicopter flights can be arranged either at the Transit Centre in Katherine (right on Stuart Highway), or in the kiosk at the campgrounds before Katherine

Gorge. Canoes are also for hire. Sitting in flat-bottomed boats with a park ranger as guide, visitors can navigate the gorges, but different boats have to be boarded above the rapids between the individual gorges.

Depending on your timetable and finances, you may explore the whole of Katherine Gorge in this way. (A hat, protective oil, and swimming gear are absolutely essential! This goes for all tours in the Northern Territory!) The more intrepid visitors can take a canoe or a kayak and paddle unaccompanied upstream.

During the rainy season, however, all waterborne activity on Katherine River sometimes has to be abandoned since the spots where one changes from one boat to the other turn into wild rapids, effectively preventing anyone from sailing through.

If the water rises even further, jet boats are used to visit the gorges instead of the normal excursion boats. Either the Visitors' Centre or the car park at Edith Falls is the starting or finishing point for one-day trips or for walks, with tents and rucksacks, lasting several days on the numerous well-marked trails through the park's wild places. The network of footpaths is 100 kilometers long and will lead you to lonely waterfalls, lagoons and Aborigine rock paintings.

Even the shortest trail will require you to be physically fit and properly equipped, but the chance of seeing so much flora and fauna is well worth the effort, and the views of the gorges are never less than spectacular.

### ON THE ROAD TO THE RED CENTRE

Riding southward on Stuart Highway again, you reach **Mataranka** ㉒ after 106 kilometers. Just beyond the town, a road forks off to the **Mataranka Homestead**. A thermal source here pumps out 16,000 liters of 34.5 °C water every minute. It feeds the crystal-clear thermal pond, in which one can bathe under palms in a tropical atmosphere (free of charge, too).

It's the ideal place to take a break from driving. The source was discovered by soldiers stationed here during World War Two. The natural pool was first enlarged for the officers and later used for touristic purposes.

The highway carries on south, and the soil and landscape gradually take on that reddish coloring so characteristic of the interior, with the sparse woodland turning to bush land. **Larrimah** ㉓ (the railway from Darwin once came here, which was supposed to connect to the Ghan in Alice.

The plan is still under discussion today), **Daly Waters** ㉔, with its historic pub and rodeo every third weekend in September, **Dunmarra Roadhouse** ㉕. Elliott and the Roadhouse Renner Springs Roadhouse are on the 600-kilometer- leg of the journey.

65 kilometers beyond Dunmarra Roadhouse, a tarred road turns off to the right to **Newcastle Waters** ㉖, a modern ghost town. Australia's last drove started

**STUART HIGHWAY (NORTH)**

0 _____ 100 km

off from here in 1988. After that, the road trains completely absorbed the job of the drovers. Besides the larger-than-life statue of a drover, you can visit the saloon, which was closed in 1975, an old store, and the post office. There are neither toilets nor fuel, or any other facilities for tourists.

The journey continues to **Elliott** ㉗ and **Renner Springs Roadhouse** ㉘. All these communities along the Stuart Highway have one thing in common: there are service stations vital in the remote north and the visitor will encounter accomodation for the night.

About 50 kilometers before you get to the Roadhouse Three Ways, you will pass **Attack Creek Historical Reserve** ㉙. In 1860, Aborigines of the Warramunga tribe forced the explorer John McDougall Stuart, after whom the highway was named, to abandon his attempt to cross the Australian continent from Adelaide to the north coast.

Another reminder of pioneer history is **John Flynn's Historical Reserve** in

*Northern Territory*

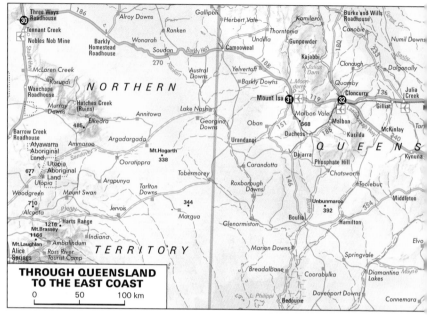

THROUGH QUEENSLAND
TO THE EAST COAST

0    50    100 km

**Three Ways** ③⓪. The Reverend John Flynn founded the Flying Doctor Service, to which, even today, many an Outback family owes its life.

### Heading Eastward for the Coast

In Three Ways, you will have to make a decision: If you follow **Stuart Highway** you will arrive at Alice Springs after a journey of some 550 kilometers, where you can enjoy the world- famous natural attractions of the Northern Territories: Devil's Marbles and Uluru (Ayers Rock); cf the chapter on Straight through the Red Centre, page 163.

If you choose to turn off at **Barkly Highway**, there will stretch 1,500 kilometers ahead of you to Townsville or 2,000 kilometers to Rockhampton – an extreme Outback trek.

You will cross the border to Queensland near the town of Camooweal. In this remote corner of the state, civilization has only a tenuous influence on the landscape.

Even some of the larger highways are encrusted with mud and dirt, and smaller roads are little more than dust tracks. With the exception of the highways, the roads in the northern interior can become impassable during the rainy season.

You will be traveling through semi-arid deserts, where the only vegetation consists of thorn thickets and dry, spiny grass, where towns are hundreds of kilometers apart, and remote cattle stations rely on voice radio for contact with the outside world. Here, neighbors live many hours' drive away and people have to be extremely self-reliant in order to survive this harsh life.

The town of **Mount Isa** ③① (662 kilometers) is the world's largest producer of lead and silver, which all originates from one single mine.

Life in this remote town, surrounded by such barren land, revolves around the mining installations, which tourists may visit. However, please do take note of the fact that advance booking for this is required.

156                    *Guidepost pages 158-159*

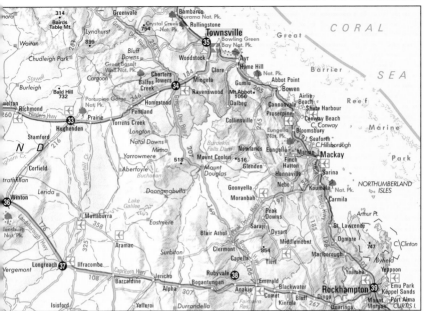

In **Cloncurry** ③②, you must finally decide whether to travel on to Townsville or to Rockhampton, for the road forks here: **Flinders Highway** runs to Richmond and then on to **Hughenden** ③③.

From Hughenden, the highway goes on to ✱**Charters Towers** ③④, once Australia's most prolific gold-mining town. Many relics of those long gone days have since been restored, for example the stock exchange building, once the scene of feverish wheeling and dealing.

Nowadays, most of the action centers around agriculture. From here, it is only another 130 kilometers to lively **Townsville** ③⑤, which lies on the sparkling waters of the Great Barrier Reef. Here you will find a scuba diver's paradise.

Rockhampton is reached along the **Landsborough Highway.** After some 450 kilometers, this seemingly endless stretch of road through the flat, monotonous Outback will take you from Mount Isa to the small Outback town of **Winton** ③⑥. This is the birthplace of Australia's

unofficial national anthem, *Waltzing Matilda*. Composed by Banjo Patterson, his tragic ballad about a tramp was first sung in public at the North Gregory Hotel in the town.

About 180 kilometers south of Winton is the town of **Longreach** ③⑦, where a monument was erected to the Outback pioneers in the ✱✱**Stockman's Hall of Fame**.

From Longreach, carry on along the **Capricorn Highway**. Rockhampton is another 570 kilometers away, on the Capricorn Highway.

You might interrupt your journey for a stop at the neighboring villages of **Anakie**, **Sapphire** and **Rubyvale** ③⑧, 60 kilometers west of Emerald, where you can try your luck searching for gems (licence required). Your chances are good, as there are huge sapphire and ruby deposits in the area.

In **Rockhampton** ③⑨ (cf page 195), the visitor finally returns to civilization after courageously following the trek through the Australian Outback.

*Northern Territory*

## DARWIN (☎ 08)

**i** **Darwin Region Tourism Association**, Beagle House, corner of Knuckey / Mitchell Sts, Tel. 89814300, a branch of the **Parks and Wildlife Commission of the Northern Territory. Northern Land Council**, 9 Rowling St, Casuarina, Tel. 89205100. Provides permits for visits to Aboriginal territory.

**▬ ⑤⑤⑤ MGM Grand Darwin**, Gilruth Ave, Mindil Beach, Tel. 89438888. **Centra Darwin**, 122 Esplanade, Tel. 89815388. **Mirambeena Tourist Resort**, 64 Cavenagh St, Tel. 89460111. **Novotel Atrium**, corner Peel und Esplanade, Tel. 89410755. **The Carlton Hotel Darwin**, Esplanade, Tel. 69800800.

**⑤⑤ Cherry Blossom**, 108 Esplanade, Tel. 89816734. **All Seasons Frontier Darwin**, Buffalo Court, Tel. 89815333. **Melaleuca Lodge**, 50 Mitchell St, Tel. 89413395 (less expensive rooms as well). **Park Lodge**, 42 Coronation Drive, Tel. 89815692.

**⑤ Banyan View Lodge YWCA**, 119 Mitchell St, Tel. 89818644. **Darwin City YHA**, 69 Mitchell St, Tel. 89813995. **Elkes Inner-City Lodge**, 112 Mitchell St, Tel. 89818399. **Overlander Caravan Park**, McMillans Rd, Berrimah (13 km east of the city), Tel. 89843025.

**✖** The Barramundi fish, which weighs up to 50 kg is a native of the waters of the Northern Territory. It is a tasty delicatessen and is definately worth a try. Other culinary specialities of the north are buffalo and kangaroo steaks. **Christo's on the Wharf**, Wharf Precinct (Stokes Hill Wharf), Tel. 89818658. Fish and seafood, prepared Mediterranean style. In the Wharf Precinct there are many other snack booths, international cuisine. **Hogs Breath**, 32 Smith St Mall, Tel. 89413333. Chain restaurant; Tex Mex cuisines and steaks. **Lindsay Street Cafe**, 2 Lindsay St, Tel. 89818631; despite its name, a real restaurant. **Magic Wok**, 48 Cavenagh St, Tel. 89813332. Meat and seafood Asian.

**▥ Indo-Pacific Marine**, Stokes Hill Wharf, Tel. 89811294, Underwater world live. Open April-Oct. daily 10:00 a.m.-5:00 p.m., Nov.-March Mon-Sat 9:00 a.m.-1:00 p.m., Sun 10:00 a.m.-5:00 p.m. Also worth seeing is the **Australian Pearling Exhibition** in the same building, which features the history of pearling and cultured pearls in the waters of Northern Australia. Mon-Fri 10:00 a.m.-5:00 p.m., Sat-Sun 10:00 a.m.-5:.30 p.m. **Fannie Bay Gaol Museum**, East Point Rd, Tel. 89998290, jail museum daily10:00 a.m.-5:00 p.m. **Museum & Art Gallery of the Northern Territory**, Conacher St, Fannie Bay, Tel. 89998201. Aborigine and southeast Asian art, history (such as information concerning cyclon Tracy), changing exhibits. Mon-Fri 9:00 a.m.-5:00 p.m., Sat-Sun 10:00 a.m.-5:00 p.m.. Entrance free (except for ehibitions) .

**Military Museum**, East Point, Tel. 89819702, daily 9:30 a.m.-5:00 p.m. The Second World War is the topic here – Darwin was repeatedly bombed by the Japanese in 1942 and was threatened by a Japanese invasion.

**Crocodylus Park**, McMillans Rd, Berrimah, Tel. 89472510.

**⚑ August:** The *Beer Can Regatta* in Darwin is Australia's craziest "regatta." The boats, which start from Mindil Beach in August, are made of empty beer and soft-drink cans.

**⛴ Bathurst** and **Melville Islands**: The only way tourists can visit these islands and their inhabitants, the Tiwis, is offered by the local tour operator **Tiwi Tours,** Tel. 89815115. A day with flight, lunch, various visits to sights and excursions costs from $A 260 / person, two days cost from $A 470.

**⛴** In the city's bookstores you can purchase the book *Bushtuckerman:* it provides an overview of the fare Aborigines can find to eat in the bush in times of necessitiy.

## FROM DARWIN TO TOWNSVILLE / ROCKHAMPTON

**⛴ Road conditions:** If you are travelling off Highway 1, then you should check the road conditions. Large parts of the stretch are unpaved. Flooding lasting days can occur during the rainy season from October to March, on the asphalted roads as well. In addition, please remember that in summer, temperatrues can often rise above 40 °C.

### ADELAIDE RIVER (☎ 08)

**▬ ⑤⑤ Adelaide River Inn**, Stuart Hwy, Tel. 89767047.

### BARCALDINE (☎ 07)

**▬ ⑤⑤ Landsborough Lodge**, Landsborough Highway, Tel. 46511100.

### BATCHELOR (☎ 08)

**▬ ⑤⑤ Rum Jungle Motor Inn**, 220 Rum Jungle Road, Tel. 89760123.

**⑤ Batchelor Caravillage**, Tel. 89760166. **Banyan Tree Caravan Park**, Litchfield Park Road, Tel. 89760330.

### BIRDSVILLE

**⚑** The little town (a pub and a handful of huts) is located some 800 km from Winton southwest of the Landsborough Hwy in the fringe of the Simpson Desert. The **Birdsville Races** are held here once a year. On the first weekend in September, thousands of visitors from all over Australia gather here. The horse races themselves aren't really that important; mostly, it is an occasion to guzzle great amounts of beer in the company of one's friends. The Outback feeling of this event is incomparable. **Warning:** Road conditions for most of the stretch are bad. In Birdsville there is very little accommodation, therefore it is suggested to bring a camper or a tent and enough provisions, – especially beer.

### CHARTERS TOWERS (☎ 07)

**Cattlemans Rest Motor Inn**, corner of Bridge and Plant Sts, Tel. 46873555. **York St Lodge and B&B**, 58 York St, Tel. 47871028.

### CLONCURRY (☎ 07)

**Wagon Wheel Motel**, 54 Ramsay St, Tel. 47421866.

### DALY WATERS (☎ 08)

**Hi-Way Inn Motel**, Stuart St, Tel. 89759925.

### EMERALD (☎ 07)

**Central Highlands & Gemfields Information Centre**, Clermont St, Tel. 49824142.

**A & A Lodge**, Clermont St, Tel. 49822355.

**Precious gem fields:** Some mines and precious gem fields in Sapphire and Rubyvale can be visited, in some you may even do a little prospecting yourself. Information at the *Tourist Centre* in Emerald and *The Bobby Dazzler* in Rubyvale, Tel. 49854170. A *fossickers licence* ( around $A 3) can be obtained in the shops and gem parks in Sapphire and Rubyvale and at the *Department of Minerals and Energy*, Clermont St, Emerald, Tel. 49824011.

### HUGHENDEN (☎ 08)

**Hughenden Rest Easi Motel**, Flinders Highway, Tel. 47411633.

### KAKADU NATIONAL PARK (☎ 08)

**Bowali Visitor Centre**, Jabiru, Tel. 89381120.

**All Seasons Frontier Kakadu Village**, Arnhem Hwy, South Alligator River, Tel. 89790166. **Frontier Kakadu Lodge & Caravan Park**, Jabiru Drive, Jabiru, Tel. 897924. **Gagudju Crocodile Hotel**, Flinders St, Jabiru, Tel. 89792800. **Gagudju Lodge Cooinda**, off Kakadu Highway, Tel. 89790145. Inexpesnive YHA rooms as well.

Kakadu National Park from above – a **sightseeing flight** offers fantastic glimpses and unusual photo perspectives. *Kakadu Air*, Jabiru, Tel. 89792411.

### KATHERINE (☎ 08)

**Katherine Region Tourist Association**, corner of Linday St and Stuart Highway, Tel. 89722650.

**All Seasons Frontier Katherine**, Stuart Hwy, Tel. 89721744. **Pine Tree**, 3 Third St, Tel. 89722533. **Palm Court Backpackers**, corner of Giles / Third Sts, Tel. 89722722. **Nitmiluk Caravan Park**, Gorge Rd (im National Park), Tel. 89721253.

**Cutta Cutta Caves**, 27 km south of Katherine on Stuart Hwy, with stalactite caves and bats. Guided tours only.

### LONGREACH (☎ 07)

**Longreach Motel**, 127 Eagle St, Tel. 46581996. **Gunnadoo Caravan Park**, Thrush Rd, Tel. 46581781.

**The Australian Stockman's Hall of Fame and Outback Heritage Centre**, Tel. 46582166, daily 9:00 a.m.-5:00 p.m. All about the Outback.

### MATARANKA (☎ 08)

**Mataranka Homestead Tourist Park**, Tel. 89754544 (motel, camping and caravan park).

### MOUNT ISA (☎ 07)

**Riversleigh Fossil Museum & Tourist Information Centre**, Marian St, Tel. 47491555 / 1300-659660.

**The Overlander**, 119 Marion St, Tel. 47435011. **YHA**, Wellington Park Rd, Tel. 4743557. **Riverside Tourist Caravan Park**, 195 West St, Tel. 47433904.

The largest mines in the world (copper, silver, tin) can be visited Mon-Fri. The underground guided tours are often booked out weeks in advance, booking at Riversleigh Centre.

### THREE WAYS (☎ 08)

**Three Ways Roadhouse** and **Caravan Park**, corner of Stuart and Barkly Highway, Tel. 89622744.

### WINTON (☎ 07)

**Winton Outback Motel**, 95 Elderslie St, Tel. 46571422. **Banjos Motel & Cabins**, corner of Manuka and Bostock Sts, Tel. 46571213.

**Lark Quarry Environmental Park** (111 km southwest), approximately 93 million-years-old dinosaur footprints. **Outback Sheep Station:** On the Lorraine Station (54 km southeast, 31 000 hectares, 23 000 sheep and 3000 cattle), you can experience the life of an Australian farmer close-up: The Robinson Family, Lorraine Station, Tel. 07-46571693, from $A 60 / person / day. Other Outback farms: Queensland Host Farms Ass, 72 Victoria Park, Kelvin Grove, Tel. 07-8326799.

*Northern Territory*

Coober Pedy: Opal Capital
of Australias Outback

# THE RED CENTRE

ON THE WAY TO ALICE
ALICE SPRINGS
ULURU (AYERS ROCK)
KATA TJUTA (OLGAS)
COOBER PEDY

## ON THE WAY TO ALICE

985 kilometers from Darwin and 24 kilometers south of the intersection of the Stuart Highway with the Barkly Highway leading to Queensland is the interesting old gold-mining town of **Tennant Creek** ❶. Still today, it recalls the days of Australia's last great gold rush in 1932. Only one of the gold mines is still operating nowadays, and the local museum exhibits many items that document the town's picturesque past.

Australia's largest opencast mine, **Nobles Nob**, is situated 12 kilometers away. A lookout point gives a plunging view into the 100-meter- deep basin.

In **Battery Hill Regional Centre** a rock crushing facility (stamper battery) and a reconstructed gold mine provide impressions of the arduous but sometimes productive labor of the gold prospector. The gold tour of the abandoned gold mines run by one of the natives is very interesting.

Legend has it that Tennant Creek was built up around the first pub to open its doors in the region. The truck carrying the building materials allegedly broke

*Previous Pages: Uluru, Ayers Rock. Left: Machine Gun Joe – as legendary as his hometown Coober Pedy.*

down in front of the said pub, and it was decided to build the houses there rather than at the creek.

104 kilometers to the south stand the **★Devil's Marbles** ❷, which really do glow as red as marbles in the evening sunlight. In Aboriginal mythology they are said to have been left behind by the Rainbow Serpent, but the more prosaic geologist sees only a series of massive boulders rounded into great balls by the effects of erosion, but no less interesting for that.

Only a short distance away is **Barrow Creek** ❸, where the weary traveler can stop and wash the dust from his mouth at the legendary *Drinker Bank*. This country pub was originally one of the eleven telegraph stations that were set up by the pioneers. From here it is only another 282 kilometers to Alice Springs. The route passes **Central Mount Stuart** ❹, which is the geographical center of Australia.

### ★ALICE SPRINGS

**★Alice Springs** ❺ is known affectionately by Aussies as Alice and is the undisputed capital of the Red Centre. It began in 1872 as a supply station for the overland telegraph line then being set up as a direct communications link between Europe and the towns of south Australia. It now has a population of 22,000.

*The Red Centre*

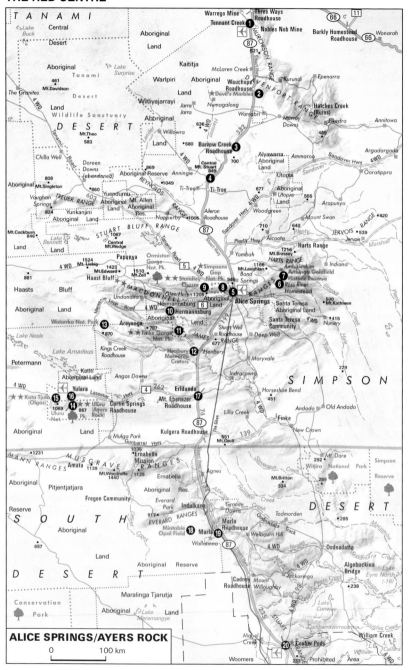

**ALICE SPRINGS/AYERS ROCK**

0       100 km

The name Alice Springs goes back to the adventurer W. Mills, who discovered a water-hole in a dried-up river bed 3 kilometers to the north of the present town.

In honor of Charles Todd, Superintendent of the Overland Telegraph project (a former south Australian Postmaster-General) Mills named the river Todd River and the town Alice Springs, after Todd's wife.

Nowadays Alice Springs is a modern, typically Australian provincial town with an economy based mainly on tourism. Although some of its importance derives from its location as the starting point for trips to Ayers Rock, it also has a number of attractions of its own.

Top of the list is the **Old Telegraph Station** north of the town, just behind **ANZAC Hill**, which offers a good view over Alice Springs.

In the center of town are the **Royal Flying Doctor Base** and the **John Flynn Memorial Church** (and museum), with informative displays on the brave and dangerous work of the flying doctors who used to fly around the Outback to their patients in prop planes (and still do in many places).

A detour to the **Araluen Centre** on Larapinta Drive provides insight into the history of the city, and has an art gallery worth seeing. Also interesting is the **\*Museum of Central Australia**, with an exhibition of natural history and history of the exploration of the Red Centre.

The life and work of Ted (actually Theodro Heinrich) Strehlow is particularly vividly portrayed. He studied and documented the culture of the Aranda people.

Born in 1908, the son of German Lutheran missionaries grew up with native playmates in the Central Australian town of Hermannsburg. An airplane museum and a pioneer cemetery are also part of the exhibits.

Worth seeing is the **\*Alice Springs Desert Park** (6 kilometers outside of the city on Lapinta Drive, daily from 7:30 a.m. - 6:00 p.m.), which opened in 1997. Three typical desert eco-systems are recreated here, and through which there runs a path. Of particular interest are the timid animals of the night in the nocturnal show, and the bird of prey show in the nature theatre (twice daily). Plan three hours for this visit. Those who are interested in the traditional art of the Aborigines will find rich pickings in Alice, with a variety of craft shops offering authentic artifacts at affordable prices, in addition to the usual kitsch.

At the **Aboriginal Arts & Cultural Centre** run by Aborigines on Gregory Terrace, the wood-carvings, bark paintings, musical instruments and weapons on display are accompanied by detailed notes on how they are made and used and their significance. To the south, **Heavitree Gap**, a narrow rocky gorge, forms a natural boundary to the town of Alice.

Throughout the year in Alice Springs, various festivals are held. The most bizarre of these is the **Henley-on-Todd Regatta** on the first Saturday in October. Boats are supposed to take part in races on the Todd River. The problem is that there is rarely any water in the river and the oarsmen, undeterred, have to run along the dry river bed carrying their boats.

### Excursions from Alice

A spectacular sunrise can be enjoyed from a hot-air balloon at dawn.

Visitors with less lofty ambitions can take to the air at a lower altitude on the back of a camel. A camel farm close to Alice offers sightseeing tours and various shorter rides on the edge of town. These camels were originally imported from Afghanistan, so that food caravans could supply Alice Springs.

The construction of the famous stretch of railway track from Port Augusta along

*The Red Centre*

the Oodnadatta Track to Alice Springs (approximately 1600 kilometers) would also have been impossible without these ships of the desert.

Aussies, who like to shorten words, paid tribute to the camels by abbreviating Afghanistan to Ghan when naming the legendary train which still travels the line between Adelaide and Alice Springs.

For tourists who are more interested in culture, there are organized Aboriginal Culture Tours. It is best to book a tour which is run and guided by the Aborigines, thus garnering insight into the philosophy and way of life of the native people, perhaps getting to know some songs and dances and learning something of how they obtain and prepare their food. But there is no obligation to taste the raw witchety grubs – fat white larvae – prized as a great delicacy by the Aborigines! Visitors hiring a car in Alice Springs

*Above: Camel Cup racing in Alice Springs. Right: The waterfalls in Kings Canyon only run following heavy rains.*

should always go for a four-wheel drive vehicle (with camping equipment if required).

The Stuart Highway and Lasseter Highway are now surfaced throughout, but it is impossible to experience the Outback to the full just by racing from place to place and ticking each place off the list.

The only way to savor a little of the pioneering spirit of the past is to take a bumpy ride along dusty tracks and dried-up sandy river beds and across the muddy water-holes.

The first opportunity to do so is a side trip into the **\*\*Eastern MacDonnell Ranges**, which are seldom frequented by tourists, but is very attractive.

The gorges along Ross Highway, **Emily Gap**, **Jessie Gap**, **Corroboree Rock** and **Trephina Gorge** are just as beautiful as those of the western Ranges. The 4-kilometer-long road to **John Hayes Rockhole** close to Trephina Gorge can only be negotiated by a four-wheel drive vehicle. The former gold-digger town of Altunga was founded around the turn of

the century and is worth a visit. The next 76 kilometers are asphalted on the way to **Ross River Homestead ❻** where you can eat, lodge, go on camel or horseback tours in the desert; but afterwards the going really gets tough. 33 kilometers of nature road runs up numerous inclines, around sharp turns, through a paradisean sylvan countryside, all the way to the ghost town of **Arltunga ❼**.

There is an information center with a lucid slide show that tells the story of Arltunga. Shortly before arriving at your destination, you will come across the **Arltunga Bush Hotel** (formerly called by themselves the "Loneliest Pub in the Scrub.")

Campgrounds with cabins have been set up next to the pub. The way back to Alice can be done (only in a four-wheel drive) on the Arltunga Tourist Drive (180 kilometers).

Not far from Alice Springs are the gorges of the **✴✴western MacDonnell Ranges.** The best known of these are **✴Simpson's Gap ❽** with its black-foot

rock kangaroos and **✴✴Standley Chasm ❾**, a narrow cleft 85 meters deep. Between 11:30 a.m. and 12:30 p.m., cameras click merrily away, when the sun's rays shine into the chasm and turn the walls of rock, containing iron oxide, bright red.

A further 85 kilometers along Larapinta Drive is **Hermannsburg ❿**, once a Lutheran mission station whose buildings now house an art gallery and tearooms (no permit required, but there is an entrance fee for the village and also for the gallery) The **Albert Namatjira Monument** commemorates the painter born in Hermannsburg in 1902. His aquarelles can be seen in Hermannsburg and in Alice Springs.

He was the first Aboriginal artist to be recognized by the Caucasians. But even he was unable to bridge the gap between black and white cultures, and he died an alcoholic in 1959 – a fate which unfortunately too often awaits many Aborigines in Alice Springs. From Hermannsburg, a byroad (passable only by four-wheel

*The Red Centre*

drive vehicles) heads into the **\*\*Finke Gorge National Park** ⑪. After a brief stop at the **Amphitheater**, which is a holy place to the Aborigines and has some impressive rock formations, you come to the amazing **\*\*Palm Valley**.

Here rare cabbage palms, which have been growing in the area since prehistoric times, are reflected in the calm waters of the Finke River, and it is worth taking time out for a walk of 2 or 3 hours.

There are several ways to get to Kings Canyon in Watarrka National Park:

Leaving Alice Springs in a southerly direction, the route leads back onto the track, as the Outback people call Stuart Highway.

At Erldunda, turn west on the Lasseter Highway towards Luritja Road some 106 kilometers to the north from Alice – a total of approximately 450 kilometers. Those who have a 4-WD at their disposal can take the far more interesting route via Namatjira Drive (West MacDonnell Ranges) or Larapinta Drive (Hermannsburg) and finally along the unpaved **Mereenie Loop Road**, which runs to the canyon after some 200 kilometers.

Because this road runs through Aboriginal land, a permit is required ($A 2, available in Hermannsburg, in Kings Canyon Lodge or in Alice Springs).

132 kilometers south of Alice Springs is a turn-off at Ernest Giles Road ( a gravel road, 4-WD required) towards Watarrka National Park. After driving 8 kilometers along Ernest Giles Road, there is a 6 kilometer detour (bumpy, unpaved road) to the **Henbury Meteorite Craters** ⑫. A shower of meteorites landed here around 4700 years ago, leaving 13 craters which can still be seen quite clearly.

**\*King's Canyon** in **Watarrka National Park**, is a valley 270 meters deep where the King's Creek has eaten into the sandstone over many centuries and formed almost vertical walls of rock. There are two trails through the densely wooded ravine and along the surrounding cliffs, with names like Lost City, Aladdin's Lamp and Garden of Eden, which give some idea of the weird rock formations to be seen. The Garden of Eden honors its name – it is a small oasis with a water source for cooling off.

Solid shoes, or at least very good sneakers, are needed for the hike. Leave before sunrise. The first leg of the walk along the edge of the canyon is very steep, and sheer torture when the sun is out.

King's Canyon to Uluru (Ayers Rock) can be reached directly via **Luritja Drive**; turn off to the west and join Lasseter Highway after 170 kilometers – a stretch of some 315 kilometers.

### **\*\*ULURU (AYERS ROCK)**

**\*\*Uluru (Ayers Rock)** ⑭, perhaps the best-known tourist attraction in Australia,

*Above: Australians are excellent equestrians.*
*Right: The cliff cupola in Kata Tjuta (Olgas).*

is 445 kilometers from Alice Springs and is easily reached along the Stuart and Lasseter Highways. This impressive mound, rising about 350 meters from the sandy plain below, was named for an Australian politician by its white "discoverers."

The Aborigines have called it Uluru for centuries. It is one of their sacred places. The land on which Uluru stands is part of the Uluru National Park, declared in 1958, and after very many years and interminable legal wrangles, the area has finally been returned to its original owners, the Anangu.

The park is now leased from the Aborigines and administered by the *Parks Australia North*.

For the Anangu, the rock is not a natural attraction inviting to tempt one's athletic prowess, rather it is a sacred spot. Rock paintings adorn many of the caves and ravines created by erosion.

According to an Anangu dreamtime mythology, Uluru was "built" by two boys playing in the mud after a heavy rainstorm. Geologists date its formation to approximately 600 million years ago.

For tourists from around the globe, Ayers Rock is the inspiration for a million photos, with its kaleidoscope of colors ranging from bright red through brown to silver gray, depending on the time of day and the weather.

At sunset the crowds gather early at the purpose-built **Sunset Viewings** to grab the best places. Because the monolith is a sacred place for the Aborigines, they do ask visitors not to climb it.

However, for those who cannot restrain themselves, please note that climbing Uluru is prohibited during the summer months between 10:00 a.m. and 6:00 p.m. and at other times when the temperature is above 38 $^0$C or when it is raining.

## **KATA TJUTA (THE OLGAS)

A trip to Uluru will leave you with a feeling of euphoria, but be sure not to miss the **Kata Tjuta (Olgas)** ⑮ 32 kilometers to the west, which are just as

The Red Centre

beautiful, and possibly even more so, and are certainly much less crowded with tourists. This collection of 36 smaller rocks is thought by the Aborigines to be giants turned to stone. The place is not overrun by hordes of tourists and a walk along one of the many trails through the Olgas evokes the sensation of being totally alone and lost in the Red Centre. The **Valley of the Winds Walk** is particularly recommended if you have the time and if you feel you are reasonably fit. The starting point for Uluru and Kata Tjuta is the **Ayers Rock Resort** in **Yulara** ⑯, a tourist town outside the National Park with shops and accommodation to suit every pocket. From Yulara it is 17 kilometers to Ayers Rock, 50 kilometers (to the Olgas and 239 kilometers on the Lasseter Highway to **Erldunda** ⑰.

### *COOBER PEDY

Back on the Stuart Highway, the road leads southward all the way. Happily, this stretch is now surfaced throughout its length.There is little to stop for on the 485-kilometer-stretch to Coober Pedy, but visitors looking for other features of Outback life should arrange a detour to the **Mintabie Opal Field** ⑱ (turnoff behind Chandler railway station or in Marla Bore). Many unsuccessful opal prospectors from Coober Pedy who think the city in the south has grown too big are now trying their luck here, usually in rather primitive living conditions.

The best place to stock up with fuel and food is **Marla** ⑲. This is most important on any trip in the Outback: be sure to fill up with fuel, food and especially water at every opportunity as the heat may well make you feel extra thirsty! *Coober Pedy ⑳ itself is still synonymous with the hard life of the Outback in the past and the spirit of the pioneers who rode their luck. Coober Pedy was originally known as the Stuart Range Opal Field, named after John McDouall Stuart,

who in 1858 was the first European explorer in the area. In this town of 5000 people everything is centered on opal, a translucent gemstone in a wonderful variety of colors.

In Coober Pedy there are people of 50 different nationalities. Many of them have built their homes in former mine shafts (calling them dugouts) because the only place to live when the temperature goes over 50 °C in the summer is underground. The best example of this Outback lifestyle is Crocodile Harry's dugout. A visit is a must, as is trying your luck in the search for opal. Anything found on the surface belongs to the finder.

Many Aborigines can be seen searching among the debris from the successful mines and tourists can follow their example (finding out who has struck lucky afterwards over a beer in the pub!), but you should always ask the mine owner's permission beforehand. A lot of visitors have been fortunate enough to boost their spending money with a lucky find.

A permit is required from the Department of Mines in order to operate a mine so if you are thinking of taking up opal prospecting in a serious way you must go through the proper channels. Another slice of life in Cooper Pedy can be found at the drive-in cinema. Before every film this message is screened: "Bringing explosives into the cinema is strictly forbidden!"

80 kilometers south of Coober Pedy is another typical feature of the Outback, the *dingo fence*. This fence protects the sheep to the south from wild dingos and is 9600 kilometers long over all. The fence requires constant maintenance, which is a full-time occupation for many rangers.

It is a further 538 kilometers to **Port Augusta** at the end of the Stuart Highway. Hardly worth an overnight stop, unless a side trip is planned from the **Pimba Roadhouse** (with a gas station) to Woomera (the military test site) and on to the nearest opal field at Andamooka.

## RED CENTRE (☎ 08)

### ALICE SPRINGS

**ℹ️ Central Australian Tourism Industry Association (CATIA)**, 60 Gregory Terrace, Tel. 89525800. Permits ($A 2) for Mereenie Loop Rd (unpaved road to Kings Canyon, 4-WD highly recommended). **Central Land Council**, 33 Stuart Highway, Alice Springs, Tel. 89516320. Permits for Aborigine territory.

🛏️ 🟢🟢🟢 **Alice Springs Resort**, 34 Stott Tce, Tel. 89526699. **Lasseters Hotel Casino**, 93 Barret Dr, Tel. 89507777. 🟢🟢 **Alice Motor Inn**, 27 Undoolya Rd, Tel. 89522322. **All Seasons Frontier Oasis Alice Springs**, 10 Gap Rd, Tel. 89511444. **Desert Rose Inn**, 15 Railway Tce, Tel. 89521411. **Diplomat Motor Inn**, corner of Hartley St / Gregory Tce, Tel. 89528977. **Larapinta Lodge**, 3 Larapinta Dr, Tel. 89527255. **Territory Inn**, Leichhardt Tce, Tel. 89522066. **Vista Hotel Alice Springs**, Stephens Rd, Tel. 89526100. 🟢 **Elke's Backpacker Resort**, 39 Gap Rd, Tel. 89528422. **Melanka Lodge**, 94 Todd St, Tel. 89522233. **Pioneer YHA**, corner of Parsons St / Leichhardt Tce, Tel. 89528855. **Toddys Resort**, 41 Gap Rd, Tel. 89521322. **Stuart Caravan Park**, Larapinta Drive, Tel. 89522547.

🍴 **Bar Doppio**, Fan Lane (off Todd Mall); inexpensive vegetarian cuisine. **Camel's Crossing**, Fan Arcade, near Todd Mall, Tel. 89525522, Mexican. **The Overlanders Steakhouse**, 72 Hartley St, Tel. 89522159. Rustical. Meat-eaters paradise; the *Drovers Blowout* can be especially recommended. Most of the larger animals of the Northern Territory are on the menu: buffalo, camel, kangaroo, crocodile, beef and barramundi.

🏛️ **Museum of Central Australia**, corner of Larapinta Drive / Memorial Ave, Tel. 89515532. daily 9:00 a.m.-5:00 p.m. **Aboriginal Art & Culture Centre**, 86 Todd St, Tel. 89523408. Run by natives. Aboriginal art, didgeridoo lessons, *Aboriginal Culture Tours* into the surrounding areas. **Royal Flying Doctor Service of Australia**, Stuart Terrace, Tel. 89521129, all about the flying doctors of the Outback. Mon-Sat 9:00 a.m.-4:00 p.m., Sun 1:00 p.m.-4:00 p.m. **Panorama Guth**, a 60-meter-long and 6-meter-high 360 degree wall painting in the city center, with scenes of life in the Outback.

🎫 The **Henley-on-Todd-Regatta**, foot-race held on the first Saturday in October in the dried-up river bed of the Todd River.

🎫 Every second Sunday morning **flea market** (not in high summer) in the Todd Mall pedestrian zone with Aboriginal arts and crafts, musical instruments and much more. The **Sounds of Starlight Theatre** is also there, a music and slide show about the Red Centre (April-Nov. Tues-Sat from 7:00 p.m.; 90 minutes). **Casino** on the city's outskeirts. **Hot air balloon rides** with champagne breakfast at dawn with *Spinifex Ballooning*, Tel. 1800-677893, and *Outback Ballooning*, Tel. 1800-809790. Short **camel rides** at the *Frontier Camel Farm* on Ross Hwy east of Alice Springs, Tel. 89530444; **Horse rides** with *Ossie's Horseback Treks*, Tel. 1800-628211 (3 hours to 2 days including camping). **Walking tours** with *Walking Tours Larapinta Trail* through the West MacDonnell Ranges, Tel. 1800-803174.

### COOBER PEDY

**ℹ️ Tourist Information Centre**, Hutchison Street, Tel. 86725298 or 1800-637076.

🛏️ 🟢🟢🟢 **Desert Cave Hotel**, Hutchison St, Tel. 86725688. 🟢🟢 / 🟢 **Opal Inn Motel**, Hutchison St, Tel. 86725054. **Radeka Downunder Motel & Backpackers**, Oliver St, Tel. 86725223. **Umoona Opal Mine**, Hutchison St, Tel. 86725288. **Underground Motel**, Catacombe Rd, Tel. 86725324. **Coober Pedy Oasis Caravan Park**, Hutchison St, Tel. 86725169.

### TENNANT CREEK

**ℹ️ Regional Tourist Association**, Battery Hill Regional Centre, Peko Rd, Tel. 89623388.

🛏️ 🟢🟢 **Bluestone Motor Inn**, Paterson St, Tel. 89622617. **Eldorado Motor Lodge**, Paterson St, Tel. 89622402. **Safari Lodge Motel**, 12 Davidson St, Tel. 89622207. Also some inexpensive dormitory-style rooms.

### WAUCHOPE

🛏️ 🟢🟢 **Wauchope Hotel**, Stuart Hwy, Tel. 89641963.

### YULARA / ULURU (AYERS ROCK)

🛏️ All accommodation is part of the **Ayers Rock Resort**, Tel. 98609099, and therefore very expensive. In descending order, from expensive to (somewhat) less expensive: **Sails in the Desert Hotel**, **Desert Gardens Hotel**, **Emu Walk Apartments** and **Outback Pioneer Hotel**. The **Outback Pioneer Lodge**, dormitory-style beds a la youth hostel, (but expensive). Camping at the **Ayers Rock Campground**, Tel. 89562055, some cabins.

🎫 The area around the 348-meter-high **Uluru** (Ayers Rock) and the **Kata Tjuta** (The Olgas) is a National Park. Ayers Rock Resort in Yulara is outside; Visitor Centre with an exhibition on on geology, fauna and flora and information about hiking in the park, sightseeing flights and tours, such as "Desert Dinner" under the stars. Tel. 89577377, daily 8:30 a.m.-5:00 p.m. The new **Uluru Kata Tjuta Cultural Centre** in the National Park, on the Uluru access road, provides information about the National Park and the people who have been living here for centuries, Tel. 89563138, daily 7:00 a.m.-6:00 p.m. Participation in a walk organized by the Anangu rangers is a must.

*The Red Centre*

171

# FROM SYDNEY TO BRISBANE

**AUSTRALIAN GRAND TOUR**
**NEW ENGLAND HIGHWAY**
**PACIFIC HIGHWAY**
**MYALL LAKES NATIONAL PARK**
**BYRON BAY**
**GOLD COAST**

## THE AUSTRALIAN GRAND TOUR

There can be no more beautiful way to say farewell to a city than to drive northwards out of **\*\*Sydney ❶** across the Harbour Bridge. The view more than justifies avoiding the newly opened tunnel and there's no toll when driving outward from the city!

One last look at the Opera House and the skyline, then many of the travelers embark on their *Australian Grand Tour* which will take them several thousand kilometers in a few weeks and finish for most of them back at the Harbour Bridge – not a bad prospect!

Times have changed in Sydney, as the first few kilometers will show. Once upon a time it was a pleasant, leisurely drive through the suburbs along the **Pacific Highway**. Now most motorists use the **Sydney-Newcastle Freeway** where No Stopping signs replace the scenic splendor that can still be enjoyed along the old road, for example, if you stop at the **Ku-ring-gai National Park**. The **\*Hawkesbury River** is a popular sailing venue for many Sydneysiders, as is **Lake**

*Previous pages: Cape Byron – the easternmost point in Australia. Left: Humor on their faces and on their t-shirts – typically Australian.*

**Macquarie** further to the north, where prices are still reasonable. Beyond the **Brisbane Water National Park** – often a rather sorry sight in the summer after the forest fires – the road passes through **Gosford ❷**, the home of **Old Sydney Town**, a replica of Sydney as it used to be (open Wed-Sun 10:00 a.m. to 5:00 p.m. and during NSW school holidays Mon-Sun).

Well worth a visit is the **Australian Reptile Park & Wildlife Sanctuary**, where one can get a close look at poisonous snakes, spiders and crocodiles. Some of the "typically Australian" animals to be found in the sanctuary (kangaroos, emus, koalas, etc.) are partially tame and may be fed and petted (daily 9:00 a.m. to 5:00 p.m.)

Further inland is one of the best wine-growing areas in Australia, the **\*Hunter Valley** (turnoff at Freeman's Waterholes). The economy was not based on wines here but on coal in the 19th century. The small towns of **Maitland**, **Singleton**, **Branxton**, **Broke** and **Pokolbin** offer plenty of opportunities for wine-tasting, with over 40 wineries normally open to visitors between 9:00 a.m. and 5:00 p.m., and after an introduction to the history of New South Wales. The main town in the Hunter Valley is **Cessnock ❸** (population 17,000), a good center for overnight

*From Sydney to Brisbane*

those who prefer to enjoy the superb coastal scenery stay on the **Pacific Highway**.

## NEW ENGLAND HIGHWAY

On this road it is 1027 kilometers from Newcastle to Brisbane. You may be in a hurry, but it's still worth taking a few detours. For instance, the road which turns off at **East Maitland** towards **Morpeth** on the Hunter River gives a good overall impression of the Hunter Valley without going far from the highway.

From the Hunter Valley the highway climbs towards the Great Dividing Range. With its rich pastures, the New England region is well-known for rearing sheep and cattle. But in **Tamworth** ❻, a town of 35,000 people, country music is the thing. At the end of January when the **Tamworth Country Music Festival** is held, the town with its huge golden guitar and Country Music Wax Museum is a big draw for music fans all round the country.

accommodation and excursions. The best time to visit is in February or March when the grapes are harvested.

The most famous inhabitant of **Maitland** ❹ was Caroline Chisholm (1808-1877), who campaigned for better living conditions for the newly arrived immigrants, who often lived in the greatest misery.

The industrial and coal mining city of **Newcastle** ❺, with a population of 260,000, is New South Wales's second city, but it suffers from being only 156 kilometers from Sydney, and travelers have many tempting alternatives in the attractive surrounding countryside.

Most people merely glimpse Newcastle on the right as they go past, although it does have some good beaches. Decision time comes 14 kilometers further north at Hexham.

Drivers in a hurry take the inland route along the **New England Highway**, but

The hilly surroundings of the nearby **Lake Keepit State Recreation Area** ❼ make it an ideal venue for hang-gliders and paragliders.

Peace and quiet (maybe good luck, too) can be found by heading out along the **Fossickers Way** to the old gold-mining town of **Nundle** ❽. This route can be used as an alternative to the highway, returning to it at Glen Innes, but it is better to stay on the New England Highway if you are planning a visit to the university town of **Armidale** ❾ 42 kilometers northeast of Tamworth. Here, too, it is easy to see why this part of Australia has been named after places in Britain; both the land and the people bear a striking resemblance to their European counterparts. **Glen Innes** ❿ (98 kilometers) has a nostalgic old-country feel about it. The local people still live as they used to mainly by gem fossicking (for sapphires). Its location, at an altitude of 1073 meters, means the nights are pleasantly cool even

*Above: Inside a wine-growing estate in Hunter Valley (Tyrell's Wines).*

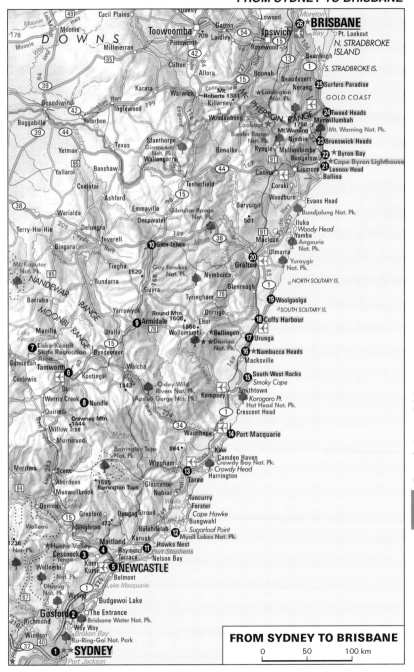

**FROM SYDNEY TO BRISBANE**

0          50          100 km

in summer, but you feel a warm climate beckoning as the road approaches Queensland. The border crossing into the Sunshine State is 112 kilometers further on beyond Tenterfield.

However different the towns along the New England Highway may be, they have one thing in common. From any one of them, it is possible to drive down through the hills of the Great Dividing Range to the Pacific Coast below. There are many secondary roads leading eastward to the coast and these detours are always a rewarding experience.

### PACIFIC HIGHWAY

If the route chosen is the Pacific Highway, there are many enjoyable side trips along the 998-kilometer-(mainly dual) carriageway that follows the coast to Brisbane. Beyond Newcastle is the lob-

*Above: Country Music Festival in Tamworth at the end of January. Right: The ferry at Mungo Brush in Myall Lakes National Park.*

ster and crayfish coast. All the way along there are stalls at the side of the road where fresh shellfish are sold. The only other ingredient needed for the perfect dinner (plus a bottle of wine from Hunter Valley) is a scenic setting; and that can be found a few kilometers away, on the shores of **Port Stephens** ⓫, called simply *the bay* by the townspeople. On the south side is the tourist resort of **Nelson Bay** and one of the loveliest beaches in the area, **Fingal Bay**. Porpoises frolic year round in the seas just off the coast.

On the other side of the bay the **Tea Gardens** (reached via a detour off the Pacific Highway, 12 kilometers beyond Karuah) have attractive promenades, marinas, a pub and a seafood restaurant.

### Myall Lakes National Park

Over the Singing Bridge is the neighboring village of **Hawks Nest**. Its normal population is 1100, but it is several times greater in the summer because it is the center for trips to the **Myall Lakes Na-**

tional Park ⑫ to the north. Myall Lakes is a popular place with Sydneysiders for renting a houseboat (hire centers in **Bulahdelah**). Visitors who fancy a holiday on the water are well advised to stock up with food, as there are only two supply depots along the shore, at Legges Camp and Bungwahl. The area can also be explored by car, by driving as far as **Mungo Brush** (23 kilometers, half of which is on unsurfaced road). To the right, the surf and the salt water lure you into the sea for a swim. To the left, the tranquil banks of the Bombah Broadwater Lake and clear, fresh water tempt you to the lake – and the two are less than a hundred meters apart. In the summer the banks swarm with campers. However, it is not difficult to escape the crowds along one of the many bushwalks. A ramble to Johnsons Beach or further on to Shelley Beach is particularly rewarding. A trip in the car up to the projection of land known as **Seal Rocks**, with its lighthouse and sandy beaches, is also recommended for the beauty of the scenery.

Just past **Mungo Brush** the lake has to be crossed by a ferry (which sails even if it has only one passenger). After disembarking, you will find an ideal spot for breakfast at **Bombah Point** (Myall Shores) before reaching Bulahdelah 16 kilometers to the west and rejoining the busy Pacific Highway.

Visitors who prefer to continue along the coast can turn off 4 kilometers beyond Bulahdelah towards **Forster** and **Tuncurry**. The two roads converge at **Taree** ⑬, famous for its fertile soil, rich agriculture and the lush State Forest nearby.

### Coastal Towns In Banana Land

Our itinerary leaves the highway again 49 kilometers further on at **Kew** and continues along the coast road to **Port Macquarie** ⑭ (population 28,000). This town has developed from a penal settlement, founded in 1821, to one of the best-known holiday resorts in New South Wales. Port Macquarie has some fine

*From Sydney to Brisbane*

beaches and historic buildings (St. Thomas's Church was built in 1821) and is a convenient place for an overnight stop, being about halfway between Sydney and Brisbane. It will give you a chance to experience the old pioneering days in **Timbertown**, a replica village near **Wauchope** (open daily from 9:00 a.m.), where the old lumberjacking days are brought back to life (daily from (9:00 a.m.). At **Kempsey** (51 kilometers) it is best to follow the signposts to **Hat Head National Park** (camping allowed at Hat Head) to **South West Rocks** ⑮, where the ★**Trial Bay Gaol** stands on a rocky headland above the shore. It was first built to house convicts and later accommodated German prisoners during the First World War. Trial Bay Gaol has now been converted into a very popular museum. Peaceful beaches and a camp site

*Above: It is not only in Grafton that the hotel-pub is an institution. Right: The road usually leads to the Great Barrier Reef on the east coast.*

lie directly in front of the prison walls. ★**Nambucca Heads** ⑯ (Beilbys Beach is the central beach) is in the heart of the banana country, with plantations lining the highway all the way to Coffs Harbour. West of **Urunga** ⑰ is the historic village of ★**Bellingen** (where the museum in Hyde Street offers a glimpse of the past) and also the ★**Dorrigo National Park** on the 1000-meter-high plateau of the same name with its tropical rain forest and many waterfalls. Or there is the challenge of whitewater rafting on the Nymboida River. **Coffs Harbour** ⑱ (population 45,000) is one of those popular seaside resorts that very few travelers can pass without stopping. The liveliest area is Park Beach with Ocean Parade immediately behind it. If you've ever wanted to get inside a banana, this is your chance, at the **Big Banana Theme Park** (right alongside the Pacific Highway to the north). The 10-meter-long concrete banana marks the entrance and one can visit the plantation and taste culinary banana specialities.

Something much more spectacular can be found 25 kilometers to the north at **Woolgoolga** ⑲ (called *Woopi* for short by the natives), where you're suddenly transported to India. Temples appear at the roadside and the climax is a replica of the Taj Mahal. If you like Indian food, Woolgoola is the place to stay.

About 60 kilometers further north, the road crosses a twin-level bridge into the inland town of **Grafton** ⑳ (population 16,500). The streets in the center are lined with great jacaranda trees (there is an annual blossom festival in October / November) and there are a number of old houses near the Cathedral and around Fry Street.

This place on the broad Clarence River has retained much of its traditional charm. The river flows along unhurriedly below the Crown Hotel, the best place to enjoy a cool beer after a hot day.

The air of calm is deceptive, though, because there are flood warning notices everywhere and the old timber houses on the bank are built on stilts for protection.

The route continues for 140 kilometers to Ballina and there is no particular reason to linger.

### *BYRON BAY

Now comes one of the best stretches of coastline – the coast road to **Lennox Head** ㉑. Just before the town, there is a lookout with magnificent views over the long beaches and a coastline which in places drops steeply to the sea.

**\*Byron Bay** ㉒, the easternmost place in Australia, is firmly in the grip of tourism. But somehow the mix is right; it is mostly young people, surfing freaks and artists who colonize the superb beaches and numerous pubs in the town. For many years its best-known resident has been Paul Hogan, famous throughout the world as Crocodile Dundee.

There's no need to use your car in Byron Bay; try some of the many walks in-

stead. The best one is to the **\*Cape Byron Lighthouse** (preferably as dusk is falling), but watch the time because the lighthouse (Australia's most easterly point) is closed from 5.30 p.m. to 8 a.m. and can then only be admired from a distance. Below it is one of the smallest and most beautiful beaches in Byron Bay, **Watego's Beach**, with good surf.

To the south of the Cape is **Tallow Beach**, which is nearly 10 kilometers long and almost deserted. This is a sharp contrast to **Main Beach** near the town center where most of the noisy resort life is concentrated.

A day on the beach should finish with a beer in the Great Northern Hotel (on the main street) or the Railway Friendly Bar, one of the nicest pubs along the east coast, with the drinking on one side and the station on the other. Perhaps that's one of the reasons why so many visitors make arrangements to arrive on the late train from Sydney.

Travelers who find Byron Bay too crowded can stay overnight at **Lennox**

*From Sydney to Brisbane*

**Head** or at **Brunswick Heads** 🔢 11 kilometers to the north. This small town at the confluence of Brunswick River and Simpson Creek is less attractive scenically but is more convenient and within easy distance from Byron Bay.

It has good beaches on both rivers as well as on the ocean and all are popular with locals and tourists.

Make the most of the peace at Brunswick Heads, 65 kilometers further north (either via **Murwillumbah** or along the coast) is the invisible border between New South Wales and Queensland, at Tweed Heads.

## GOLD COAST

**Tweed Heads** 🔢 in New South Wales and its sister town **Coolangatta** in Queensland are at the southern end of the Gold Coast. Both have a wide variety of tourist attractions and accommodations. Passing through **Burleigh Heads** (with

*Above: Byron Bay lighthouse.*

fine beaches), you come to **Surfers Paradise** 🔢, the main center on the controversial Gold Coast. It is one of the favorite destinations for Australian (and Japanese) tourists and paid dearly for its popularity in the 1970s when the development boom went out of control, leaving many once fine beauty spots over-built and spoiled.

It is difficult, if not impossible, to restore charm to any place once builders and property speculators move in, especially when there has been a slump in the economy, such as happened here.

Sadly, on the Gold Coast, all that glitters is not gold under the blazing Queensland sun. The seemingly endless stretch of sand (42 kilometers) is matched by row upon row of high-rise blocks which cast long shadows over the sands in the late afternoon.

The Gold Coast has a better reputation for its excellent golf courses (around 20) and many enjoyable theme parks: **Movieworld**, **Dreamworld**, **Wet & Wild** and especially **Sea World**, where entertainment is provided by regular dolphin shows and performing whales.

Attractive animal parks are **Currumbin Sanctuary** in Currumbin / Tugun and especially the more tranquil **Fleays Wildlife Park** in West Burleigh. The Gold Coast is the place for visitors looking for fun, a touch of luxury and plenty of variety.

Those who prefer peace and quiet can find complete contrast in the tranquil hinterland, only an hour's drive away. Farmland and rain forest with many waterfalls are the main features of the landscape along the arc of steeply towering mountain ranges (such as McPherson Range), where there are numerous national parks.

**\*Lammington National Park** is particularly lovely, with beautiful bushwalks. Whichever way your decision leads you, the journey northward leads to at **\*Brisbane** 🔢, the capital of Queensland.

### ARMIDALE (☎ 02)

🛏 ⊖⊖ **Armidale Regency Hallmark Inn**, 208 Dangar St, Tel. 67729800.

### BRUNSWICK HEADS (☎ 02)

🛏 ⊖⊖ **Harbour Lodge Motel**, Tweed St, Tel. 66851851. **Heidelberg Holiday Inn**, The Terrace, Tel. 66851808.

### BYRON BAY (☎ 02)

ℹ **Tourist Centre**, 80 Jonson St, Tel. 66858787.

🛏 ⊖⊖⊖ **Byron Bay Holiday Inn**, 45 Lawson St, Tel. 66856373. ⊖⊖ **Sunseeker Motel**, 100 Bangalow Rd, Tel. 66857369. **Byron Bay Beach Club**, Bayshore Dr, Tel. 66858000. ⊖ **Backpackers Holiday Village**, 116 Jonson St, Tel. 66858888 or 1800-350388. **Backpackers Inn**, 29 Shirley St, Tel. 66858231. **Belongil Beachhouse**, Childe St, Tel. 66857868.

📷 **Street markets** every Sunday, new age hippie flair; Byron Bay and Brunswick Heads, every second Sunday in the village The Channon north of Lismore, every fourth Sunday in Lismore and Bangalow.

### CESSNOCK (☎ 02)

ℹ **Tourist Centre**, Turner Park, Aberdare Rd, Tel. 49904477.

### COFFS HARBOUR (☎ 02)

ℹ **Visitor Information Centre**, Rose Ave / Marcia St, Tel. 66521522.

🛏 ⊖⊖⊖ **Novotel Opal Cove Resort**, Pacific Highway, Tel. 66510510. ⊖⊖ **Caribbean Motel**, 353 High St, Tel. 66521500. ⊖ **Aussitel Backpackers**, 312 High St, Tel. 66511871. **Coffs Harbour YHA**, 110 Albany St, Tel. 66526462.

### GLEN INNES (☎ 02)

🛏 ⊖⊖ **New England Motor Lodge**, Church St, Tel. 67322922.

### GOLD COAST (☎ 07)

ℹ **COOLANGATTA**: **Tourist Centre**, Beach House Plaza, Tel. 55367765. **SURFERS PARADISE**: **Gold Coast Tourism Bureau**, Cavill Mall, Tel. 55384419.

🛏 **COOLANGATTA**: ⊖⊖ **Coolangatta Ocean View**, Marine Park / Clark St, Tel. 55363722. ⊖ **Sunset Strip Budget Resort**, 199 Boundary St, Tel. 5599 5517. **SURFERS PARADISE**: ⊖⊖⊖ **Gold Coast International**, Gold Coast Hwy / Staghorn Ave, Tel. 5592 1200. ⊖⊖ **Iluka Beach Aesort**, corner Esplanade / Hanlan St, Tel. 55399155. ⊖ **Surfers Central Budget Accom.**, 40 Whelan St, Tel. 55384344. **Surfers Paradise Backpackers Resort**, 2837 Gold Coast Hwy, Tel. 55924677. **TWEED HEADS**: ⊖⊖ **Homestead Tweed**, 58 Boyd St, Tel. 55361544. ⊖ **Tweed Billabong Holiday Park**, Holden St, Tel. 55242444.

🏛 **Minjungbal Aboriginal Centre**, South Tweed Heads, Kirkwood Rd, Tel. 55242109, daily,10:00 a.m.-4:00 p.m.

📷 **Theme parks**: Entrance to all parks is $A 42, unless otherwise stated. Transport is free with *Surfside Buslines*, Tel. 131230, or $A 12 / day from the hotels with the *Gold Coast Tourist Shuttle*, Tel. 1300-655655. **Dreamworld**, Pacific Hwy, Coomera, 17 km north of Surfers Paradise, Tel. 1800-073300, 10:00 a.m.-5:00 p.m.. Disneyland in miniature, **Movieworld**, Pacific Highway, Oxenford, Tel. 55733999, 10:00 a.m.-5:00 p.m., all about movies. **Sea World**, Sea World Drive, Main Beach, Tel. 55882205, 10:00 a.m.-5:00 p.m., dolphin and whale shows. **Wet'n'Wild**, Pacific Hwy, Oxenford, north of Surfers Paradise, Tel. 55732255, 10:00 a.m.-5:00 p.m., water fun, $A 22.

📷 **National Parks** Lamington, Mount Warning, Border Ranges and Nightcap, hiking. Information: Tweed Tourism, Murwillumbah, Tel. 02-66721340.

📷 **Warning**: Pickpockets are drawn to the great numbers of holiday makers on the Gold Coast!

### HAWKS NEST (☎ 02)

🛏 ⊖⊖ **Beachfront Motor Inn**, 15 Beach Rd, Tel. 49970324. ⊖ **Hawks Nest Beach Caravan Park**, Booner St, Tel. 49910239.

### LENNOX HEAD (☎ 02)

🛏 ⊖⊖ **Santa Fe**, 8 Byron St, Tel. 66877788. ⊖ **Lennox Beach House**, 3 Ross St, Tel. 66877636.

### MYALL LAKES (☎ 02)

ℹ **Great Lakes Information Centre**, Little St, Forster, Tel. 65548799.

### NAMBUCCA HEADS (☎ 02)

ℹ **Tourist Information**, Pacific Hwy, Tel. 65686954. 🛏 ⊖⊖ **Miramar**, 1 Nelson St, Tel. 65687899. **Scotts B&B**, 1 Ocean St, Tel. 65686386. ⊖ **Backpackers Hostel**, 3 Newman St, Tel. 65686360.

### NEWCASTLE (☎ 02)

ℹ **Tourist Information**, 92 Scott St, Tel. 49299299. 🛏 ⊖⊖ **Noahs on the Beach**, Shortland Esplanade, corner Zaara St, Tel. 49295181. ⊖ **Newcastle Beach YHA**, 20 Pacific St, Tel. 49253544.

### PORT MACQUARIE (☎ 02)

ℹ **Information Centre**, Clarence St, Tel. 65831293. 🛏 ⊖⊖ **Aquatic**, 253 Hastings River Drive, Tel. 65837388. **Port Pacific Resort**, 6 Clarence St, Tel. 65838099.

⊖ **Lindel Travellers Hostel**, 2 Hastings River Drive, Tel. 65831791. **Beachside Backpackers YHA**, 40 Church St, Tel. 65835512.

🏛 **Sea Acres Rainforest Centre**, on Pacific Drive,Tel. 65823355

### .SOUTH WEST ROCKS (☎ 02)

🛏 ⊖⊖ **Costa Rica Motel Resort**, 134 Gregory Ave, Tel. 65666400.

### TAMWORTH (☎ 02)

ℹ **Tourist Centre**, Peel St, Tel.1800-803561.

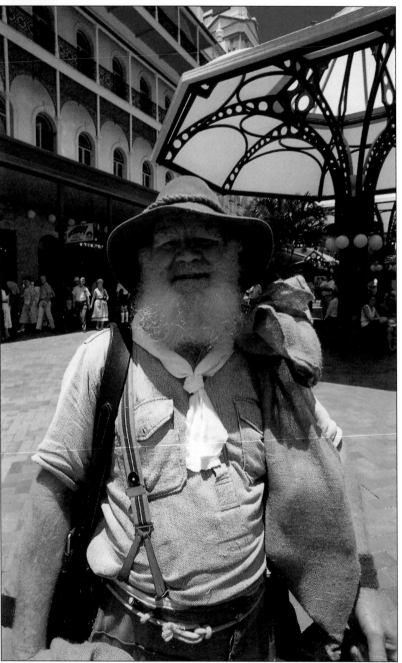

# FROM BRISBANE TO TOWNSVILLE

## BRISBANE
## ISLANDS AND MOUNTAINS IN
## THE ENVIRONS OF THE
## SUNSHINE COAST
## GREAT BARRIER REEF
## WHITSUNDAY ISLANDS

### *BRISBANE

**\*Brisbane's** birth was far from auspicious. In 1770 Captain Cook sailed right past, on his way up the coast, and in 1779 Matthew Flinders could find nothing exciting in Moreton Bay.

In 1823, John Oxley, the Surveyor-General, took a different view when the convict settlement in Sydney began to get overcrowded, and Sir Thomas Brisbane, the Governor of New South Wales, sent him north to find a suitable place for another penal colony.

The first contingent of convicts arrived only a year afterwards, but a shortage of water and disputes with the Aborigines later forced them to abandon the settlement at Redcliffe. They moved 30 kilometers up-river to the site where the city of Brisbane now stands.

The penal colony was closed in 1839 and the land was released for settlement in 1842, laying the foundations of the new state which gained independence in 1859 and was named Queensland.

Brisbane has remained a village for the last 150 years, or so they used to say

*Previous pages: A delicacy – fresh seafood. Left: The metropolis of Brisbane has retained its village charm, as demonstrated by this Brisbaneite.*

mockingly in the rest of the country. Today, the capital of the Sunshine State (with more than 1.5 million inhabitants) is one of Australia's favorite cities.

Its year-round mild climate, reasonable rents and enviable holiday areas close to the city (the Sunshine Coast to the north and the Gold Coast to the south) are attracting more and more people to live there.

Tourists can enjoy a visit as well, though they will look in vain for the elegance of Melbourne or the atmosphere of Sydney.

The center of this city of over a million people extends along the banks of the **Brisbane River**, which forms a backdrop to every view.

Not surprisingly, Brisbane is also a city of bridges, including Merivale, William Jolly, Victoria, Captain Cook and the splendid Story Bridge, best seen from Bowen Terrace in the New Farm precinct.

### City Tour

The morning commuter traffic flows over **Story Bridge ❶**, while rowers ply their oars on the Brisbane River underneath.

A ferry leaves from the **Holman Street ❷** mooring in the Kangaroo Point precinct approximately every ten minutes

*City map page 188, Guidepost pages 201-203*

187

*From Brisbane to Townsville*

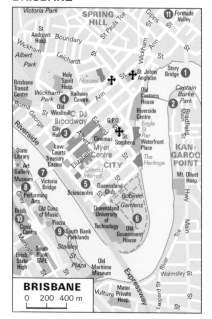

**BRISBANE**
0   200  400 m

for the Riverside Ferry Terminal at the edge of the city center. Leaving a little later, you may pass a paddle-steamer which leaves The Pier several times daily on river cruises.

The **Old Customs House** (1889) on the opposite river bank can be recognized from afar by its green cupola; there is a lovely art gallery there.

The adjacent **Riverside Centre** is the ideal spot for a mid-morning snack or lunch, for there are sandwich shops and numerous food stalls with a wide range of international cuisine.

It is best to avoid the rush hour between noon and 1:00 p.m. when the place is full of business people and secretaries!

An alternative at lunchtime is **King George Square** in front of the **City Hall** ❸ (built between 1920 and 1930), a venue for many musical and theatrical productions. This is also the start of the **Heritage Trail** (information sheet obtainable

*Right: Evening ambience on King George Square with City Hall in the background.*

tainable from the Visitors' Bureau), which passes through the **Central Business District** (CBD) to 39 of the city's historic buildings.

This recommendable walk demonstrates how Brisbane has achieved a perfect balance between old-world charm and modern design.

The oldest building in the city is the **Old Windmill** ❹ (in Wickham Terrace), built in 1828. Its name is misleading, however. The convicts had to compensate for the lack of wind by sheer muscle power.

Most of the old buildings are in **George Street**: the **Treasury Casino**, built between 1885 and 1926 in the style of an Italian palace, the **Queensland Club** on the corner of Alice Street, the two-story **mansions** of 1890, now with a restaurant and shopping mall, and **Parliament House** (1865).

Running parallel to it is Queens Wharf Road, where the **Old Commissariat Store** (1829) is located. The adjacent **Brisbane Sciencentre** ❺, a technological museum, has exhibitions one can touch and with which one can experiment.

A stroll through the **Botanical Gardens** ❻ (at the end of George Street), where **Old Government House** stands, takes you back again to the Brisbane River.

From here, there is a footpath along the river to Edward Street, leading back a few blocks further to the **Queen Street Mall**.

This pedestrianized zone is the heart of the CBD. A pleasant interlude can be spent under the awnings of the cafe-restaurants in the mall's center.

The other side of the Brisbane River is reached via the **Victoria Bridge** ❼. Culture buffs are spoilt for choice at the **\*Queensland Cultural Centre** ❽ (Victoria Bridge / South Bank).

In addition to the **Queensland Museum**, which shows you at a glance all you should know about the state, and the

\*Queensland Art Gallery, which is well worth a tour, there are regular concerts and plays in the Performing Arts Complex.

Nearby the South Bank Parklands ❾, venue of the 1988 World Expo and now an attractive recreational park by the inner city, stretches along the Brisbane River.

The 16 hectares of grounds comprise tropical parks, an artificial bathing lagoon with sandy beach, a Wildlife Sanctuary, Maritime Museum and an IMAX movie theater with a gigantic screen (3-D movies, among others).

It is possible to stroll through an arts and crafts market or relax in the sundry cafes, restaurants and pubs - most offer seating outside. Numerous fire-eaters, living sculptures and street musicians supply entertainment.

A bicycle and footpath runs from South Bank Parklands to Story Bridge. At times it runs directly along the cliffs of the Kangaroo Point precinct (River Sculpture Walk). There is a splendid view from here of Brisbane's illuminated skyline – from this distance, nothing remains of its "village-like charm." There are regular events and exhibitions held in the Brisbane Exhibition & Convention Centre ❿. A large part of the city's night-life is played out in Fortitude Valley ⓫ ("The Valley"). Brisbane's little Chinatown stretches to the northeast of CBD, between Wickham Street and Ann Street, where there are also numerous pubs and restaurants.

### Islands and Hills Around Brisbane

The surroundings of Brisbane offer contrasting attractions. The coast beckons to the east, and the city is surrounded on the other three sides by hills.

For many of the inhabitants (*Brisbaneites*), \*North Stradbroke Island ⓬ is the favorite spot for week-ending. Straddie has beautiful beaches and a number of bushwalks. The island is reached by ferry from Cleveland or Redland Bay. Overnight accommodation is

*From Brisbane to Townsville*

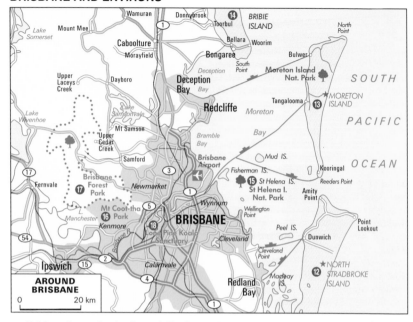

available and camping is allowed. Further north is **\*Moreton Island** ⑬, connected to the mainland by car ferry from Redcliffe.

In **Moreton National Park** there is one of the highest sandhills in the world, the 280-meter-high **Mount Tempest**. The waters around Cape Moreton are celebrated fishing grounds for marlin (all the year round), but the culinary specialty of the area is the Moreton Bay bug, a type of lobster.

Another island option is **Bribie Island** ⑭ 60 kilometers to the north, which is connected to the mainland by a bridge.

**St. Helena Island** ⑮ is at the estuary of the Brisbane River and was used as a prison from 1867 to 1932 (tours run from Brisbane).

A trip into the hinterland means a trip into the hills: from **Mount Coot-tha** ⑯ (6 kilometers), where the attractions are the Botanical Gardens and the Planetarium, there is the best panoramic view of Bris-

*Right: Koala in Lone Pine Koala Sanctuary.*

bane. In **Brisbane Forest Park** ⑰ along Mt. Nebo Rd, there are some very good areas for a picnic near to Bellbird Grove.

Southwest of the city's center is the **Lone Pine Koala Sanctuary** ⑱ (12 kilometers). This park is one of the best known of its kind. Visitors can see, feed or even fondle some 60 species of birds, kangaroos and, most famous of all, over 100 koalas, nearly all of which were born in the sanctuary, not caught in the wild.

Contrary to popular belief, koalas are not bears; they are marsupials, which carry their babies in pouches just as kangaroos do. Koalas are not found anywhere else in the world. Be careful though; they may look cuddly but they can scratch! The best time for a visit is around 2:30 in the afternoon when the koalas are fed on eucalyptus leaves. This is incentive enough for them to open their eyes, even though they need about 18 hours' sleep a day. Lone Pine can only be reached by boat (with Miramar Cruises daily from 1:00 p.m. from North Quay in the CBD, Tel, 07-32210300).

## FROM BRISBANE TO TOWNSVILLE

Tourists turning their back on *Brisbane **❶** and heading north are on the brink of an adventure. Whatever destination they have in mind, Highway 1 – called the Bruce Highway as it runs through Queensland – is the road to take.

After just 300 kilometers the Sunshine Coast tempts travelers to linger awhile. At Rockhampton (640 kilometers) comes the start of the Great Barrier Reef, with its spellbinding coral islands.

Anyone in the mood for a touch of Robinson Crusoeism can "go underground" on one of the innumerable islets. Others may prefer the Outback, in which case they can turn off westward near Rockhampton into the unending bush country near Emerald, Longreach and Winton.

It's almost impossible to bypass Mackay (975 kilometers) on the Hibiscus Coast and the Whitsunday Island group (1120 kilometers) without stopping off. Then relish your last taste of city life Queensland-style at Townsville (1371 kilometers) and Cairns (1717 kilometers).

From Ingham to just behind Cape Tribulation on the coastal cliffs there is a luxuriant growth of rugged rain forest, followed by sparse savannah which stretches to the tip of the peninsula.

Behind Cooktown / Laura the voyage continues through sparsely populated country. The journey through Cape York Peninsula (only in 4-WD vehicles and not during the rainy season between December and April) is a challenge, for several river courses must be crossed.

Queensland's entire length, from south to north will have been crossed by the time one reaches Cape York, and some 2,800 kilometers traveled since leaving Brisbane. Following the long, usually strenuous drive, many tourists find the view of close by (but not accessible from here) Papua-New Guinea to be a meager

reward. But the following applies in Queensland: the trip is the goal – and there are enough rewarding stops along the Queensland coast.

### SUNSHINE COAST

Before leaving the multi-lane **Bruce Highway** beyond Landsborough in the direction of **Caloundra** towards the coast, one should drop by the *Glass **Mountains National Park ❷**.

In 1770 Captain Cook himself was impressed by this region of 13 mountains – all the result of volcanic activity which took place 20 million years ago.

It has excellent bushwalking and climbing. Anyone can reach the top of Mount Ngungun in just two hours, to be rewarded with a splendid view.

Mount Beerwah and Mount Tibrogargan are both rather difficult to climb; good physical condition and some mountaineering experience are required. And you should not tackle Mount Coonowrin (or Crookneck) at all unless

*From Brisbane to Townsville*

you are a very experienced mountaineer.

The inland region of the Sunshine Coast also has its share of sights to admire: the **Big Pineapple** sculpture marks the entrance to the **Sunshine Plantation** ❸, about 8 kilometers south of Nambour.

A ride on the Sugar Cane Train elucidates a great deal about fruit and nut farming. The world's largest ginger factory in **Yandina** ❹ offers tours of its facilities. Look for signs along Highway 1.

In contrast to the Gold Coast further south, the **Sunshine Coast** is still fairly peaceful and relaxed, except during the months of December and January.

Unfortunately, in the south, around **Maroochydore** and **Alexandra Headland**, increasing numbers of concrete blocks are being constructed.

In **Noosa** ❺, on the fine north end of the Sunshine Coast, care is being taken with the style. The hinterland is being built slowly, but most hotels and holiday

*Above: Fraser Island, the world's largest sand dune.*

apartments do have 2–3 stories. Noosa is comprised of the center Noosa Heads and the "suburbs" of Noosaville and Tewantin to the west as well as Sunshine Beach in the southeast.

At the end of the 1970s Noosa was still a well-kept secret known only to hippies and surfers. Since then, although it has been discovered by the rich and beautiful people from Sydney and especially Melbourne, it is still worth a visit.

During the day, Noosa Main Beach with its sun-worshippers is where it all happens, but those who like peace and quiet (and surfers who find the waves superior waves) prefer the beaches to the east, such as Sunshine Beach (lifeguards on duty), Marcus Beach and Peregian Beach. In the evening people meet in the (pricey) restaurants and bars along Hastings Road.

When the beach begins to pall, *Noosa National Park (477 hectares, under conservation protection) to the east, on a promontory surrounded by rain forest and low shrubberies is not far away. It has some spectacular walks along the wild, rocky coast (Coastal Track and Alexandria Bay Track) to protected bays.

Laguna Lookout reveals magnificent sunsets over the entire hinterland of the Lakes District (an ideal area to rent a houseboat) and the small towns of Noosaville and Tewantin.

Noosa is a favorite starting point for the trip to Fraser Island (instead of Hervey bay, more to the north), and "discover" ★**Cooloola Coast** ❻ north of Noosa along the way.

The island and the coast are part of the Great Sandy Beach Region and are encompassed by ★**Great Sandy National Park**. ★★**Fraser Island** ❼ is the world's largest sand island with a surface of 184,000 hectares.

A four-wheel drive is a must for both the island and the Cooloola Coast on account of the soft sand. A day trip to Noosa is not really worthwhile, as the journey is simply too long.

One to three over night stays will give you better opportunities to visit the island in any case (permit required).

There is a ferry from Noosa at Tewantin over the Noosa River, and then a drive along the 40 Mile Beach towards Rainbow Beach. There is a 4-WD trail which runs more inland from Boreen Point or Kin Kin.

Ensure you have adequate maps and enquire carefully about the tides – some parts of the coast are only accessible at low tide.

At **Inskip Point** north of Rainbow Beach there is a car ferry to Fraser Island. The landscape is similar to that found on Cooloola Coast: a seemingly endless beach one the east coast, **75 Mile Beach**, serves as a "highway" for the 4-WD vehicles; and many freshwater lakes and trails in the dense rain forest of the interior.

Bathing there is not recommended on account of the sharks and the dangerous undertows, but one can cool off all the better in the lakes. Hotel-style accommodation is available at the lovely Kingfisher Bay Resort on the west coast as well as on the east coast in Eurong, Happy Valley and Dilli Village.

There are also several camping sites, most of which are under the administration of the National Parks and Wildlife Service.

In Happy Valley and Eurong, food and gas is very expensive – therefore it is best to bring your own provisions over to the island from the mainland.

**Hervey Bay** ❽, lies 34 kilometers north of the Bruce Highway at Maryborough, is also a popular departure point for trips to Fraser Island. A day trip is worth while. Hervey Bay comes to life between the middle of August and the end of October, when large numbers of humpbacked whales regularly surface in the bay. A number of small firms have interesting ★★**whale watching tours** on their program.

**Bundaberg** ❾ is mainly known for its rum distillery (tours available) and Bundy is much-loved and drunk throughout the country. This town of 50,000 people is also the point of departure for trips to the southernmost islands of the Great Barrier Reef.

Ships and hydroplanes leave Port Bundaberg to Lady Musgrave Island. ★**Lady Elliott Island** ❿ can be reached from Bundaberg by plane. The latter has a resort for its guests.

For ★**Lady Musgrave Island** ⓫ (a national park), on the other hand, you will have to stock up on provisions and drinking water, and if you wish to spend the night, a permit is required.

These islands can also be accessed from the *Town of 1770*. In that case, leave Bruce Highway about 180 kilometers north of Maryborough (keep an eye out for the signs) and drive on uncovered roads to the coastal towns of **Agnes Water** and **Seventeen Seventy** ⓬ ("1770"). This is where Captain Cook first set foot on Queensland territory, in May 1770.

*From Brisbane to Townsville*

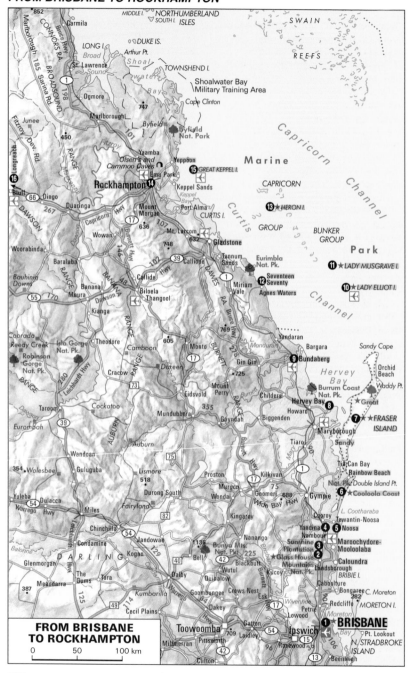

FROM BRISBANE
TO ROCKHAMPTON

0          50          100 km

Secluded beaches are a feature of both of these lovely and peaceful resorts beaches.

### Sugar Cane and Dream Islands

Traveling along the Bruce Highway, it is easy to see that you are now in the **Sugar Cane Region**. The road is bordered by cane fields right up to Townsville.

Sugar, or white gold, pays the bills for many towns along the Queensland coast and still ranks higher than tourism as a source of revenue.

Everywhere there are sugar refineries which can be visited during the harvest season from the end of June till about November. Some cane fields are burnt just before harvesting and it pays to take care on the Bruce Highway when passing these fires.

**Gladstone** is the center for trips to **⋆Heron Island ⓭**. This 17-hectare coral cay is everyone's idea of a south-sea island and is one of the best places in the world for skin-diving. The only accommodation is in a luxury resort that is beyond the average budget; day trips are no longer available.

Just before Rockhampton, the road crosses the Tropic of Capricorn. Driving into the city, the visitor is welcomed by a Brahman bull to this, the *beef capital* of Australia.

**Rockhampton ⓮**, 40 kilometers from the coast, has little in common with the other coastal cities. It seems much more like a typical provincial Queensland town of the interior., dry, hot and conservative.

Do find time to visit the **Dreamtime Cultural Centre**, a vivid portrayal of the traditions and culture of the Aborigines.

The **Capricorn Coast** from Emu Park to Byfield National park in the north is worth a visit, for it has tranquil beaches and rain forest – perhaps using the coastal town **Yeppon** (32 kilometers northeast of Rockhampton) as a base. The island group **Keppel Islands** is offshore of the

coast. The easiest access is to **Great Keppel Island ⓯** (14.5 square kilometers). It has found favor particularly with the backpack tourists and families on account of its inexpensive lodging, beautiful beaches and attractive hikes. It also caters to day trippers: from Rosslyn Bay close to Yeppon there are many shuttle launches leaving for the island.

Visitors who want a real taste of the Outback should catch the Greyhound Bus from Rockhampton to **Longreach ⓰**. The journey takes them past small and seemingly forgotten settlements, through endless kilometers of arid bush.

In 1988 the **⋆⋆Australian Stockman's Hall of Fame** and Outback Centre was completed opposite the airport to honor the hardy people of the Outback.

Visitors continuing along the coast do not have to travel far from Rockhampton before they have the chance to cool off with a tour of the **Olsen's and Cammoo Caves**, famous for their stalagmites and stalactites.

The following 334-kilometer-stretch between Rockhampton and Mackay can certainly be described as the most boring of all the coastal routes in Queensland.

### Eungella National Park and Cape Hillsborough

Around the town of **Sarina ⓱** (40 kilometers south of Mackay, the beautiful beaches are uncrowded and ideal for relaxation after a long car journey.

**Mackay ⓲**, known as the *Sugar Capital of Australia* because of its five sugar refineries, has nothing spectacular to offer, but the relaxed atmosphere invites the tourist to take things at a leisurely pace, visiting, for instance, Queens Park with its beautiful walks and Orchid House.

From **Mount Oscar** there is a good view over the city and the port. The best beaches are north of the city center.

On hilly **Brampton Island ⓳** 32 kilometers off the coast at Mackay there is an

*From Brisbane to Townsville*

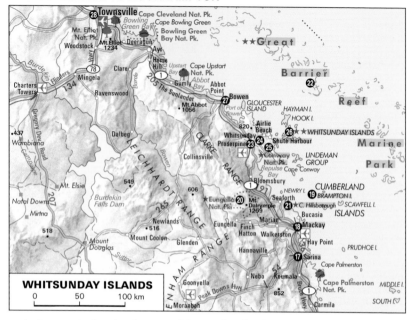

WHITSUNDAY ISLANDS
0    50    100 km

exclusive resort – but do take note of the fact that day trippers are not allowed to visit here.

The most popular attraction in the region is ★**Eungella National Park ⑳** – and not just for nature-lovers. The park is 85 kilometers west of Mackay in the Clarke Range area and has a most unusual combination of tropical and subtropical vegetation. This is the home of the duck-billed platypus, and also of the much less popular leeches which tend to ambush park visitors by dropping from the leaves onto the arms and legs of people walking below. Only small sections of the 500 square kilometers of park are accessible along marked trails. Most of these trails start from the Ranger's office on Broken River. Another national park, on the coast this time, is ★**Cape Hillsborough ㉑** (turning off the Bruce Highway beyond Fairleigh, 55 kilometers from Mackay). Here there are a number

*Right: One of the numerous lifeguards on the Great Barrier Reef.*

of walks through the bush, crossing over dense rain forest in some spots. Wandering down Butterfly Valley in the winter, the walker is beguiled by clouds of these beautiful creatures.

Visitors during the Australian summer (beginning in November) can go to Turtle Lookout to watch turtles coming on land to lay their eggs in the sand. The offspring hatch in January and wander off into the water. The view over the steep cliffs along the shore and the islands in the Hillsborough Channel is breathtaking.

The beaches on the eastern coast of Australia are covered with little balls of sand after the ebb. They are produced by the sand bubbler crab, which digs about under the sand for food and then spits up the indigestible grains of sand. This phenomenon can be frequently observed at Cape Hillsborough.

### ★★GREAT BARRIER REEF

The ★★**Great Barrier Reef ㉒**, one of the great natural wonders of the world, extends almost all the way along the coast for a distance of around 2000 kilometers, covering an area of more than 350,000 square kilometers.

It is estimated that some 2000 species of fish and over 50 different birds live on and from the reef. Coral polyps in the millions (over 400 different species) have shaped the reef into a living microcosm for over 15,000 years. This has led to the formation of over 600 islands of varying sizes, some of which are accessible to visitors.

Many of the resort islands advertised as being on the Great Barrier Reef are not actually part of the reef at all, but they are no less beautiful for that.

Although the reef was given protected status in 1975, the growth of the coral and thus its continued existence is at risk from environmental pollution and the expansion of tourism.

Visitors should follow some simple rules. Do not break off or take away any coral. Wear rubber shoes when walking on the reef. Do not move stones or rocks in the water to avoid cutting yourself on the sharp coral or even stepping on the relatively rare but lethal stone-fish.

If you cut or injure yourself on the reef, contact a doctor immediately, even for minor cuts, as there is a risk of infection. Sun burn risk is especially high; do wear a t-shirt and long pants or leggings.

The **Great Barrier Reef Marine Park Authority** which is responsible for administering the Marine Park has its headquarters in Townsville (Flinders Street East). It is the place to go for all the necessary information, maps and entry permits for specially protected areas.

### **WHITSUNDAY ISLANDS

Ever since Captain James Cook discovered the beautiful tropical islands of the Whitsundays in the 1770's, people come to visit this beautiful region. Today, **The Whitsunday Islands**, are one of the

greatest tourist attractions in Australia, with over 560,000 visitors a year (it is the third busiest tourist destination in Queensland).

There are numerous activities to be enjoyed on the Whitsundays, such as sailing, diving, or exploring the coral.

At **Proserpine** ㉓ it is better to leave the Highway and turn off towards the coast.

It is 25 kilometers to **Whitsunday City** ㉔, formed in 1987 from the settlements of Airlie Beach, Cannonvale, Jubilee Pocket and Shute Harbour. It used to be a tranquil and sleepy little area, but now there are noisy hordes of mainly young holiday makers in all the beer gardens and pubs, especially at **Airlie Beach**.

There is a wide choice of entertainment and accommodation. During the day, diving courses and sailing trips are among the attractive offers.

The road to **Shute Harbour** only 10 kilometers away passes through **\*Conway National Park** ㉕ (238 square

*From Brisbane to Townsville*

kilometers). Until the last ice age, its volcanic rocks were joined to what are now the Whitsunday Islands.

The park can be explored along a number of trails. Information is obtainable from the ranger, opposite the camp site.

Because there are so many yachts, launches and catamarans using it as a starting point for tours of the Whitsundays, Shute Harbour is one of the busiest harbors in Australia. People with privately owned boats are often willing to take hitch-hikers with them on these trips.

Captain Cook first sailed through the **\*\*Whitsunday Islands** ㉖ in 1770. 200 years later they have begun to develop into the second most popular holiday area in Australia after the Gold Coast.

Millions of Australian dollars – and Japanese yen! – were poured into the building of resorts and harbor installations so that every tourist would find

*Above: Whitehaven Beach on Whitsunday Island is one of the most attractive beaches east of Shute Harbour.*

something to their taste on the islands. The Whitsunday Group is made up of 74 islands, almost all of which have national park status.

Seven islands have been opened up to international tourism. Most of them are quite expensive, even though they have been classified in the mid-price range. Sometimes the all-inclusive package tour can be slightly less expensive.

**South Molle Island**, 20 minutes from Shute Harbour, though somewhat overcrowded, is still ideal for a family holiday. The resort has many leisure facilities and is not too up market. The island's beaches, many of which are very stony, are linked by a network of paths right through the national park. Don't miss the view from the highest point on the island, Mount Jeffreys.

**Daydream Island**, 5 kilometers from Shute Harbour, is perfect for a day trip, being so close to the mainland. It has a wonderful combination of white sand and green rain forest. The resort is located in the south of the 2- kilometer-long island.

Separated from it by a narrow channel is **Long Island** (11 kilometers long but only 2 kilometers wide), a place for people who like something quieter. It is just off the coast and is reached by ferry from Shute Harbour.

Three resorts, all not too expensive by Whitsunday standards, offer accommodation. Along the 13 kilometers of trails you can go looking for wallabies, giant goana lizards and bats. From various points there are glorious panoramas over the Whitsunday Islands.

The island beaches which face the mainland are sandy, but those on the ocean side tend to be stony and the strong winds can sometimes make them very uncomfortable.

The least typical of all of the Whitsunday Islands is **Hamilton Island**. Over the past few years a town has grown up up on this island which is a giant holiday complex offering the same attractions as the Gold Coast.

An international airport, accommodation for 1,500 visitors, a marina for 400 yachts, artificial beaches and the biggest freshwater pool in Australia are just some of the features which set it apart from the other islands. There is even a service which arranges weddings in a tiny chapel under the palm trees. This is very popular with Japanese couples.

Although Hamilton Island does not have national park status, there are walks through unspoiled natural surroundings.

The **Passage Peak Walk** meanders along a beautiful path to the island's east coast. Visitors who cannot afford to stay at the resort (or don't wish to) have a choice of various day excursions starting from Shute Harbour.

On **Lindeman Island**, at the southern end of the Whitsunday Group, a Club Med Resort has been established. There are 20 kilometers of marked trails through the hilly interior leading to good sandy and coral beaches.

Launches leave for the island from Shute Harbour. The most northerly island in the Whitsunday Group is also the most exclusive.

*From Brisbane to Townsville*

The **Hayman Island Resort**, the only accommodation on the island, is one of the most luxurious hotels in Australia. Its proximity to the reef attracts divers from all round the world.

**Hook Island**, however, the second largest island in the Whitsunday Group, is far more reasonably priced (camping possibilities) and is very popular with divers and snorkerlers.

Its magnificent northern beaches are the perfect point of departure for tours exploring the Great Barrier Reef.

There is no resort accommodation on **Whitsunday Island** itself, but what it does have is the most beautiful beach in the whole group.

**\*\*Whitehaven Beach** is a snow-white fringe of sand 6 kilometers long, with **Whitsunday Peak** (438 meters high) towering above it – sheer heaven! It is far from easy to tear yourself away from such a paradise and return to the mainland.

*Above: Eyeball to eyeball with the fascinating underwater world.*

**To Townsville**

After this you can make good time all the way to Townsville. Fields of sugar cane border the Bruce Highway and there is really nothing worth stopping for.

Even **Bowen** ㉗ (population 8,000) can be given a miss, unless you're looking for a job. Every summer people from around the world come to help with the harvest and earn money for their travels. For relaxation they join the tourists on the beach at Rose, Murrays or Horseshoe Bay not far from the town center. If you still haven't seen any wildlife parks, then spend one or two hours in the **Billabong Sanctuary** about 15 kilometers before Townsville. A number of animals native to Queensland live here: koalas, wombats, fresh- and salt-water crocodiles, naturally various kangaroos that let themselves be fed. Even cassowaries, those large cursorial birds, can be seen. After covering 1371 kilometers from Brisbane, you finally reach **Townsville** ㉘, the largest tropical city in Australia.

## BRISBANE (☎ 07)

**Brisbane Tourism**, Elizabeth St, Tel. 32218411. Information booth in the Queen St Mall and in City Hall. **North Stradbroke Island**, Junner St, Dunwich, Tel. 34099555. **Queensland National Parks and Wildlife Service**, 160 Ann St, Tel. 32245641. **Royal Automobile Club of Queensland** (RACQ), 190-194 Edward Street, Tel. 33612444.

Details concerning **markets, bar music** and other **events** can be read in the *Courier Mail*, Brisbane's leading daily newspaper; the best is the Thursday editon, in the *What's On* supplement.

⊟ ⊛⊛⊛ **Conrad International Treasury Casino Hotel**, corner of William / George St, Tel. 33068888. **Brisbane Hilton**, 190 Elizabeth St, Tel. 32342000. **Quay West Brisbane**, 132 Alice St, Tel. 38536000. **Royal Albert Boutique Hotel**, corner of Elizabeth / Albert Sts, Tel. 32918888.

⊛⊛ **Albert Park Hotel**, 551 Wickham Terrace, Tel. 38313111. **Gregory Terrace Motor Inn**, 397 Gregory Terrace, Tel. 38321769. **Metropolitan Motor Inn**, 106 Leichhardt St, Tel. 38316000. **Ryans on the River**, 269 Main St, Kangaroo Point, Tel. 33911011. **South Pacific Palms Motel & Holiday Apartments**, corner of Bowen Terrace / Langshaw St, New Farm, Tel. 33582366.

⊛ **Backpackers Courtney Place**, 50 Geelong St, East Brisbane, Tel. 38915166. **Balmoral House**, 33 Amelia St, Fortitude Valley, Tel. 32521397. **Brisbane City YHA**, 392 Upper Roma St, Tel. 32361004. **Yellow Submarine Hostel**, 66 Quay St, Tel. 32113424.

**Breakfast Creek**: The old **Breakfast Creek Hotel** (1889) on the corner of Kingsford Smith Drive and the stream is one of Brisbane's most popular pubs (attractive beer garden and good steaks). Across the way, in the shopping and restaurant complex **Breakfast Creek Boardwalk** are many take-away joints and a good seafood restaurant. **Brunswick St**, Fortitude Valley: a gold mine for restaurants and cafes; such as the **California**, 376 Brunswick St, good for breakfast, around the corner are many Asian restaurants and a food court in **Chinatown**. **Southbank Parklands**: More restaurants, snack bars and take-away joints. **Cafe Tempo**, 181 Boundary St, West End, a good, inexpensive Italian restaurant. **City Gardens Cafe**, Botanical Gardens, daily 9:00 a.m.-5:00 p.m., a peaceful oasis not far from the CBD. **Boardwalks**, South Bank, Tel. 38461880. **Customs House Brasserie**, Queen St, Tel. 33658921, lovely view of the river. Tea or proper meals, Tues-Sat, open evenings as well.

**Paddington Tavern**, 186 Given Terrace, Paddington, pub with beer garden and live music on Friday evenings. Close by is the disco / night-club **Metro**, 61 Petrie Terrace. Numerous pubs and night-clubs with live music in **Fortitude Valley**, partially the center of the gay scene. The formerly infamous area has changed for the better – but do be prudent late at night.

⊞ **Queensland Cultural Centre**: South Bank, comprises the **Queensland Performing Arts Complex**, Tel. 38407192, with theater and concert halls, the **Queensland Art Gallery**, Tel. 38407303, daily 10:00 a.m.- 5:00 p.m., with an extensive collection of Australian art and the **Queensland Museum**, Tel. 38407555, daily 9:30 a.m.- 5:00 p.m., with a collection displaying the social and natural history of Queensland.

**Queensland Maritime Museum**, Stanley St (on the edge of the South Bank Parklands), Tel. 38445361, daily from 9:30 a.m.-5:00 p.m., seafaring exhibition on the dry-dock built in 1881.

**Parliament**: When in session. you can cast a glance at the politicians and the goings-on from the Public Gallery. Otherwise there are daily tours of the building at 10:30 a.m. and 2:30 p.m., corner of Alice and George Streets, Infos Tel. 32267111.

**Brisbane Festival**: Art festival with a street parade, every two years (even years).

**Brisbane River**: A trip on the public ferries (CityCat or Inner City Ferries) is inexpensive. Information on routes and prices at *Transinfo*, Tel. 131230. Or try a real river cruise on one of the two paddle-wheel steamers *Club Crocodile River Queen*, which cast-off from Eagle St Pier in the city. Bookings Tel. 32211300. *Mirimar Cruises* cast-off daily every morning on the North Quay for a river cruise to Lone Pine Koala Sanctuary (approximately $A 20 without entrance).

**Markets**: Saturdays in Brunswick St in Fortitude Valley; Sundays at the Riverside Centre as well as Eagle St Pier in the city; in the Southbank Parklands Fridays 5:00 p.m.-10:00 p.m. (Lantern Markets) and Saturdays and Sundays during the day (Craft Village).

**Lone Pine Koala Sanctuary**: Every overseas tourist seems to have come to pet a koala, but there are some other Australian animals here as well. Jesmond Rd, Fig Tree Pocket, 11 km west of Brisbane. Tel. 33781366, daily 8:00 a.m.- 5:00 p.m.

## FROM BRISBANE TO TOWNSVILLE (☎ 07)

During the reainy season (beginning of Dec.-end of Feb.) there is heavy rainfall on the coast and there are often **floods** in the interior. Many streets become impassable. Before starting out, it is recommended that you enquire about the conditions at the Royal Automobile Club of Queensland (RCAQ).

*From Brisbane to Townsville*

## AGNES WATER

🛏 💲💲 **1770 Holiday Cabin Retreat**, Lot 26, Round Hill, Tel. 49749270.

## BILLABONG SANCTUARY

📷 15 km south Townsville on Bruce Hwy, daily 8:00 a.m.-5:00 p.m. Not a tourist park with koala petting zoo; good animal demonstrations. Plan on spending 2-3 hours there.

## BUNDABERG

ℹ **Visitor Information Centre**, 271 Bourbong St, Tel. 41522333 or 1800-060499.

🛏 💲💲 **Bundaberg Coral Villa Motor Inn**, 56 Takalvan St, Tel. 41524999. 💲 **Cane Village Holiday Park**, Twyford St, Tel. 41551022.

📷 **Lady Musgrave Barrier Reef Cruises**: Shop 1, Bundaberg Port, Tel. 1800-072110.

## CALOUNDRA

🛏 💲💲 **Kawana Waters International Motor Inn**, 18 Nicklin Way, Kawana Waters, Tel. 54446900. **Ocean Views Motor Inn**, 115 Bulcock Street, Tel. 54911788. 💲 **Shearwater Holiday Units**, 79 Edmund St, Kings Beach, Tel. 54911744.

## CAPE HILLSBOROUGH

🛏 💲💲 **Cape Hillsborough Resort**, Tel. 49590262.

## EUNGELLA NATIONAL PARK

🛏 💲💲 **Broken River Mountain Retreat**, Tel. 49584528.

## FRASER ISLAND

🛏 💲💲💲 **Kingfisher Bay Resort**, Tel. 1800-072 555. 💲💲 **Eurong Beach Resort**, Tel. 41279122. **Fraser Island Retreat**, Happy Valley, Tel. 41279144. **Yidney Rocks Cabins**, Tel. 41279167. 💲 **Dept of Environment & Heritage Camping Areas**.

📷 *Air Fraser Island* undertakes **sightseeing flights** over Hervey Bay and the southern part of the long extended island; in the right season, one can observe whales. Tel. 41253600.

## GLADSTONE

ℹ **Gladstone Area Information Centre**, Marina Ferry Terminal, Bryan Jordan Drive, Tel. 49729922.

🛏 💲💲 **Sundowner Chain Motor Inn**, corner of Far St/ Dawson Highway, Tel. 49724322.

## GREAT KEPPEL ISLAND

🛏 💲💲💲 **Great Keppel Island Resort**, Tel. 49395044. 💲💲 **Keppel Haven**, Tel. 49336744.

💲 **YHA Backpackers Village**, Tel. 49275288.

## HAMILTON ISLAND

🛏 💲💲💲 **Hamilton Island Holiday Inn**, Tel. 49469999.

## HERON ISLAND

🛏 💲💲💲 **Heron Island Resort**, Tel. 49781488.

## HERVEY BAY

ℹ **Tourist Information**, 63 Old Maryborough Road, Tel. 41244050 oder 1800-444155.

🎫 **Ferry connection** from Hervey Bay: from Mary River Heads to Wanggoolba Creek and to Kingfisher Bay, from Urangan Boat Harbour to Moon Point. Bookings at the Central Booking Office: Tel. 41241300. In addition, a rapid catamaran plies between Urangan and Kingfisher Bay; day trippers may use the amenities of the resort; Tel. 41255511. From Rainbow Beach: Inskip Point to Hook Point, Tel. 54863154. Car drivers require a *vehicular permit* ($A 30 before departure or $A 40 on the island). Available in the branch offices of the Dept of Environment & Heritage, in Hervey Bay and also at car rental companies and ferry companies. There is a fee for the camping grounds in the national parks as well (approximately $A 4 per person per day)

🛏 💲💲 **Playa Concha Resort**, 475 Esplanade, Torquay, Tel. 41281555. **Reef Motel**, 410 Esplanade, Tel. 41252744. 💲 **Beaches Backpackers**, 195 Torquay Tce, Tel. 41241322. **Point Vernon Caravan Park**, 26 Corser St, Tel. 41281423.

📷 Information and bookings for numerous **Whale Watch Cruises**; (from approximately mid-August to mid-October) at the Tourist Office or Whale Watch Centre in Urangan, Tel. 1800-358595.

## MACKAY

ℹ **Information Centre**, 320 Nebo Road, Tel. 49522677. **RACQ** (Automobile Club), 214 Victoria St, Tel. 49572918.

🛏 💲💲 **Four Dice Motel**, 166 Nebo Rd, Tel. 49511555. **Marco Polo**, 46 Nebo Rd, Tel. 49512700. 💲 **Larrikin Lodge YHA**, 32 Peel St, Tel. 49513728.

📷 **Caution**: In the period between October and April (Australian summer), dangerous, highly poisonous marine stingers appear north of Mackay in the waters off the (mainland) beaches: one single contact could be fatal! Bathers should avoid swimming outside the marked protective zones at this time. However, the beaches on the offshore islands of the Great Barrier Reef are relatively safe!

If despite all precautions you have contact with a stinger: many beaches have mail-box like containers, in which there is a bottle with (blue tinted) vinegar. Generously pour the vinegar on the affected part and seek immediate medical attention!

### MAROOCHYDORE / MOOLOOLABA

**Maroochydore Tourism & Travel**, Sixth Ave, Tel. 54791566. **Mooloolaba Tourism Sunshine Coast**, 126 Alexandra Pde, Tel. 54777311.

**Beach Motor Inn**, 61 Sixth Ave, Tel. 54437044.

**Waterfront Resort**, David Low Way, Tel. 54484488.

**Maroochydore YHA**, 24 Schirrmann Drive, Tel. 54433151.

**Maroochy Palms Caravan Village**, 319 Bradman Ave, Tel. 54438611.

A glimpse under the water's surface is afforded by **Underwater World**, On the Wharf, Mooloolaba, Tel. 54442255.

### MARYBOROUGH

**Fraser Coast / South Burnett Regional Tourism Board**, 388-396 Kent St, Tel. 1800-444155. **Maryborough Tourist Information Centre**, 30 Ferry St, Tel. 41214111.

### NOOSA

**Noosa Heads Tourist Centre**, Hastings Street, Tel. 54474988.

**Noosa Junction Tourist Centre**, Shop 5, The Oasis, 20 Sunshine Beach Road, Tel. 54473755.

**Sheraton Noosa Resort**, Hastings St, Tel. 54494888.

**Noosa Haven Motor Inn**, 119 Noosa Parade, Tel. 54499211. **Chez Noosa Resort Motel**, 263 David Low Way, Tel. 54472027.

**Halse Lodge YHA**, 17 Noosa Drive, Tel. 54473377.

**Noosa Backpackers**, 9-13 William St, Tel. 54498151.

**Peregian Beach Caravan Park**, 215 David Low Way, Peregian, Tel. 54481223.

In August: **Gympie Country Music Muster** (in Gympie).

In September: the **Noosa Jazz Festival.**

In November: the hinterland **Woodford Folk Festival**, famed throughout Australia (near Blackall Range).

### RAINBOW BEACH

**Dept of Environment & Heritage**, Rainbow Beach Rd, Tel. 54863160, daily 7:00 a.m.-4:00 p.m. Vehicular permits for Fraser Island.

### ROCKHAMPTON

**Capricorn Tourism**, The Spire, Gladstone Rd, Tel. 49272055.

**RACQ** (Automobile Club), 134-136 William St, Tel. 49272255.

**Dept of Environment & Heritage**, Yeppoon Rd, Tel. 49360511.

**Club Crocodile Motor Inn**, corner of Albert & Alma St, Tel. 49277433.

**Rockhampton Court Motor Inn**, 78 George St, Tel. 49278277. **Rockhampton YHA**, 60 MacFarlane St, North Rockhampton, Tel. 49275288.

### SEVENTEEN SEVENTY

**Captain Cook Holiday Village**, Tel. 49749219.

### WHITSUNDAY ISLANDS

**Information Centre**, 277 Shute Harbour Rd, Airlie Beach, Tel. 49466665 or 1800-801252.

**Dept of Environment & Heritage**, Shute Harbour Rd, Tel. 49467022.

There are ferries and boats to the Whitsunday Islands from Shute Harbour, cruises also begin in Mackay. If you are not travelling in the Australian summer and during the season (until the end of January, around Easter and June / July), try getting to one of the islands from Airlie Beach on "stand by." Information on this at the Information Centre in Airlie Beach.

**AIRLIE BEACH: Mediterranean Resorts**, Golden Orchid Drive, Tel. 49466391.

**Backpackers by the Bay**, 12 Hermitage Drive, Tel. 49467267.

**Club Habitat YHA**, 394 Shute Harbour Rd, Tel. 49466312 or 1800-247251.

**Airlie Cove Resort Van Park**, Shute Harbour Rd, Tel. 49466727.

**BOWEN: Whitsunday Sands Resort**, Horseshoe Bay, Tel. 47863333.

**DAYDREAM ISLAND: Daydream Island Resort**, Tel. 49488488.

**HAYMAN ISLAND: Hayman Island Resort**, Tel. 49401234.

**HOOK ISLAND: / Hook Island Resort**, Tel. 49469380.

**LONG ISLAND: Club Crocodile Long Island Resort**, Tel. 49469400.

**Palm Bay Hideaway Resort**, Tel. 49469233.

**Whitsunday Wilderness Lodge**, Tel. 49469777.

If you can afford it, the best way to discover the waters is with your own (chartered) boat. This is known as bareboat charter. Here are some contact addresses for companies specializing in this type of activity: *Australian Bareboat Charters*, Tel. 49469381; *Whitsunday Escape*, Tel. 1800-075145; *Whitsunday Rent a Yacht*, Tel. 1800-075111. However, on none of the resort islands may you bring your own food and drink!

*From Brisbane to Townsville*

# FROM TOWNSVILLE TO CAPE YORK PENINSULA

**TOWNSVILLE**
**CAIRNS**
**DAINTREE / CAPE TRIBULATION**
**NATIONAL PARK**
**CAPE YORK PENINSULA**

## TOWNSVILLE

The double city **Townsville-Thuringowa ❶** (a distortion of the German place name "Thüringen") is, with its 140,000 inhabitants, the largest tropical Australian city. Cairns, further to the north, cannot be beaten as a tourist magnet, but Townsville is the undisputed center of industry, economy, business and administration in the north.

City founder Robert Towns, a businessman from Sydney, recognized this strategic location and laid the cornerstone of the city's development. The products of cattle-raising, mining and sugar cane cultivation were shipped from here, often to Asia. Townsville is also an important scientific center, particularly for marine research – the city is the seat of the James Cook University and the Great Barrier Reef Marine Authority has its headquarters here.

With several stately historical buildings and a lively, unrushed ambience, Townsville does indeed have charm, but it is its surrounding areas that are particularly alluring: the gold digging towns of Charters Towers and "almost ghost town"

*Previuos pages: Member of the Tjapukai Dance Theatre. Left: Crocodiles are part of everyday life in some waters.*

of Ravenswood, the offshore isle Magnetic Island and the Great Barrier Reef just 2 hours boat-ride away (cf page 197).

The **\*reef HQ** combines tourism and research and is well worth a visit. A successful attempt has been made to simulate the actual situation and evolution of a living coral reef, with approximately 100 species, in a huge pool containing 2.5 million liters of water. A second pool (with 750,000 liters of water) is home to various predatory fish, such as reef sharks and others, barramundi and conger eels. 27 smaller aquariums, video films and short lectures round off the program presented to visitors. The **\*Omnimax Theatre** shows three to four films a day. The films are projected onto a domed screen, giving the impression of being smack in the middle of the action. Most impressive!

The **\*Museum of Tropical Queensland** has a new, ultra modern location next to the reef HQ. It covers the areas of technology, natural history and the history of North Queensland; the focal point of this exhibition are items from the wreck of the *Pandora*, which sank in domestic waters in 1791.

The lively center of the city is the harbor promenade known as **The Strand**, **Flinders Street** and palm-fringed **Flinders Mall**. The Percy Tucker Re-

*From Townsville to Cape York Peninsula*

## NORTH OF TOWNSVILLE

0        50        100 km

*Guidepost pages 218-219*

gional Gallery, the Customs Building, the Post Office and the former Queen's Hotel which line Flinders Mall are a reminder of the heady days of the gold rush in nearby Ravenswood and Charters Towers which have left traces of sudden wealth in Townsville too.

**The Mall**, the city's pedestrian zone, is not very different from other Australian shopping streets, except on Sundays when traders from all round the region come to display their colorful wares and crafts at the Flinders Mall **Cotters Market**. Townsville's night-life offers a wide variety of live music and theater, especially at the **Townsville Civic Theatre** and the **Entertainment & Convention Centre**. The international yacht marina and the casino at the Sheraton Hotel are also worth a visit. The beach promenade **The Strand** is being refurbished; soon there will be cafes and restaurants, piers and a swimming enclosure in which one can swim in summer without fear of the dangerous jellyfish.

The finest view over the city is from **Castle Hill**, a red granite hill 290 meters (950 feet) high. Not part of the reef but only 8 kilometers (5 miles) off the coast is ★**Magnetic Island ❷**, a popular destination for a day trip.

This granite and coral island was discovered by Captain Cook in 1770. As his ship sailed past, there were problems with the compass which they blamed on what they assumed to be magnetic rocks on the island. That was the reason for naming it - or misnaming it - Magnetic Island.

**Picnic Bay** is the main town on the island. The ferries from Townsville berth here and buses take you to the main places of interest. There are many small resorts along the east coast to **Horseshoe Bay**, the largest bay on the island, and ideal for all kinds of water sports. Alma, Arthur and Radical Bays offer excellent

*Above: The southern cassowary is particularly prolific on the northwestern coast.*

swimming and snorkeling, plus some lovely bushwalks. The highest point on the island is **Mount Cook**, reaching a height of 500 meters, and which can be climbed from Nelly Bay.

### Heading for Cairns and Port Douglas

As we resume our journey northwards back on the mainland, fields of sugar-cane still dominate the landscape. In **Ingham ❸**, sugar is the only source of income. Without its fertile soil, this region would just be a blank space on the map. For the last hundred years Ingham has always been the place with the highest sugar production in Australia. The white gold is shipped from the **port of Lucinda**, some 6 kilometers off the coast, where container ships are loaded with sugar from the longest loading jetty in the world. **Victoria Mill**, the largest sugar refinery in the land (4 million tons of sugar are processed per year), guides visitors through its facilities during the harvest season from June to October.

*From Townsville to Cape York Peninsula*

If you prefer a more varied landscape, 48 kilometers away to the west is the ★**Wallaman Falls** ❹ in **Lumholtz National Park**, where Australia's highest waterfall gushes into the Herbert Gorge from an impressive height of 305 meters. There are many viewing points from which to take in its splendor.

The sleepy fishing village of **Cardwell** ❺, 52 kilometers north of Ingham, is a good starting point for trips to ★★**Hinchinbrook Island** ❻. The hilly island, with its 40,000 hectares it is Australia's largest island national park, was a part of the mainland until approximately 10,000 years ago. At the end of the ice age, the valley which separates the island mountain from today's coastal range filled with water. This created **Hinchinbrook Channel**, which is lined with mangrove forests, in which salt-water crocodiles and dugong (manatees) live. Behind

tower mountains covered with rain forest. The backbone of the southern part of the island is formed by sheer projecting granite cliffs, the highest of which is the 1121-meter-high **Mount Bowen**. A breathtakingly beautiful and unspoilt landscape – except for the establishment of some hiking paths and a small resort in the extreme northeast, the island has been shielded from civilization.

From the resort at Cape Richards, you can walk to **Shepherd Bay** or **Macushla Bay**, but unless equipped with a proper insect repellent, you will be accompanied by the more irritating island inhabitants – sand flies and mosquitoes. The 32-kilometer ★★**Thorsborne Trail** along the east side of the island is among the most popular of Australia's bushwalks (only for hikers in good condition and with bush experience). The necessary permit should be obtained 6-8 weeks in advance, as only a limited number of hikers are admitted. Permits and further information (for example, concerning camp sites) can be obtained at the Reef and Rainforest

*Above: A day trip to Magnetic Island. Right: Sugar cane harvest.*

Centre in Cardwell. All provisions and camping equipment (camping stoves – fires are not permitted) must be brought with you. The ferry from Cardwell to Hinchinbrook Island offers cruises to the east side of the island during the season (approximately April to November) and drops off or picks up hikers there.

On the mainland going north is the **Edmund Kennedy National Park**, with many waterfalls, fresh water pools and very varied vegetation. A small 22-kilometer-long stretch of road leads to **Murray Falls**, a particularly beautiful place situated a few kilometers to the north of the Edmund Kennedy National Park.

**Tully ❼**, located in the aptly named coastal strip between Ingham and Cape Tribulation known as the Wet Tropics, is said to be the place with the highest rainfall in Australia (an average of 4267 millimeters annually). This area should be avoided between December and April, in what is rightly called the wet season, unless you are embarking on a sporting venture on the **Tully River**, which is one of the best places for whitewater rafting in the Southern Hemisphere. The ride by rubber dinghy is a wet one, but so much fun that it is now the top attraction of the whole region.

Beyond Tully, it is best to turn off Highway 1 towards Mission Beach, where the tropical vegetation of the rain forest extends right down to the 12-kilometer-long beach. The first white explorers set off in 1848 from Tam O'Shanter Point on an expedition to the north and began the colonization of northern Queensland.

The entire coastline here is known as Cassowary Coast. Signposts warning drivers of the presence of this strange, emu-like running bird (it can't fly) with a horn on its blue head are as frequent here as kangaroo warnings elsewhere in the country.

**Mission Beach ❽** itself is named after an Aborigine mission founded in 1914, and consists of three communities, Mission Beach, Wongaling Beach and South

*From Townsville to Cape York Peninsula*

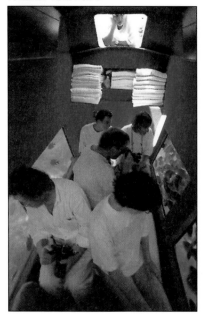

Mission Beach. There are numerous hotels, resorts and caravan parks that serve as bases for excursions into the surrounding area. A section of the beach in Mission Beach has been cordoned off by nets to prevent the jellyfish-like stingers from floating in, so that swimming here in summer, when these creatures float in, is possible. Several Rain Forest Walks, which inform visitors about the rain forest, have been laid out around Mission Beach. Information can be had at the Visitor Centre at the northern end of Mission Beach.

Mission Beach's main importance nowadays is as a center for excursions to the **Family Islands**. Of the eight islands, only Dunk Island and Bedarra Island are accessible to tourists. 75 per cent of the dense tropical rain forest on **\*Dunk Island** ❾ is protected by national park status. The island full of peace and plenty, as

*Above: On a tour of discovery with the semi-submarine. Right: By train to Kuranda.*

it was called by the Aborigines, is the largest of the Family Islands. Its symbol is the blue Ulysses butterfly.

The best way to explore the island and see many of its 100 resident species of birds is by following a circular trail 10 kilometers long, which also leads up **Mount Kootaloo** (271 meters high). Beaches and water sports are the other attractions of Dunk Island.

Accommodation is available at the resort, but it is expensive. Somewhat more simple in style, but less expensive is an overnight stay at the camp site of the National Parks & Wildlife Service (permit is required). There are several ferry crossings a day from Clump Point.

On **Bedarra Island** ❿ more to the sout, there is an exclusive resort. The sinfully expensive cost of an overnight stay buys one peace and tranquility, for day trippers are not allowed on the island.

Back on Highway 1, sugar, still contained in the canes that grow as far as the eye can see, is still the center of attention. In **Mourilyan** ⓫, a whole museum is lovingly devoted to it. In **Innisfail**, a nine-day Sugar Festival is held in its honor in September / October. Angling trips on the North and South Johnstone Rivers and a visit to the nearby Nerada tea plantation (the only one in Australia) are the other attractions of the area.

Further north is **Wooroonooran National Park** ⓬ which contains the highest mountain in Queensland, **Mount Bartle Frere** (1622 meters).

The climb is possible but arduous, especially as only those areas around the **\*waterfalls** which are in the 320 square kilometers national park are accessible.

### CAIRNS

346 kilometers after leaving Townsville, we arrive in **Cairns** ⓭, which owes its name to a former Governor of Queensland, William Cairns. A good 100 years have gone by since then

*From Townsville to Cape York Peninsula*

and William would hardly recognize his namesake, the northernmost city in Queensland. The jumping-off point for the tourist trek to northern Queensland, this city of almost 100,000 people is developing increasingly as a sort of Gold Coast of the North. Entertainment and shopping possibilities are ever growing, but this has taken the toll of the local color. Along **The Esplanade** on the waterfront with its many hotels, cafes and restaurants, the crowds are of many nationalities. Diving enthusiasts from all round the world arrange to meet here so the atmosphere is lively and cheerful for most of the day.

Cairns also has a **School of the Air**, a radio station which gives lessons to the children of the Outback. Under the same roof (at 1 Junction Street) is the **Royal Flying Doctor Service**. It is worth taking a stroll through the **Botanical Gardens** (Flecker Park).

Cairns itself does not have any appropriate bathing beaches, it is necessary to go to one of the Northern Beaches (Palm Cove is especially attractive) or Port Douglas. The warnings in summer (approximately October to April) concerning the dangerous jellyfish apply here as well. Those not wishing to use a hotel pool or the bathing areas in the hinterland should take a day trip to **Green Island ⑭**, a small coral bay where the beaches are safe for swimmers. For snorkeling or scuba diving you might wish to take a trip to the Great Barrier Reef. Excursions of every type are offered everywhere in Cairns. Someone will try to sell you a trip or a cruise in every single type of accommodation, from a backpacker hostel to the big hotels. If you are in the mood for a stroll after dining or shopping, then head for **The Pier Marketplace**.

Also very popular is a trip by train from Cairns to **Kuranda ⑮**. This otherwise rather quiet settlement of 800 people in the Atherton Tablelands comes to life on Wednesdays, Thursdays, Fridays and especially Sundays when there is an attractive and colorful alternative market featuring local crafts and Aborigine art. The

train runs twice in the morning. Early birds should ask about the milk train which goes on week-days only. It is less crowded and the tickets are cheaper. You can also catch it from the restored station at **Freshwater**.

The journey covers a distance of 34 kilometers and takes about an hour and a half. The line took five years to build and was opened as the main link between the coast and the interior in 1891.The return trip to Cairns should be done with the brand-new ★**Skyrail** cable train. It leaves from opposite the railway station in Kurunda, and carries passengers on a 7.5-kilometers journey over the **Barron Gorge National Park**.

There are two stops on the way with little wooden piers that conveniently lead through the by and large untouched vegetation of this rain forest. The terminus of

*Above: Snorkelers start off from Port Douglas to the Great Barrier Reef. Right: On the northern tip of Australia, red sandy paths lead up to Cape York.*

the Skyrail in Smithfield is also where the ★**Tjapukai Cultural Theme Park** is located. In the **Tjapukai Dance Theatre**, Aborigines display their culture in a blend of modern showbiz and traditions going back thousands of years.

The show lasts all day. You should set aside approximately two hours to visit the other attractions of the park (spear and boomerang throwing, a reconstructed Aborigine village). The park is open daily from 9:00 a.m. to 5:00 p.m.

In the hinterland of Cairns, in the ★**Atherton Tablelands**, are the crystal-clear maare (crater lakes) ★**Barrine**, ★**Eacham** and the artificial **Lake Tinaroo**, but a car is needed to get there. If Cairns is too hot for you, then you will enjoy the climate in and around ★**Atherton** ⓰.

The area lies at an altitude of 700 meters above sea level and is a few degrees cooler than the coast, and not nearly as humid.

In Atherton, pay a visit to Fascinating Facets and its Crystal Cave. In the (artifi-

cial) caves, crystals of all shapes and colors are displayed: Australian opals can be purchased at a good price in the shop there.

South of Lake Tinaroo and Yungaburra is the **Curtain Fig Tree**. A ficus has completely covered two trees with its rhizomes, creating a somewhat bizarre 10-meter-curtain.

Taking the Captain Cook Highway along the coast, we come to **\*Port Douglas** ⑰, which has developed over the past few years into a quieter alternative to Cairns, mainly because of its golden, palm-fringed **Four Mile Beach**.

Port Douglas is also an important center for day excursions to the Great Barrier Reef (on the *Quicksilver*, for example).

To enjoy a very different kind of breakfast, you can drink your coffee among birds and butterflies in The **\*Rainforest Habitat** (Wednesdays and Sundays, 30 A\$ including the entrance fee).

Under a special canopy in this park, there is a stretch of tropical rain forest close enough to touch. The wildlife to be seen ranges from koalas to crocodiles, so it is best to have your camera at the ready.

## \*\*DAINTREE AND CAPE TRIBULATION NATIONAL PARK

After passing through **Mossman** ⑱, and the impressive **\*Mossman Gorge** in Daintree National Park, it is possible to make a detour to the little town of **Daintree** ⑲.

From here, **\*cruises** on small ships along the **Daintree River** are available. Tip: book the first tour of the morning – that way you will see more animals. Those going towards Cape Tribulation and Cooktown must cross the river with the **Daintree River Ferry** (runs daily from 6:00 a.m. to midnight).

Caution: there are crocodiles in many of the rivers of northern Queensland. It is imperative to heed the crocodile warning notices.

If you miss the last ferry at Daintree River, wait until the next morning. The locals will be happy to regale you with

*From Townsville to Cape York Peninsula*

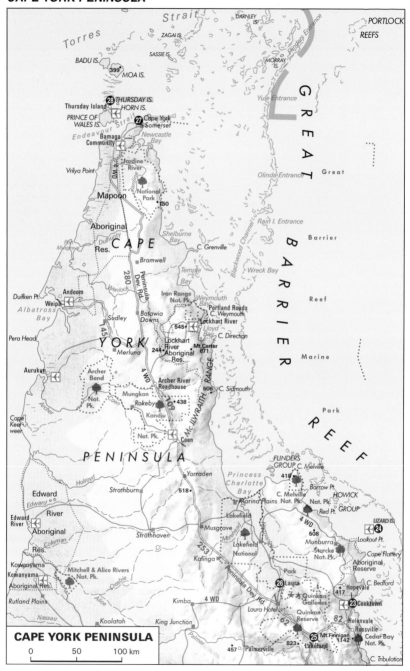

**CAPE YORK PENINSULA**

0        50        100 km

true stories (!) of travelers who tried to swim across the river but who sadly never made it across to the other shore.

In the coastal strip between Daintree River and Cape Tribulation, rain forest still dominates the scene, but there is no longer any remote wilderness along the road. **★★Daintree National Park ㉠**, along with the other rain forests of the Wet Tropics, has been on UNSECO's World Heritage List since 1989 on account of its importance in earth's prehistory, its precious flora and fauna and its especial beauty.

The stretch to **Cape Tribulation ㉑**, mostly asphalted now, can be driven without problems with normal vehicles in the dry season (enquire at the rental car company whether they will allow the drive to Cape Tribulation with their car!) At **Noah Creek**, there is a wide wooden path running through the coastal rain forest, at Cape Tribulation there is a path from the parking lot to a lookout at the Cape – both are rather overrun in the dry season. Between Cow Bay (approximately 11 kilometers north of the ferry) and Cape Tribulation there are numerous accommodation possibilities in all price categories.

The **Bloomfield Track** leads northward. From here, only four-wheel drive vehicles are allowed, and during the rainy season all traffic comes to a standstill. At any rate, you should once again inquire about the road conditions at one of the lodges in Cape Tribulation National Park. Remember that local inhabitants have a great deal more experience driving on these roads than you might have.

The ford over the **Bloomfield River**, just before the Aborigine mission of **Wujal Wujal**, is the only one that has been reinforced with concrete.

Nevertheless, you should be very careful when the swollen river covers it with

water. You can easily lose your sense of direction driving over the water, and suddenly land in the river. The Aborigine village itself is one of the so-called dry settlements where no alcohol may be drunk or sold. This applies to tourists as well!

To slake your thirst, you need only drive as far as **Helenvale ㉒**. Within a radius of several hundred kilometers, there is no better option than the *Lions Den Hotel*, the sort of typical Outback pub you see in picture books.

From there it is another 32 kilometers to Cooktown (on a partly surfaced road). Along the way, you will pass **Black Mountain**. The origin of its black rocks is uncertain. Some say it the color comes from black algae that once covered the mountains. Numerous tourists who have tried to "climb" these mountains have died in the stone labyrinths.

### CAPE YORK PENINSULA

On his first voyage of exploration in 1770, Captain Cook was forced to anchor

*Above: Deep-sea fishing.*

*From Townsville to Cape York Peninsula*

*i*

off the coast of northern Queensland because the hard coral of the reefs had damaged his ship, the Endeavour.

The repairs were carried out in a sheltered bay, where the town of **Cooktown** ㉓ now stands. The best view over the offshore islands is from **Grassy Hill**, where Queensland's oldest lighthouse still shines through the night.

Around 100 kilometers north-east of Cooktown is **Lizard Island** ㉔, another Paradise island on the Great Barrier Reef which is surrounded by magnificent coral reefs.

Should the coastal road from Cape Tribulation National Park be closed, or if you do not have a four-wheel drive, then you can reach Cooktown via the inland road over Mount Carbine and Lakeland.

At **Lakeland** ㉕, we reach the Peninsula Developmental Road leading to **Laura** ㉖. At **Split Rock**, 13 kilometers south of the town, there is a bush path leading to Aborigine rock paintings. They are called the **\*\*Quinkan Galleries** for the figures portrayed there with long, thin arms and legs.

From Laura the journey continues northwards through the **Cape York Peninsula**, where nature still survives in its original state.

However, If you plan to continue your drive, do enquire in Laura about the road conditions. During the wet season, the stretch is often not passable for months, even for those with a four-wheel drive.

To reach **Cape York** ㉗, you have to drive another 700 kilometers, cross more than 50 rivers and curse the terrible roads every inch of the way.

At the end of the journey, Papua New Guinea appears within reach (130 kilometers away), but there is no access to it from here.

The islands of the **Torres Strait** do, however, belong to Australia. The largest and best-known of these is **Thursday Island** ㉘, which is connected to Cairns by plane or to Cape York by ferry.

## NOTH QUEENSLAND (☎ 07)

**Risk of epidemic**: Signs along the road warn of the risks of transporting certain plants into other areas. In the area around Cairns, the *papaya fruit-fly* was first discovered in 1995. As a result, a gigantic area in Queensland was quarantined. It is forbidden to most fruits from this area. If you do so anyway, the fruit will be taken from you and destroyed. (This does not apply to preserved, dried or frozen products).

**Crocodile Warning**: It is imperative that you heed these warnings along the North Queensland rivers – there really are crocodiles here!

### ATHERTON TABLELANDS

**Kookaburra Lodge**, corner of Oak St and Eacham Rd, Yungaburra, Tel. 40953222. **Lake Tinaroo Pines Motel & Caravan Park**, Lake Tinaroo, near the dam, Tel. 40958232. **Atherton Backpackers**, 37 Alice St, Atherton, Tel. 40913552. **On The Lake Eacham Caravanpark**, Lakes Drive, Yungaburra, 2 km south of the lake, Tel. 40953730.

### CAIRNS

**Tourism Tropical North Queensland**, corner of Fogarty Rd / Esplanade, Tel. 40513588; many booking agencies for tours and cruises. **Gulf Savannah Tourist Organisation**, 55 McLeod St, Tel. 40514658. **RACQ** (Automobile Club), 112 Sheridan St, Tel. 40514788. **Dept of Environment & Heritage**, 10-12 McLeod St, Tel. 40523096.

**Cairns Hilton**, Wharf St, Tel. 40502000. **Radisson Plaza**, Pierpoint Rd, Tel. 40311411. **G'Day Tropical Village Resort**, 7 McLachlan St, Manunda Tel. 40537555. 5 km from the center; quiet location. **Reef Palms Motel**, 41 Digger St, Tel. 1800-815421. **Floriana Guesthouse**, 183 The Esplanade, Tel. 40517886. **Gone Walkabout Hostel**, 274 Draper St, Tel. 40516160. **Uptop Downunder Backpackers**, 164 Spence St, Tel. 40513636.

For **bathing**, try Green Island and the lovely Northern Beaches, located north of Cairns: Machans, Holloways, Yorkeys Knob, Trinity, Kewarra, Clifton, Palm Cove and Ellis Beach.

### CARDWELL

**Reef & Rainforest Centre**, Bruce Hwy, Tel. 40668601. Operated by the Dept of Environment & Heritage; permits for the Thorsborne Trail on Hinchinbrook Island.

### COOKTOWN

**Sovereign Resort**, corner of Charlotte / Green Sts, Tel. 40695400. **Hillcrest Guesthouse**, Hope St, Tel. 40695305. **Pam's Place Backpackers**, Charlotte St, Tel. 40695166. **Tropical Breeze**

Tourist Park, Charlotte St / McIvor Rd intersection, Tel. 40695417.

James Cook Historical Museum, corner of Helen and Furneaux Sts, daily 9:30 a.m.-4:00 p.m.

### DAINTREE NATIONAL PARK / CAPE TRIBULATION

All addresses on Cape Tribulation Rd, unless otherwise stated. Daintree Wilderness Lodge, 13 km north of the ferry, Alexandra Bay, Tel. 409 89105. Coconut Beach Rainforest Resort, 32 km north of the ferry, Cape Tribulation, Tel. 40980033. Rainforest Retreat, 10 km north of the ferry, Cow Bay, Tel. 40989101. Crocodylus Village (YHA), Buchanan Creek Rd, Cow Bay,12 km north of the ferry, Tel. 40989166. Idyllic location, in the rain froest. PK's Jungle Village, Cape Tribulation, Tel. 40980040.

### GREAT BARRIER REEF

Excursions to the reef and the islands of the Great Barrier Reef with catamarans from Cairns, Palm Cove and Port Douglas: Quicksilver, Tel. 40995500.

### HINCHINBROOK ISLAND

INGHAM: Hinchinbrook Visitor Centre, corner of Bruce Highway / Main St, Tel. 47765211. Dept of Environment & Heritage, 11 Lannercost St, Tel. 47761700. Mon-Fri 9:00 a.m.-4:00 p.m. Permits for camping in the National Parks and for the Thorsborne Trail on Hinchinbrook Island.

Hinchinbrook Island Resort, Tel. 40668585 and 1800-777021.

### INNISFAIL

Paronella Park Heritage Gardens: romantic little castle, built by Catalan immigrants, and which is surrounded by a tropical park. The detour from Bruce Hwy is well worth it: 19 km southwest of Innisfail near the town of Mena Creek. Daily 9:00 a.m.-5:00 p.m. There is a small camp-ground beside the park.

### KURANDA

Kuranda Rainforest Resort, corner of Greenhills Rd / Kennedy Hwy, Tel. 40937555. Kuranda Caravan Park, off Myola Rd, Tel. 40937316.

### LAURA

Aboriginal Rockpaintings: Many galleries in sandstone cliffs bordering the valley of the Little Laura River southwest of Laura, with Abroginal rock paintings. The land is privately owned; overnight accommodation in the Jowalbinna Bush Camp (simple cabins and campground). Tours to the rock galleries are offered. Information and booking Tel. 40515777. Arrival via Laura; from Laura only with a four-wheel drive vehicle.

### MAGNETIC ISLAND

Frequent ferry connections (10-14 times per day) from Townsville and cruises to the Great Barrier Reef are offered by Sunferries, Tel. 47713855.

Arcadia Hotel Resort, 7 Marine Parade, Arcadia, Tel. 47785177. Magnetic Retreat, 11 Reuben Trc, Arcadia, Tel. 47785357. Magnetic Island Tropical Resort, Yates St, Nelly Bay, Tel. 47785955. Marshalls B&B, 3 Endeavour Ave, Arcadia, Tel. 47785112.

### MISSION BEACH

Mission Beach Information Centre, Porters Promenade, Tel. 40687099.

Castaways Beach Resort, corner of Pacific Parade / Seaview St, Tel. 40687444. Eco Village Mission Beach, Clump Point, Tel. 406587534. Mission Beach Resort, corner of Cassowary Drive / Wongaling Beach Rd, Tel. 40688288. Treehouse YHA, Bingil Bay Rd, Tel. 40687028, one of the loveliest YHA's in Australia.

### PORT DOUGLAS

Tourist Information, 23 Macrossan St, Tel. 40995599.

Sheraton Mirage Hotel Port Douglas, Port Douglas Rd, Tel. 40995888. Archipelago Studio Apartments, 72 Macrossan St, Tel. 40995387. The White House, 19 Garrick St, Tel. 40995660. Port Douglas Backpackers, 8 Macrossan St, Tel. 40994883. Port O'Call Lodge YHA, Port St, Tel. 40995422. Four Mile Beach Caravan Park, Barrier St, Tel. 40985281.

### TOWNSVILLE

Townsville Information Centre, Bruce Hwy, Tel. 47783555. Information kiosk in the Flinders St Mall. Sheraton Townsville & Casino, Sir Leslie Thiess Drive, Tel. 47222333. Aquarius in the Beach, 75 Strand, Tel. 47722455. Seagulls Resort at the Seafront, 74 Esplanade, Tel. 47213111 o. 1800-079929. Southbank Motor Inn, 23 Palmer St, Tel. 472 1474. Civic House, 262 Walker St, Tel. 47715381. Reef Lodge, 4 Wickham St, Tel. 47211112. Rowes Bay Caravan Park, Heatleys Parade, Tel. 47713576.

reef HQ (formerly the Great Barrier Reef Wonderland), 2-68 Flinders St East, Tel. 47500800, daily 9:00 a.m.-5:00 p.m., fantastic underwater world in a living coral reef exposed to the sun.

### UNDARA

On Hwy 1 250 km southwest of Cairns: the Undara Lava Tubes, discovered in 1984. Molten lava flowing down the mountain through the river beds caused a 126-long-tunnel to form, hardening the exterior shell; inside the lava continued to flow. They may only be visited on a tour, on account of the very fragile ecosystem. Accommodation in the Lava Lodge in converted railway wagons. Information / bookings: Lava Lodge, Mt Surprise, Tel. 40971411 and 1800-990992.

*From Townsville to Cape York Peninsula*

## AUSTRALIA'S FLORA

The most famous of Australia's trees is the eucalyptus (gum tree), a deciduous tree with some 700 varieties – more varieties than any other deciduous tree – which has adapted well to the very diverse climatic zones and soils found in Australia. Ghost gums, with their typical white trunks, sometimes appear to grow directly out of the red rocky cliffs of Central Australia's ravines. In the snow-covered wintry uplands of South Australia and Tasmania, the stocky snow gums often snuggle close to the ground.

Near rivers and tributaries, the river red gums rise with their wide-sweeping crowns. Mallee, a low-growing eucalyptus shrub, covers extensive stretches of South Australia. Jarrah (the mahogany gum-tree), red tingle, marri (a red gum)

*Previous pages: Aboriginal rock paintings at the Quinkan Galleries. Above: A Snow gum tree. Right: A spiny ant-eater forages for food.*

and the towering karri (one of the blue gums) grow only in the south-west of Western Australia.

The last, with the mountain ash or eucalyptus regnans in Victoria and Tasmania, are among the world's tallest trees: they can reach heights of up to 70 or even 90 meters.

The tea-tree belongs to the genus Melaleuca, which "delivers" tea-tree oil. Cork is manufactured from the bark of the paper-bark tea-tree.

Wattles are heavily represented by 800 varieties, from shrubs to towering trees.

Proteas are noticeable for their singularly-formed partially-glowing colored inflorescence, with many individual clustering blooms. Typical of the genus Banksia is the somewhat thicker, brush-like tuber; Grevillea and Hakea have a cylindrical shape with longish hooks, whereas Dryandra displays large fleshy blooms.

The beach casuarina (from a fancied resemblance of the branches to the feathers of the cassowary bird), is known in Australia as beef-wood or oak, an evergreen which grows to a height of 2 to 3 meters and has thin branches and needle-sharp leaves. It is often planted as a windbreak to help hold the soil in place.

Grass-trees are often found in the hardwood forests; out of their stocky trunks, often charred by bush fires, grow bushels of green pointy grass. Ancient palm-ferns and southern beeches are relics from the Mesozoic period.

## AUSTRALIA'S FAUNA

The duck-billed platypus, with its thick, dark-brown fur, duck-bill and webbing, is high on the list of Australia's curiosities. It belongs to the subclass monotremata (one vent), which is considered to be the transitional form between reptiles and mammals. Thus the platypus combines many of the reptile's characteristics, such the cloaca (a single

vent for genital, urinary and digestive organs); it is oviparous, having the characteristics of mammals – milk glands, pelt warmbloodedness. The heel of the male bears a hollow spur connected to a poison-secreting gland; this spur is probably used as a weapon. The platypus lives in Australia's eastern waters.

Another representative of the monotremata is the porcupine or spiny ant-eater, of the genus Echidna, which can be found everywhere, and which feeds on ants and termites. It is about the size and form of a hedgehog.

Marsupialia, an ancient subclassification of mammals with some 40 species, have filled all of Australia's ecological niches. The pouch is characteristic of the marsupial. The abdominal pouch is sustained by means of two bones of a peculiar structure, which defend the abdominal viscera from the pressure of the young as these increase in size during their mammary or marsupial existence. The young are born as embryos, and crawl from the birth canal into the pouch, where

they firmly suck on a teat and, depending on the species, will continue developing inside the pouch for the next 2 - 7 months. The young can leave the pouch, but return to nurse in times of danger. A female can simultaneously nurse an embryo in her pouch and a young animal which has already outgrown the pouch. An interesting aspect of the marsupial reproduction system is that in drought years, a pregnancy can even be put on "hold"; growth of the fertilized ovum is stopped and does not continue until the somewhat older sibling has left the pouch. The most famous of all the marsupials is represented on the Australian coat of arms along with the emu: the kangaroo. There are some 250 species, ranging from the almost 2-meter-tall great red kangaroos to animals the size of rats. Wallabies are smaller as a rule, and differ from kangaroos by their long narrow head and big ears.

Aboreal marsupials spend most of their time searching for food in the tree-tops. Among these are the koalas. They feed exclusively on 12 varieties of eucalyptus

*Flora and Fauna*

leaves. The flying squirrels are tree inhabitants as well. With the aid of the skin along the side of their bodies, they can sail from branch to branch high in the forests among the towering tree crowns. Possums, which also live in trees, feed both on flower buds and fruits as well as on smaller animals and birds. The common possum species, which is the size of a cat, has now encroached as far as the suburbs and into big city parks.

The wombat, (also known as badger), a compact, stocky animal which can weigh some 35 kilos, is a herbivore and digs tunnels under the earth like a mole. The wombat has a general resemblance to a small bear. The bettong, a mouse-sized animal, feeds on the nectar of blossoms, thereby pollinating the Banksias and Grevilleas with its long, brush-like tongue. Other representatives are the rat-sized potoroo or kangaroo-rat and the numbat or banded ant-eater, which live in South and Southwestern Australia.

The Australian ornithological world comprises some 720 species, of which 600 are nesting birds. It is interesting to note that more than 60 per cent of these nesting birds brood only in Australia. The colorful parrots are really most striking. Budgerigars, usually called budgies for short, also originated here in Australia.

The Australian bush resounds to the mocking laughter of the kookaburra, the arboreal kingfisher – also known as the laughing jackass. Much more melodic is the clear ringing call of the bell-bird. The lyrebird, an outstanding voice imitator, resembles a pheasant when it spreads its beautiful lyre-shaped tail at mating time. The nondescript male bower bird attempts to win a wife for himself in another way: he builds alleys with branches which he decorates with findings (preferred color: blue). The second heraldic

beast, the emu, a member of the Cursores who reaches 1.80 meters, is as incapable of flying as the helmet cassowary who makes his home in north-east Queensland and New Guinea, the mallee fowl in South Australia and the bush turkey. The two last-named animals, as large as pheasants, need the warmth of this environment to incubate their eggs. Frogs are the only amphibians represented in Australia. On the other hand, the reptile world has representatives in abundance. The most widely distributed are the lizards. There are 5 families with 500 varieties, such as geckos, agamas, thorny devils and frill-necked lizards. The largest are the goannas (iguanas). The giant goanna can reach 2.5 meters in length.

Dangerous animals: of Australia's 165 varieties of snakes, 25 are considered dangerous for man; several, such as the taipan and the fierce snake (also called inland taipan) are counted amongst the most poisonous in the world. The bite of the brown snake can also be deadly, as can that of the black snake, the death adder or the copperhead. The fierce snake has been sighted only in remote regions of Central Australia. Snakes such as the black snake, on the other hand, are found in wood and bush areas (even in the outskirts of large cities) of Australia's thickly-settled south-east. General safety measures for traveling in the bush: wear stout ankle-high boots and long trousers, stamp firmly on the ground and stay on the path.

In the tropical waters of North Australia one must beware year-round of the salt water crocodiles. They often move upstream with the tides and conceal themselves far from the sea in distant rivers and water holes in the North, and in brackish and even fresh water. Before bathing in the sea or in watering places, the visitor is advised to obtain information on the crocodile danger from the local residents. Camping or long walks near the shore as well as angling in crocodile

*Right: A profusion of colors – the rainbow iris and Banksia blossoms.*

waters is also better left alone. Unlike the ubiquitous salt water crocodile population which also obtains in South-East Asia, the somewhat smaller sweet water crocodile (Crocodylus Johnsonii) is found only in North Australia. It is said not to be dangerous to man.

Great caution is recommended in the case of several types of spiders: both the funnel web spider, which is most often found in the moist eastern area, and also the redback spider, indigenous to the drier regions. Both enjoy living in dark corners in sheds or barns. A funnel web spider's bite can be fatal, if serum is not administered. The hunting spider with its body the size of a hand and black hairy legs admittedly looks fearsome but is none the less harmless. Nor are the inshore waters free of danger. Most types of sharks avoid men; some (the white pointer shark, the tiger shark and the hammerhead shark), however, are known aggressors. Particularly in the cooler waters of South and East Australia, water sportsmen are aware of the risks of attack. Other dangerous, potentially deadly denizens of the deep are the sting ray; the stonefish disguised as a stone, the attractive black-and-white-designed oblong mussel appearing as a cone-shell, and the little blue-ringed octopus.

In the entire North of Australia, somewhat north of Coral Bay on the west coast and Rockhampton on the east coast, highly poisonous jellyfish make sea bathing impossible in the rainy season (October to May). They are called box jellyfish, sea wasps or common marine stingers. The jellyfish prefer to stay near the beach, but they also appear in the river estuaries' brackish water, their meter-long tentacles almost invisible in the water. Contact with the skin is extremely painful, in the worst case fatal. Many beaches in the vicinity of coastal resorts have protected stinger-free enclosures with nets, where swimming is possible during the jellyfish season. Outside these zones one should never put even a toe in the water. Seek information as to the current situation at the site.

*Flora and Fauna*

## RURAL LIFE IN AUSTRALIA

Most Australians still prefer to cling to their rugged coastline and big cities rather than venture into the rest of the country, commonly referred to as "the bush," which is an all-encompassing expression used to describe farms, country towns and tiny settlements outside the main capital cities – Sydney, Melbourne, Brisbane, Perth, Adelaide and Hobart.

It takes in harsh deserts, lush rain forests, vast open plains where sheep are numbered in millions, and thousands of kilometers of wheat country.

Farm machinery outlets, grocery stores and hotels dominate the main streets of most small provincial towns.

Farmers travel for hundreds of kilometers to do the weekly shopping, drink in the pub with their "mates," play a game of cricket or go to church.

*Above: Forest fires often erupt in summer.*
*Right: Flocks of sheep in the Outback.*

Schoolchildren stand in the early morning in small groups beside the highway waiting for a bus to take them into the regional high schools.

In the real Outback children are sent away to boarding school or study with "School of the Air" (by radio), but for many, long bus trips to and from school are the routine.

In Western Australia the main settlement is in the fertile southwestern corner where kangaroos appear to outnumber human residents.

Drivers are warned to watch out for kangaroos and wombats; take your eyes off the road for a minute and you could be staring into the eyes of a very frightened kangaroo or wallaby.

The animals appear to be magically drawn to the headlights of passing cars.

Nature does not make it easy for the farmers to use the land. One of the major problems is the native animals.

In some places, it would appear that kangaroos have reached what the farmers consider plague proportions, for the kan-

garoos ravage the feed that has been set aside for the farm animals, leaving them short of food. The kangaroos are hunted with spotlights and guns. Although some controlled culling is carried out under government supervision, it is fiercely contested by animal rights activists.

Australia has always been full of conflicts of this kind, between the farmer and native or introduced animals.

Foxes hunt sheep in vast areas of the Victoria highlands where farmland and native bush meet, and the farmer is constantly pushing back the boundaries of the encroaching bush.

Rabbits, an introduced species which has frequently reached plague proportions in Australia's recent history, like to graze along with the sheep, but unfortunately, there is seldom enough feed for both of these species. Earlier in this century, therefore, farmers in Western Australia erected what was thought to be a "rabbit-proof fence" to keep the pests away from their sheep and wheat farmland.

Spanning thousands of kilometers, this fence was really of more symbolic than practical value.

Most rural people in the isolated southwest corner of Australia make their income from an unforgiving land, and a relentless climate – from jobs ranging from work on the huge wheat and sheep farms, the timber industry, small farms and the sea.

In recent years, some wine-growers have succeeded in cultivating their vines along the Swan River Valley outside Perth, and in the southwest.

As the visitor travels towards the north, the towns grow further and further apart and the road signs indicate distances of more than one thousand kilometers to places with names such as Broome and Derby.

Here the red earth yields nothing but spinifex grass, and the soil is certainly not something people take for granted in this country.

During the last big drought, which parched a large part of the continent for

*Rural Life*

several years in the early 1980s, an ironic rural humor became evident. In the Wimmera wheat belt of western Victoria, residents reportedly put up signs which read, "Danger. Field Crossing Road."

It was a grim joke, but farmers were never sure on which side of the roadway they would find their topsoil each day.

As the heat of the day abated, the dry hot gusts picked up whole paddocks of soil in a swirl of wind and dumped their load kilometers away.

Families could only stand and watch the product of years of labor swept away on the wind.

Many farmers lost all their sheep in the big drought, but others managed to survive by driving their flocks of hundreds of sheep along the roadways.

Drovers lived on the road for several long and dreary months at a time, often only taking with them a couple of horses

and a handful of well-trained sheepdogs to help them keep the flock in order.

Some towed a caravan to provide shelter while their wives and children stayed behind alone on the family property to maintain what was left of their livelihood – perhaps a few chickens, the homestead and the fences.

When the drought finally broke, the farmers worked for weeks through the night to replant the soil with crops to replenish the earth.

Apart from drought, the other chief threat is fire. Bushfires strike without warning, usually at the end of a very long summer when the earth is parched and the days are long.

It is a threat most Australians outside the main cities have learned to live with. Every small rural community has an emergency strategy, a plan of action to be taken in case the worst should indeed happen.

In 1983, great fires swept through large parts of eastern and central Australia. In those fires even some outlying parts of

*Above: Water holes signify life in these isolated areas. Right: Foothills of the Stirling Range in Western Australia.*

228

Melbourne and Adelaide were threatened, and a number of small communities were completely wiped out by the raging fires.

In 1984 as well, fire destroyed countless acres of woods in New South Wales, in the environs of Sydney, especially in the Blue Mountains and in the Royal National park.

After the big bushfires, it is truly miraculous to witness just how quickly the Australian families begin to rebuild their homes and replant their gardens and shrubs again.

The bush takes on a lush green appearance, and within a few years it is almost impossible to tell where the fire had raged, for the the native gum trees and hardy shrubs grow back with a greatly renewed vigor to cover the area.

And with the new growth come the native birds and animals which abound in the Australian bush.

The kookaburras, brightly colored parrots and parakeets, as well as the kangaroos, wallabies, possums and, in certain areas, the koalas, all return once again to thrive in the areas formerly destroyed by fire.

The high country of the Great Dividing Range, which runs between the coastal strip and the interior of most of southeast Australia, is a haven for native wildlife.

In this territory, the highest peaks and a plateau are covered in snow for up to four months of the year, creating a totally different environment from that found on the remainder of the continent. The snow gums growing here provide but scant shelter from the fierce storms which can spring up in this area in less than half an hour.

The cattlemen who graze their herds here in summer have built huts which have withstood many seasons, and which have occasionally saved the life of a skier who strayed from the well-tended ski-trails in winter. There is, however, increasing pressure from environmentalists to return the high country to its original condition; to remove the huts and to revoke the summer grazing rights.

*Rural Life*

229

## SPORT AND GAMBLING

On the first Tuesday of every November, Melbourne hosts an event which neatly encapsulates Australia's twin obsessions of sport and gambling.

The Melbourne Cup is much more than a horse-race, although ostensibly that is what brings almost 100,000 people to the Flemington Racecourse for the day.

The Cup is a folk festival, costume party, bacchanalian carnival, and, almost as an afterthought, a sporting occasion.

Some dutiful sports fans gather to watch a group of relatively ordinary race-horses plod over 3200 meters for the biggest prize purse in the country, others come for the fun and exhibitionism of dressing up in outlandish clothes and getting very drunk – but all of these spectators come to share in the spending spree.

It is said that the Melbourne Cup is the race that stops a nation – there is a public holiday in Victoria and even the Federal Parliament in Canberra ceases its deliberations for the slightly more than three minutes' duration of the race .

A country so remote from the rest of the world was bound to develop its own brand of sport. Australian Rules football – a hybrid game which gives nods of acknowledgment to Irish football and rugby, which has a host of idiosyncratic touches and a jargon all its own - keeps the majority of Australians occupied during the winter months.

The game, with which cricket players were originally meant to keep fit for their summer sport, was created around 1850 in the gold fields of Victoria. A national competitive sport has developed from this modest beginning, with participants from all the five mainland states.

The strongest teams with the most enthusiastic supporters come from the states in which the new rules and the actual game's beginning were developed. Victoria, South Australia and Western Aus-

*Above: Australian Rules football is a typical hard-fought Australian sport. Right: Lawn bowling is much more peaceful.*

tralia took to Aussie Rules with gusto, but New South Wales and Queensland preferred to remain faithful to rugby.

Rugby, in both its league and union versions, is the dominant winter sport in those two states, although the Australian Football League has teams from other parts of the continent in its ranks.

The AFL Grand Final, held at the Melbourne Cricket Ground in September, regularly attracts more than 100,000 spectators, and is arguably the nation's pre-eminent sporting occasion.

Cricket is the main summer sport, and international contests against teams representing the home of the game, England, are the most passionately fought.

Australia and England battle for a tiny trophy known as The Ashes, which commemorates the first time the fledgling Antipodean colony defeated the mother country in a cricket test match in England.

In 1882 when Australia beat England by seven runs, an obituary appeared in the Sporting Times that read: In affectionate memory of English Cricket.... RIP. NB The body will be cremated and the ashes taken to Australia."

By a circuitous route some bails were burnt, put in a velvet bag and then moved to a very small not very attractive urn and the whole kit and kaboodle ended up in Lord's museum from which it never moves.

The most widely played of all sports are netball, a static form of basketball, and lawn bowls. Australia's golf courses are among the finest in the world, its tennis players among the most successful. For a nation with such a relatively small population, international success has been by far disproportionate.

The sport that is perhaps the quintessential Australian activity, surfing, had its genesis in the national commitment to sun, sand and sea. Surf carnivals are a celebration of traditional Aussie values and pleasures.

Lifesaving clubs – voluntary organizations originating from the need to look after the safety of countless thousands of

beachgoers – compete in events ranging from beach sprinting and marching contests to surfboat racing.

The surf carnival also spawned a burgeoning professional sport – the iron-man contest – which requires outstanding general fitness and excellence in swimming, surf-ski paddling and beach running.

Australia is one of only three countries to have been represented at every summer Olympics since 1896, and the only nation in the southern hemisphere to have hosted the Games, which were held in Melbourne in 1956 and in Sydney in 2000.

Many of the nation's greatest international triumphs seem to have been in or on the water, such as the 1983 capture at Newport, Rhode Island, of yachting's America's Cup, the first time the US had been defeated in more than a century. Swimming has always been one of the nation's strong points.

*Above: Windsurfing is becoming more and more popular, but surfing is still number one. Right: ... along with sailing.*

Superlative buildings which were constructed for the 2000 Olympic Games in Sydney (the Olympic grounds are at Homebush Bay) include the Sydney International Aquatic Centre, Sydney Superdome, Australia's largest sport hall (20,000 spectators) and, of course, Stadium Australia (110,000 spectators).

Skiing is quite an exclusive sport in Australia. The season is extremely short (only mid-June to mid-September) and the costs are much higher than in Europe. Attractive ski areas are in Victoria (Mount Buller) and in New South Wales (Mount Kosciusko)

Australia has its share of bizarre sports, many originating in the tropical far north of the country, where the weather seems to have a strange effect on people. Alice Springs, in the hot and dry heart of Australia, is home to the annual Henley-on-Todd Regatta on the Todd River. This is the Red Centre's idea of a watersports extravaganza, all the more fascinating because the river is totally dry. Teams from all over the country construct "boats" made of plywood and paper and race them (hoisting the bottomless craft off the ground and running frantically) along the sandy bed of the Todd. The throng which gathers to watch the events contributes to the success by noisily cheering their favorites.

Beer tends to go well with some of Australia's more colorful sporting occasions. The dusty Queensland Outback town of Birdsville has a permanent population of about 50 people, but once a year that number swells to as many as 20,000 when the crowds flock to the Birdsville Cup horse race.

Its fame has less to do with the race or the quality of the field (broken-down nags struggling around a rough track of sand and red dust) than with the social activities associated with it.

The so-called Picnic Race Meeting is another Australian staple, once-a-year event at ramshackle little country tracks that engender remarkable enthusiasm. These are true family occasions, usually accompanied by a carnival of sorts, with children's rides and sideshow spectacles.

Perhaps the most delightful of these is the New Year's Day meeting at Hanging Rock in Victoria, with races held in an extremely picturesque setting right at the base of the famous, brooding rock.

The inhabitants of Queensland have concocted a few bizarre sports, among them the Cane Toad Races - a popular recreational activity in the far north. Cane Toads were introduced to Queensland's sugar cane fields to act as potential agents against pests.

These very poisonous animals, who also happen to reproduce at an incredible rate, turned out to have developed into a right rural nuisance.

One might expect Australia to excel at competitive boomerang throwing, this being the country where the weapon originated, but the Americans generally claim the main prize at the international events.

Folklore has it that Australians would

gamble on two flies walking up a wall – and it is true that most Australians love nothing more than a bet.

Gambling is part of the national ethos. Australia's unique contribution to gambling, the game known as two-up, is now played in the country's casinos, but until recently it was legal to play two-up only on the day reserved for the commemoration of Australia's war dead, Anzac Day.

A simple heads-or-tails coin tossing game, two-up was played in the trenches during the First World War and became inseparably connected with the image of Australians at war, and a much-loved institution.

What may well be the oddest of odd "sports" – and one which also satisfies the Aussie passion for gambling – is held annually in a New South Wales country town. The football pitch is marked with numbered squares, for each of which people buy a ticket. A cow is then let loose on the field ... and the lucky winner is the person in whose square the cow chooses to defecate.

*Sport and Gambling*

### ETERNAL RIVALS

Australia's two biggest cities, Sydney and Melbourne, are famous for their long-standing rivalry. Sydneysiders are proud of their city's beauty; the magnificent harbor, the splendid beaches and the sunny skies. On top of that, they would say it is lively and fun – much the same way, perhaps, as they would describe themselves.

Melburnians, on the other hand, would call Sydney's vitality brash, loud, noisy, superficial and American. Melbourne, they say, is gracious and European, with a cosmopolitan population dedicated to the pursuit of culture and good food.

Up in Sydney, they're supposed to believe that Melbourne is dull and gray and that the people only enjoy art and theater simply because they have nothing better to do.

*Above: The glow of the modern skyline of Melbourne. Right: The brightness of Sydney's famous symbol.*

The truth, as always, lies somewhere in the middle. In reality, with each city boasting populations of over 3 million from countless countries, Sydney and Melbourne are splendidly cosmopolitan and exciting places to live. Both contain fine art galleries, restaurants, theaters, ballet companies and orchestras. The two cities are much closer in style than their residents may like to think.

Melbourne does have a European air – the outdoor cafes, the little alleys and cobbled lanes in the central city that you have to hunt to find. And Sydney does have a more hedonistic feel to it, seemingly devoted as it is to sun, sailing, surfing and the outdoors. The big difference, though, between the two metropolises is that Sydneysiders probably don't think about Melbourne very often at all.

The traditional Melbourne - Sydney rivalry is found mostly south of the Murray River, which forms the boundary between New South Wales and Victoria.

During the Gold Rush, in the 1850s, Melbourne boomed. People's sudden

wealth was translated into fine buildings, elegant boulevards and high culture.

Towards the end of the 18th century, when the economy slumped, Sydney started to expand and Melbourne never really forgave it. Melbourne could never compete with Sydney's obvious physical attractions and when it could no longer boast that it was the biggest city – the financial, intellectual and cultural heart of the country – this is when the inferiority complex started to grow, slowly but surely.

Sydney doesn't feel that it has to compete. It quite simply doesn't even think about it. Sydneysiders are confident in the knowledge that they live in the country's largest city, a city set on a magnificent harbor and blessed with regular sunshine. From a tourist's point of view, Sydney probably does seem more interesting. But save a bit of time for Melbourne. Its attractions are not as obvious, but they are almost more beguiling.

With the tree-lined street and the Victorian buildings, it's easy to imagine what Melbourne was like when it was one of the great 19th century cities of the world. The city center is much more intact than Sydney's, which suffered for quite a long time from an "if it's old, rip it down" mentality.

Sometimes one just wants to grab Melbourne people and shake them every time one hears someone begin: "The trouble with Sydney " or "Compared to Sydney", one just wants to shout "Forget Sydney! It's forgotten you. It just gets on with being Sydney. It doesn't give a damn what you think of it. If you don't like it, don't go there." And those who don't like it should not go there.

Whenever one sees Melburnians lounging at pavement cafes, huddled over a cappucino reading the weekend newspapers, strolling along the Yarra riverfront or the Esplanade at St Kilda, or tucking into pasta in some tiny restaurant down a lane, one is reminded of the astute but anonymous observer who said in 1910: "Melbourne rises to greatness the moment it forgets itself."

## OVERDOING THE SUN

At the beginning of every summer the New South Wales State Cancer Council publishes the latest statistics and trends for skin cancer, a disease which is very prevalent in Australia. Year by year the figures become increasingly alarming: "Australia has the highest rate of skin cancer in the world. There are 140,000 new cases every year."

A thousand Australians die annually from skin cancer. In most cases the condition is caused by overexposure to solar radiation." Be very, very careful when traveling in Australia. It is not worth risking your future health just to get a good suntan.

There is continuing controversy in Australia about the fast-growing hole in the ozone layer and the consequent rise in ultra-violet radiation, which is consid-

ered to be primarily responsible for the incidence of skin cancer and mainly affects the countries of the Southern Hemisphere close to the South Pole. The increased cancer risk, particularly for fair-skinned Aussies, is casting a dark and threatening shadow over the bright sunshine of the summer months which begin at the end of October.

To Australians, the sun is a national institution, but this is now beginning to crumble. After the weather forecast, for instance, burn times are now read out regularly. These tell you how long you can safely stay out in the sun at midday the next day without risking sunburn – generally much less than one hour.

Roadwork gangs (the celebrated flagmen) and other high-risk employment groups are issued with free sun cream, sun hats and sunglasses along with their pay. Many schoolchildren are not allowed to walk home from school in the middle of the day – their parents collect them in cars in order to protect them from the sun.

*Above: Many Aussies still underestimate the danger of too much sun. Right: Nature has its own form of protection.*

People living north of a line from Sydney to Adelaide are most at risk. Cancer experts agree that the disease will not reach a peak for another few years yet. Young people who have spent half their childhood playing on the beach and on their surf boards will then be moving into the predicted high-risk group.

Despite these figures, which are extremely alarming for Australians, there has been very little response to the problem so far from the tourist industry. Even Queensland (officially called "Australia's Sunshine State") is continuing to promote its 364 sunny days a year, the Sunshine Coast and the pleasures of a beach holiday.

On Sydney's Bondi Beach, still one of Australia's showpieces, brown is still beautiful and the official slogan "White is beautiful" has so far totally failed to make any impact. It is mainly tourists from Europe, many of them fair-skinned, who visit Australia in summer for sun and sand. They may not be staying very long, but should still protect themselves carefully from the sun. Ann Jones, Information Officer at the New South Wales State Cancer Council, advises: "Avoid outdoor activities and intense sunlight between 10:00 a.m. and 3:00 p.m. Always wear a long-sleeved T-shirt made of non-translucent material. Use a water-resistant sun cream with a factor of 15 plus. This cream is obtainable anywhere in Australia and is much cheaper than in Europe. Also wear something on your head that shades your face and neck." This type of protection is the only reasonably sure way of avoiding the increasing dangers of overexposure to the Australian sun and also preventing the really severe headaches that accompany long hours in the sun without a hat.

Detailed information for travelers to Australia on the subject of skin cancer risks and tested sun products offering genuine protection can now be obtained from the privately financed New South Wales State Cancer Council, 2nd Floor, Angus & Coote Building, 500 George St., Sydney 2000, NSW 2001, Tel. (02) 2648888.

*Overdoing the Sun*

## METRIC CONVERSION

| Metric Unit | US Equivalent |
| --- | --- |
| Meter (m) | 39.37 in. |
| Kilometer (km) | 0.6241 mi. |
| Square Meter (sq m) | 10.76 sq. ft. |
| Hectare (ha) | 2.471 acres |
| Square Kilometer (sq km) | 0.386 sq. mi. |
| Kilogram (kg) | 2.2 lbs. |
| Liter (l) | 1.05 qt. |

## TRAVEL PREPARATIONS

### Entry and Customs

All visitors to Australia require a passport, which must be valid for at least another three months after their return journey. They also need a visa, which must be applied for before the journey. Only holders of Australian or New Zealand passports are exempt from this rule. An ordinary visitor's visa is valid for up to three months (free of charge).Most travel agencies are hooked up to the ETA – electronic transfer authority for distributing visas, so that the visitor can automatically obtain a visa when booking a flight, provided that he books on one of the 30 airlines listed and he shows his passport. There may be a processing fee. Applying for a visa via the Australian Embassy is the most complicated, lengthy and expensive method of all. A form must first be obtained a from the Australia Service, (an SAE must be provided) as well as a declaration of the purpose of the visit, for personal or business reasons). Then duly filled-out form must be sent, with a photograph, passport, and another SAE to the visa section of the Australian Embassy (or taken there personally, if there is a rush). The granting of a visa can take between two and three weeks, and costs approximately thirty-five USD. Visa application forms can be obtained

from the following embassies, among others:

**Britain**
The Australian High Commission
Australia House
Strand London WC2B 4LA
**USA**
The Australian Embassy
1601 Massachusetts Ave. NW
Washington DC 20036
**Canada**
The Australian High Commission
Suite 7010
50 O'Connor Street
Ottawa KIP 6L2

Additional information pertaining to visa requirements and entry can be obtained at www.immi.gov.au.
Vaccinations are not required for entry into the country, unless the visitor has been staying in an area with yellow fever less than six days before entry. To guard against insects and disease entering the country, the interior of every airplane coming from abroad is fumigated before landing at an Australian airport. Even though this is said to be completely harmless to humans, it is still advisable to breathe through a handkerchief. Some airlines introduce insect spray via the air-conditioning system.

All visitors over 18 have the following allowances: $A 5000 in cash, 250 cigarettes or 250 g of tobacco and 1.125 liters of alcohol may be imported duty free. In addition, adults may bring untaxable goods up to a value of 400 $A; children under 18, goods up to a value of 200 $A. Travel items for personal use can be brought in duty free. There is a strict import ban on groceries, vegetable and animal products as well as weapons and drugs.

### Travel to Australia

Most visitors to Australia travel there by air. If coming from Europe, you have two choices: the shorter route, timewise, is across Asia (stopovers in Bangkok or

Singapore). The alternative route is across the Atlantic, North America and the Pacific, with stopovers in Hawaii or Polynesia. This, of course, is the normal route for North American travelers. Luggage allowance is 32 kilograms, campers and cyclists take note!

Even though 90 per cent of all tourists first set foot on Australian soil in Sydney, there are direct international flights to Melbourne, Adelaide, Perth, Cairns, and Townsville. There are also some economical charter flights from Japan and Southeast Asia to Brisbane and Darwin.

While many airlines fly to Australia, the national carrier is Qantas, which offers excellent service. Telephone numbers are given below for reservations, those marked * being toll-free.

**Britain**
169 Regent Street, London, Tel.: 0345 747767*

**Canada**
1055 Dunsmuir Street, Suite 1714, Four Bentall Centre, Vancouver, Tel.: 684 8231. Provinces of Alberta and British Columbia: Tel.: 800 663 3411*. Rest of Canada: Tel.: 800 663 3432*

**New Zealand**
154 Queen Street, Auckland, Tel.: 79 0306
DFC Harbour Tower, Jervois Quay and Hunter Street, Wellington, Tel.: 73 8378

**Singapore**
300 Orchard Road, Tel.: 737 3744

**USA**
6151 West Century Boulevard, Los Angeles, Tel.: 800 227 4500*

### Currency and Exchange

The Australian dollar ($A) is the national currency. There are no restrictions on bringing in or taking out currency. However, if you bring in more than $A 5000, or a higher amount in another currency you will have to report this to the Cash Transaction Report Agency (CTRA). Credit cards such as American Express, Bankcard, Carte Blanche, Diners Club, Mastercard, and Visa are accepted all over the country in place of cash (strongly recommended for car hire). In remote places, understandably, cash payment will be preferred, so always make sure you have some handy. Travelers' checks can be exchanged easily in all large towns.

*Caution*: If you decide to change currency at Sydney International Airport, be prepared for a considerably less favorable exchange rate than in the city. If possible, make sure you already have some cash and small change on hand when you arrive, so that you will not need to change any money until you get into town.

### Climate and Best Time to Travel

The one big difference is that Australia's seasons are exactly the opposite of those in the northern hemisphere.
*Summer:* December through February
*Fall:* March through May
*Winter:* June through August
*Spring:* September through November.

Even within the country itself there are marked variations in climate. The north (especially in Queensland and the Northern Territory, north of the Tropic of Capricorn) enjoys a warm, tropical climate all year round. The rest of the country is situated in the temperate zone.

When planning your trip, you should bear in mind that the north has a wet season from November through April. Many roads are flooded during that period and may be impassable. During this period, dangerous marine stingers appear in the waters along the mainland coast of Queensland, and you should only bathe from protected beaches that have been cordoned-off with nets (cf page 220). The offshore islands of the Great Barrier Reef, however, are free of this jellyfish hazard. During the wet season in the north, extremely high humidity makes traveling uncomfortable. The drier winter months there are far more pleasant for holidaying. However, many tourists are disappointed when they travel through the south during the winter. Sydney can experience cold weather and even frost at that time of year, and in Melbourne you will definitely have to be prepared for storms and rain. On the credit side, this means that perfect skiing conditions can be enjoyed in the mountains of New South Wales and Victoria.

Winter is, without doubt, the best time to travel in the Outback, as summer temperatures may rise above 50°C. Summing up, the dilemma of choosing a season is one you must face alone. Whichever time you decide on, there will be some region of Australia that will lure you with a promise of "the best time to be there."

### Clothing

In general, follow the rule of dressing casually even for an official appointment (exceptions are business lunches or dinners, and restaurants in the higher price categories). There are two reasons for this: the Australians' relaxed attitude towards such matters and the generally extremes of temperature. Signs proclaiming "*No Shirt, No Shoes, No Service*" are a way of combating the outgrowths of this all-too casual way of life, and mean that customers must wear at least a T-shirt (with sleeves: tank tops not included in this category) and shoes (no so-called *thongs*, or beach sandals).

In the winter months (June through August) it may become unpleasantly cold, and not just at night. At that time of year, you should pack pullovers and jackets, as well as good shoes (which are necessary at any time in Australia, if you intend to wander even a few hundred yards off the paved roads). In the north, however, you will be perfectly comfortable all year round in very light clothing. Winter in the center of the country sometimes brings a frost at night, while day-time temperatures remain fairly high as usual. *Important:* As a protection against UV rays, which are gradually becoming more

intense over the years (due to the break-up of the ozone layer), it is absolutely essential to take sunglasses and a sun hat. Protective oils with a sun screen factor of 15 plus can be obtained everywhere in Australia and are not at all expensive. It is also advisable to wear a T-shirt while snorkeling to avoid getting a bad sunburn on your back. For bathing trips to the coral islands of the Great Barrier Reef, a good tip is to wear rubber or plastic shoes when bathing, to protect your feet against unpleasant cuts from the sharp coral, which could easily cause infection.

### Airport Taxes

In Australia, as in many countries, departure can bring a nasty surprise. The Australians have spared their tourists the nuisance of handling: your airline will have already bankrolled the necessary cash (27 $A per person over 12 years of age) at the time you purchased the ticket. This means that you can catch your flight home without having to run around the airport.

## TRAVELING IN AUSTRALIA

### By Air

In 1990, the Australian government deregulated air transport in the country. This process of liberalization caused prices to plummet, and several new air-carrier companies were created. Besides *Quantas* (www.quantas.com.au), *Ansett Australia* (www.ansett.com.au) also offers flights. The resulting competition is extremely fierce and generates a constant stream of special offers and reduced fares from which the customer can only benefit. If you are planning on taking only a few flights within Australia, you should buy your special tariff ticket in Australia (standby or last-minute tickets can also be obtained). A connecting flight within Australia is sometimes included in the price of a ticket – ask your travel agent.

However, if you want to take a larger

number of flights, it is well worth buying an air pass (which must be bought in your home country before your departure). This will give you a discount of between 25 and 50 percent of the usual tariff, depending on the carrier.

The pass is valid for a specific number of flights within a stipulated period of time. All airline companies offer these passes, but not all of them cover the whole of Australia.

Ask about fly-drive deals. The interstate airlines can also arrange car rental for you in-flight on certain routes; Sydney-Canberra, for example.

*Tip*: The route between Sydney and Melbourne is the most fiercely contested by the various carriers: tickets for off-peak periods, (sometimes night flights) are occasionally available at a special tariff of 99 $A.

### By Bus

Australia is covered by a dense network of bus routes. All large cities are connected by service several times a day. The *Greyhound Pioneer* busses travel the entire Australian mainland (with the exception of Western Australia) as do the *Mac Cafferty's* busses. Both operators offer various bus passes that are restricted to rides in specific areas and / or to a certain time period.

Information: Greyhound Pioneer throughout Australia around the clock, Tel:132030, www.greyhound.com.au; Mac Cafferty's: 07-46909888, www.maccaffertys.com.au. If you are planning to travel through the country by bus, inquire at your home travel agent about a bus pass; it is sometimes cheaper that way.

### By Train

Australia is certainly not a great country for train travel, although the trains that do run are usually classics in their own right.

The *Indian Pacific* operates between Sydney and Perth via Adelaide. The journey takes three nights or a total of 65

hours. There are two departures a week each way and tickets cost from $A 410.

The *Ghan* runs between Adelaide and Alice Springs twice a week. The journey takes 20 hours and ticket prices start from $A190. The *Ghan* also services from / to Melbourne or Sydney via Adelaide to Alice Springs once a week.

*The Sunlander* links Brisbane and Cairns three times a week and *The Queenslander* services the same stretch once a week, taking about 32 hours in each case (*Sunlander* from $A 170; *Queenslander* first class couchette car only, from $A 420).

If you want to travel by train only, you may obtain an Austrailpass at a good price from *Rail Australia* (for a period of between 14 and 90 days); this can be purchased outside Australia and at the train companies in the capitals of the Australian states. Further information on the Internet: www.gsr.com.au. The train companies of some of the Australian states (New South Wales, Victoria and Queensland) offer rail passes valid only in their territory. Inquire at Tel: 132232 (Australia-wide).

### By Car

In common with Britain, New Zealand, Japan and some other Asian countries, traffic in Australia drives on the left-hand side of the road. American and Canadian drivers will experience some initial problems on Australian roads. However, you can dispense with an international driver's license as your national driver's license will be valid for up to one year in Australia. *Important*: Always carry a reserve can of fuel in your car, as well as a container of water, a jack and a spare wheel. You can obtain detailed information and road maps, as well as help in emergencies, from the various automobile associations (addresses in the relevant guideposts), which you may call on free of charge if you are a member of an automobile association in your own country (don't forget your membership card!). All the larger international car rental companies are represented in Australia, but you will fare better financially if you book in your home country.

Many of the local companies may offer better prices, but using them could be a disadvantage in an emergency: If you do not allow enough time when returning your car before your departure, difficulties that crop up in calculating the invoice may take some time to clarify, in which case you will have to pay the total amount asked. However, with an international car hire company you may be able to settle disputes even when you get home.

Another idea worth considering is buying your own car: There is always a wide range of used cars on offer at Kings Cross in Sydney. Insurance may be a problem, though, as more and more companies are refusing to issue short-term policies to tourists. *Problem*: If you are pressed for time, shortly before departing, you may fail to get the price you ask when reselling your car, or you may not even be able to sell it at all.

You should be extremely careful when driving at night. Kangaroos are attracted by headlights, and will often run into a vehicle at top speed. Ideally, you should avoid night driving altogether. Whether driving by day or night, be careful when meeting traffic coming towards you on a gravel-surfaced road in the Outback. The life-expectancy of a windscreen can be extremely short.

Fuel is cheaper than in Europe, but more expensive than in North America, and prices vary from state to state. They range from 0,68 $A and $A 1,00.

There is a 60-kph speed limit in built-up areas, and on country roads 100 kph is the limit.

For British, though not perhaps for North American drivers the distances between cities are easy to under- or overestimate. The scale on maps can be misleading, and stretches of road of 1000 km

or more, with practically no sign of human habitation, are far from being a rarity. This must be taken into account when planning your trip.

Remember, too, that our summer holidays are winter holidays in Australia, and the days are short there. Before heading out on rough Outback tracks, inquire about the state of the road either at the local police station, the Automobile Club, or in a pinch at the nearest gas station or pub.

Many roads are impassable for months even with a four-wheel drive. In the northeasern part of the country, some tracks crossed by large rivers are open only from June / July until October.

### On Foot

You will really only want to discover the inland regions on foot; but do take every precaution. Although one becomes accustomed relatively quickly to driving on the left-hand side, pedestrians, especially at blind corners, always look the wrong way. You are advised always to cross at street traffic lights.

### Major Highways

**Sydney to Melbourne**: Hume Highway runs through the interior (879 km), from which you can branch off into the mountains of New South Wales and Victoria (Snowy Mountains and High Country).

The coastal route is more beautiful, following Princes Highway (1045 km) through or near numerous coastal towns and good beaches, and offers side-trips to Wilsons Promontory and Phillip Island.

**Sydney to Adelaide**: There are many alternative routes: Great Western, Mid Western, Sturt, Ouyen Highway, and Highway 12 provide access to the interior on a basically western route (1390 km), and is the one you should take if time is short.

Alternatively, you can stay on the Sturt Highway (1410 km) and, before reaching

Adelaide, take a long, pleasant break in Mildura on the Murray River. If you wish to include a visit to Canberra in your trip, start out on Hume Highway and then continue on Sturt Highway (1426 km) westward. Should you hanker after the solitude of the Outback, the best road to take is the Mitchell and Barrier Highway (1670 km; stop at Broken Hill) right into the interior.

**Sydney to Brisbane**: You have a choice of two routes for this trip. The Pacific Highway (Highway 1; 998 km) takes you along the coast with interesting stops at Myall Lakes, Port Macquarie, Coff's Harbour, and especially the area around Byron Bay. On the inland route, the Pacific, New England, and Cunningham Highways (1017 km) take you north via Hunter Valley, Tamworth, and Armidale.

**Melbourne to Adelaide**: The most spectacular route is along the coast. On Princes Highway (901 km) there is a turning for the Great Ocean Road, which takes you along one of the most fascinating stretches of coastline in the country. Western and Dukes Highways (734 km), which take you to the towns of Ballarat and Ararat, still have some of the gold rush atmosphere about them. There is also the possibility of a trip into the beautiful Grampians (Gariwerd) region. The Murray River is the big highlight of the second leg of the route on the Calder and Sturt Highways (950 km).

**Adelaide to Brisbane**: This route is not for timid drivers. You will see very few humans but a great many kangaroos, emus, and parrots along Barrier, Mitchell, Oxley, Newell, and Cunningham Highways (2040 km).

**Adelaide to Alice Springs**: As it is now properly surfaced along its entire length, Stuart Highway (1529 km) has lost much of its once-daunting reputation although, for most of the way the route still takes you through lonely Outback, and it is definitely worth taking a break at

Coober Pedy (where, if you are lucky, you just might happen to stumble across an opal).

**Adelaide to Perth**: At the start, the only available route takes you across the seemingly endless Nullarbor Plain on the Eyre Highway. In Norseman the road divides. The Great Eastern Highway leads you through the gold-mining towns of Kalgoorlie and Coolgardie to Perth (2706 km). The other route, on the South Coast and South Western Highways (3222 km , takes you into a magnificent coastal region, well away from the gold towns.

**Perth to Darwin**: This route is still the greatest motoring challenge for travelers in Australia. It must be said that a vehicle that is perfectly equipped and technically in tip-top condition is absolutely essential for the trip, especially if you start out on the Great Northern Highway (4236 km) which is the inland route. The much more attractive coastal route follows the Brand and North West Coastal Highways (4366 km). After that, both routes lead to Darwin on the Victoria and Stuart Highways.

**Alice Springs to Darwin**: The second leg of Stuart Highway goes northward to Darwin (1488 km . A detour worth making is via Lasseter Highway (244 km) to Yulara (Uluru / Ayers Rock) and a stop at Alice Springs.

**Darwin to Townsville**: Leave Stuart Highway at Tennant Creek in an easterly direction and aim for the Queensland coast using the Barkly and Flinders Highways (2508 km).

**Brisbane to Cairns**: You should definitely allow a few extra days when traveling along Bruce Highway (1705 km), as there are islands, bays, and beaches to visit from every town. This is Australia at its picture-book best, although the Great Barrier Reef itself is not visible from the highway.

### Distances

Sydney-Melbourne. . .  879 km/527 mi
Melbourne-Adelaide . .  734 km/440 mi

*Guidelines*

Adelaide-Perth . . . 2706 km/1623 mi
Perth-Darwin . . . . 4236 km/2541 mi
Darwin-Alice Springs 1488 km/892 mi
Alice Springs-Adelaide 1529 km/917 mi
Darwin-Cairns. . . . 2882 km/1729 mi
Cairns-Brisbane . . . 1705 km/1023 mi
Brisbane-Sydney . . . . 998 km/599 mi

## PRACTICAL TIPS

### Accommodation

All over Australia there are hotels in all price categories. Outside the large cities, however, you will usually find you are limited to motels for overnight stops. For those traveling on foot, a good network of backpackers' accommodation has been built up over the last few years: YHA (youth hostels) , no age restrictions, on-the-spot membership possible; the hotel chain Backpacker Resorts of Australia (VIP) and Nomads. There are also hundreds of independent hostels. They all offer dormitories, and often basic single and double rooms.

Information for nature lovers driving through the country without a tent: almost all caravan parks and camping grounds offer cabins or on-site vans (mobile homes). Lodgings range from simple huts to vacation homes with kitchen and bath. Prices are between A$ 30 and A$ 80 per night, though in top locations and in the peak season they can go a little higher.

Accommodation categories:

$ *Budget*: up to $A 50 (frequently accommodation in youth hostels and backpacker lodges; often in dormitories; in simple motels, double rooms).

$$ *Moderate*: $A 60-130 (prices for a double room per night, mainly in motels).

$$$ *Luxury*: over 130 $A (prices for a double room per night, mainly in hotels of the international class). Note: These rates were accurate in mid-2000. Some establishments may have put up their prices, so that they have moved up into the next price category. In tourist attractions like Ayers Rock, prices can double.

### Alcoholic Drinks

As a rule, these are served in pubs from Mondays through Saturdays from 10:00 a.m. to 10:00 p.m., with beer naturally being most popular, followed increasingly closely by Australian wine (usually of very good quality).

On Sundays, different states have different laws. The sale of alcohol in shops is restricted to special bottle shops.

### Banks

As a rule, banking hours are Monday through Thursday from 9:30 a.m. to 4:00 p.m., and Friday from 9:30 a.m. to 5:00 p.m. Only a few banks are open on Saturdays.

When making trips into the Outback or other remote areas, it is advisable to take a plentiful supply of cash (cf Currency and Exchange).

### Business Hours

Shops are generally open Monday through Friday from 9:00 a.m. to 5:00 or 6:00 p.m. The same hours apply to post offices. Shops are open Saturdays 9:00 a.m.-4:00 p.m; in the big cities the department stores and some shops in the city center are open from 10:00 a.m. to 16:00 p.m.

All over town, there are small grocery shops which often sell provisions. They are open daily until late at night, some are even open around the clock.

### Country and Politics

The Commonwealth of Australia is part of the British Commonwealth and consists of the six sovereign states of New South Wales, Victoria, Tasmania, South Australia and Queensland, as well as a number of territories including Australian Capital Territory and Northern Territory.

The position of the Sovereign, the Queen, as Head of State is recognized in the persons of her representatives who are appointed on the advice of the party in power at the time the office falls vacant. At the top is the Govenor-General, while each state has its own governor.

Prime ministers and cabinets are appointed, nominally, by the Queen's representatives and are answerable to the Senate and the House of Representatives.

*Area*: approximately 7.7 million square kilometers, which makes Australia the smallest continent.

*Extent*: from west to east approximately 4000 km, from north to south approximately 3300 km. The northernmost point of Australia is Cape York, the easternmost is Cape Byron, the most southerly is South East Cape, and the most westerly is Steep Point.

The highest mountain is Mt. Kosciuszko, which reaches a height of some 2229 meters.

*Population*: about 17 million (of these only about 1 per cent of the population are Aborigines). But the vast majority of the population lives in the cities on the eastern and southern coasts, so the average density is highly misleading.

*Population density*: 2 people per sq km.

*National flag*: Four large white stars and a smaller white star on a blue ground symbolize the Southern Cross constellation discovered by James Cook in 1769. A small Union Jack is in the top left-hand corner.

*National anthem:* "God Save the Queen" was the national anthem here, as in England, until recently. "Waltzing Matilda" was rejected as inappropriate, being the story of a thief's suicide, and "Advance Australia Fair" was adopted; set, curiously, to the tune of "God Bless the Prince of Wales."

### Electricity

The voltage in Australia is 240/250 volt, AC, at 50 Hz. You will need three-pin plugs for wall sockets. As a rule, European electrical appliances can only be used with an adaptor, and only the larger hotels provide universal sockets, though only for electric razors. Better and more expensive hotels have fixed hair driers in the rooms. All sockets have a switch that must be turned on to activate the current.

### Embassies in Canberra
### The British Embassy
Commonwealth Avenue
Yarralumla
Canberra ACT 2606
Tel: 06-2706666
### The Embassy of the United States
Moonah Place
Canberra ACT 2600
Tel: 06-270-5000
### The Canadian High Commission
Commonwealth Avenue
Canberra ACT 2600
Tel: 06-273-3844

### Food and Drink

In major Australian cities, an interesting evolution of the gastronomic scene has occurred since the 1980's, often due to the beneficial influence of various ethnic specialties introduced by immigrant groups. Melbourne and Sydney, with their thousands of restaurants and cafes, top the list as an unrivaled Mecca for the enthusiastic gourmet, followed closely by Adelaide. Perth, Darwin and Brisbane also offer a rich palette of excellent dining facilities. There is little differentiation between a restaurant and a cafe in Australia. A cafe is usually smaller, with a more modest decor. One can both drink a coffee there or eat lunch and dinner, and that rather well in the big cities. Some provincial towns in Victoria, New South Wales and South Australia offer excellent restaurants to which the spoiled big city dweller flocks. In the areas in which wine is cultivated, one generally dines well, too: Hunter Valley in New South Wales, in the Yarra Valley and on the Mornington Peninsula near Melbourne, in Barossa and Clare Vally near Adelaide as well as in Swan Valley near Perth.

However, outside of these regions and

tourist centers, there still stretches a culinary desert, and the traveller must make do with take-out and fast food. The range varies from hamburgers to meat pies and milk shakes, which become quite monotonous after a few days. But there is quite a positive exception: in many coastal towns there is a rich variety of freshly-caught fish and seafood. Over the whole country, it is generally true to say that pubs offer a choice of good, solid meals, which represent value for money. If you like meat, you will nearly always eat well, but vegetarians will sometimes have no choice but to resort to the salds offered everywhere.

Not all restaurants have a license to sell alcoholic drinks, but Australia has come up with an excellent innovation: Bring Your Own, meaning that you can bring your own wine or beer to "BYO" restaurants. The waiters will be happy to serve you your own drink with your meal, although it is possible that they will charge a little extra on the bill (per glass).

Australians must be world champions of the barbecue. Facilities for grilling food are standard equipment in every home, as well as on camping sites and in many parks (sometimes even with gas).

Australian wine, which is often of the finest quality, is one of the drinks steadily gaining in popularity, but top of the list is still beer, which is always served cold and in small glasses (without much head). In the Outback beer is sometimes served with a thin layer of ice.

*Foster* (blue can) and *Victoria Bitter* (VB) are drunk all over the country. In Queensland, you will be served *Castlemaine XXXX* (Four X). In Western Australia, the most popular brand is *Swan*.

You can order your beer in one of three ways: in a can, in a small bottle called a "stubby," or in a large glass, called a "schooner." If you are out with friends, then take a "jug" (1 liter). Glasses and jugs are always taken from the fridge.

## Holidays

Each individual Australian state has a number of public holidays. For example, major horse-racing events in each state are public holidays. The following are public holidays throughout the country:
*New Year's Day* (1 January)
*Australia Day* (26 January)
*Good Friday*
*Easter Monday*
*ANZAC Day* (25 April)

The *Queen's Birthday* is a movable holiday, always on a Monday in June, and usually combined with the previous weekend, although Queen Elizabeth's real birthday is in April.
*Christmas Day* (25 December)
*Boxing Day* (26 December)

## Medical Facilities and Insurance

Australian hospitals and medical practitioners are well up to international standards of excellence.

There are no unusual health risks for travelers, barring snakes, spiders, scorpions, and aquatic hazards (cf. page 225).

In addition, there are mosquitos which can transmit malaria (rare), and various other types of fever, such as dengue fever and Ross River fever.

These infections must be be cured properly, but they do not cause complications or leave any lasting effects.

The best prevention is an effective insect repellent.

Since there is always the possibility of falling ill on a journey, however, it is essential to take out private health insurance before your visit, including accident insurance, otherwise you might have to pay for medical treatment yourself.

## Post Offices

Three post boxes usually stand near the post office, one for local mail, one for out-of-town Australian mail and one for overseas mail.

Air mail letters usually reach their destination in a few days. Post offices are usually open from 9:00 a.m, to 5:00 p.m. In smaller towns there is usually a store attached.

### Telephoning

In Australia, there are four different area codes: 02 for New South Wales, 03 for Victoria and Tasmania, 07 for Queensland and 08 for South Australia, Western Australia and the Northern Territory.

All the telephone numbers following these area codes are composed of 8 digits.

Local calls in Australia from a phone booth cost 40c, and 25c from a private connection (hotels determine their own fees). Unfortunately, it is not possible to determine by oneself what a local call is, for even under the same area code, the call is usually a long distance call. Dial 12552 for information. Long distance calls within Australia cost Mon-Fri from 07:00 a.m. to 7:00 p.m. a maximum of $A 2.80 (at a distance of more than 745 kilometers), and a maximum of $A 1.60. Numbers beginning with 1800 are free call numbers. International calls can been be made quite easily, even from phone booths. The country dialing code can be looked up in the directory. This code is followed by the usual local dialing code minus the first zero if appropriate.

*Exception*: Red telephones are for local calls only. The costs for international calls with the *Telstra* phone company are very high.

A pre-paid phone card from some other telecommunications company (such as EZI Rate, Tel: 1800-817639; Unidial, Tel: 1800-737011) is significantly cheaper (between $A 0.35 and $A 0.60 per minute).

Phone cards can be purchased at student travel agencies and Internet cafes. Cellular phones will work if registered at 018018111.

The emergency services number is 000 all over Australia.

To call out of Australia, dial 0011 followed by the country code.

### Tipping

This is handled in much the same way as in Europe and the United States. Tipping is only necessary in higher category restaurants (about 10 per cent of the bill). Even after a taxi ride, a tip is not expected – but it will certainly not be refused.

### Time Zones

Australia has three different time zones: Eastern Standard Time (EST) is applicable in New South Wales, Australian Capital Territory, Victoria, Tasmania, and Queensland. In South Australia and in the Northern Territory the clocks are set for Central Standard Time (CST), while Western Australia uses Western Standard Time (WST).

From October through March, all states, except Queensland, Western Australia and the Northern Territory, switch to summer time. Depending on the time of year, and the state, Australian time is eight to ten hours in advance of central European time.

### Weights and Measures

While Britain and the USA have retained, or partially retained, the imperial system of weights and measures, Australia has fully adopted the European metric system, so that distances and speeds (on road signs) are given in kilometers.

Should you decide to buy an older vehicle for traveling around, be careful: do not over- or underestimate distances, as your speedometer and distance meter will be in miles instead of kilometers.

Remember that weights are in grams and kilos, and temperatures in centigrade.

### INFORMATION ON AUSTRALIA

General information on Australia can be obtained by writing to the Australian Tourist Commission (ATC):

*Guidelines*

There is good information on the individual states on the Internet:

**All Australia:** www.australia. co;

**New South Wales:** www.tourism.nsw;

**Victoria:** www.visitvictoria.com;

**Australian Capital Territory**: www. canberratourism.com.au;

**Tasmania:** www.toursim.tas.gov.au

**South Australia**: www.visit-southaustralia.com;

**WesternAustralia**: www.westernaustralia.net;

**NorthernTerritory**: www.nttc.com.au;

**Queensland**: www.queensland-holidays. com.au

### Australian National Parks and Wildlife Service

There are more than 2000 national parks and nature conservation areas in Australia. Information can be obtained from the main offices in the individual states:

**New South Wales**:

National Parks & Wildlife Service 43, Bridge St, Hurstville NSW 2220 Tel: 02-95856533

**Queensland**: Department of Environment & Heritage Naturally Queensland Shop, 160 Ann St, Brisbane 4000, Tel: 07-32278187

**South Australia**:

Department of Environment, Heritage & Aboriginal Affairs, 77 Grenfell St, Adelaide 5000, Tel: 08-82041910

**Victoria**:

Parks Victoria, information by telephone only, Tel: 131963. A small selection of information is available at the Information Centre des Dept. of Conservation and Natural Resources (NRE), 8 Nicholson St, East Melbourne 3002, Tel 03-96378080.

**Northern Territory**:

Parks and Wildlife Commission, main office: Goyder Centre, 25 Chung Wah Terrace, Palmerston, NT 0831, Tel: 08-89995511. Information booth in the Dar-

win Regional Tourist Information Centre in Darwin

**Western Australia**:

Dept. of Conservation and Land Management (CALM), 50 Hayman Rd, Como, WA 6152, Tel: 08-93340333; web site: www.calm.org.au

**Tasmania**:

Dept. of Enviroment and Lanf Management, sub-dividision, Parks & Wildlife, 134 Macquarie Street, Hobart 7000, Tel: 03-62338011

### LANGUAGE

#### Aussie Slang

Even travelers to Australia whose native language is English will spend the first few days wondering if they are hearing correctly.

On the other hand if your English is not good, you may really have problems.

One of the problems may be the individual Australian vocabulary, called Aussie slang.

Here are a few words and expressions you will come across during your trip to Australia:

*avo* . . . . . . . . . . . . . afternoon
*barbie* . . . . . . . . . . . . barbecue
*billy-tea* . . tea brewed over a campfire
*bloodyot* . . . . . . cold, rainy weather
*booze, turps, rosiner* . . . . all kinds of
. . . . . . . . . . . . . alcoholic drink
*bonzer* super, good, cxcellent, great
*breckie* . . . . . . . . . . . . breakfast
*brew* . . . . . . . . . . . . a cup of tea
*bunyip* . . . Aboriginal mythical being
*bush* . . . . everywhere outside the city
*cardigan* . . . . . . . . . . . . . jacket
*chooks* . . . . . . . . . . . . chickens
*dodger*. . . . . . . . . . . . sandwich
*drongo* . . . . . . . . . . . . . . idiot
*dunny* . . toilet, lavatory, (esp. outside)
loo, john
*esky* . . . . . . . . . . . . . . ice box
*full* . . . . . . . . . . extremely drunk
*G'day* . . . . . hallo, good morning etc.
*good onyer!* . . . . well done! carry on!

| | |
|---|---|
| *grog* | any type of liquor |
| *jug* | 1 liter of beer in a mug |
| *Kiwi* | New Zealander |
| *laughing jackass nick* | name for the Kookaburra bird |
| *lube* | drink |
| *motza* | a packet of money |
| *Mr. Say-so* | the boss |
| *mozzies* | mosquitos |
| *nippy* | cold, wet weather |
| *nobbler* | glass of schnapps |
| *Oz* | abbreviation for Australia |
| *poms* | the English |
| *quack* | doctor |
| *rapt* | satisfied |
| *righto!* | O K ! Agreed! |
| *sammich* | sandwich |
| *sheila* | a young Australian woman |
| *shivoo* | party |
| *shout* | to pay for a round of drinks |
| *shove it!* | go away! get lost! |
| *sleever* | large beer |
| *sling* | tip |
| *snags, snorkers* | sausages |
| *snort* | a drink, usually beer |
| *strides* | trousers, pants, jeans |
| *stockman* | cattle driver, cowboy |
| *stubby* | small bottle of beer |
| *tea* | hot evening meal |
| *telly* | television |
| *that's a peg!* | that's the tops! |
| *up a gumtree* | in difficulties |
| *not to know* | what's going on or what to do |
| *to get bushed* | to get lost |
| *tucker time* | mealtime |
| *the wet* | rainy season in the north of the country |

The following words are mainly well-known terms derived from the Aborigine languages:

| | |
|---|---|
| *corroboree* | Aborigine ceremony |
| *didgeridoo* | long, wooden wind instrument |
| *dillybag* | a bag woven out of natural fibers |
| *dreamtime* | the creation period in Aboriginal mythology |
| *gibber-gunyah* | cave dwellings of original inhabitants |
| *nulla-null* | a Aborigine club weapon |
| *walkabout* | a ritual walk, performed by the Aborigines |
| *willy - willy* | hurricane in the Outback |

## AUTHORS

**Peter Hinze**, Project Editor and main author of this book, first visited Australia about 15 years ago – and tried his luck looking for opals in the Outback. His fascination for the fifth continent and for Sydney has endured. Since visiting, he has made a name for himself as a freelance journalist and photographer in Germany by publishing numerous travel reports. He lives in Munich, where he works for a major weekly magazine. He also edited the Nelles Guide *New Zealand.* He wrote the following articles for this book: *Sydney, Australia's Secret Capital; From Sydney to Melbourne; Melbourne, Cosmopolitan Metropolis; Adelaide, South Australia's Tranquil Capital; From Brisbane to Townsville; From Townsville to Cape York Peninsula; Overdoing the Sun.*

**Anne Biging**, an economist and journalist, has traveled regularly and extensively in Australia for the last ten years. She has written countless articles about life and travel in Australia. She wrote for this book *Perth, the Tranquil Southwest* and *From Perth to Darwin*

**Marc Marger** has traveled all over Australia on several hitch-hiking trips, and feels just as much at home on the beaches of Queensland as in Tasmania's mountain terrain. He is the authour of the articles *Tasmania, Australia's Green Island* and *From Melbourne to Adelaide.*

**Andrea Brown** studied ethnology and psychology in Munich and Sydney. She came to know the Fifth Continent up close, as the only woman working on an Outback construction site, picking apri-

*Guidelines*

cots on the Murray River and frying hamburgers in Darwin. She is well known as a best-selling author of woman's novels and wrote the chapter *History of Australia).*

**Ulf Marquardt**, a radio journalist from Hamburg, discovered his love for Australia as a surfer on the country's beaches. This globetrotting journalist wrote *Australia's Wild North.*

**Wolfgang Koch** took a degree in chemistry but has spent the last few years studying ethnology and languages. He is an experienced travel guide and mountaineer. The authour of the article on *The Red Centre,* he is particulalry interested in the Outback and Aboriginal culture.

**Uwe Seidel**, a free-lance journalist in Berlin, used his first trip to Australia to trace his roots, and then kept going back for more. The result has been numerous travel guides and publications including a dictionary of Aussie slang. He is the author of the chapters *From Brisbane to Townsville* and *From Townsville to Cape York Peninsula.*

**Lesley Darlington**, a free-lance journalist, specializes in writing about travel. She is Australian and lives and works in Sydney. She wrote *From Adelaide to Perth f*or this book.

**Anne Dehne** has been living in Melbourne since 1989. Researching for travel guides led her to discover the multi-facets of the Fifth Continent, which she has made her home. She thoroughly re-worked and revised this edition of *Nelles Guide Australia* and wrote the *Flora and Fauna* feature

**Fiona Gillies,** a Sydney-born journalist living in Melbourne is the author of the article *Eternal Rivals.*

**Gary Walsh** is a travel journalist from Melbourne with a great love of sport. He wrote *Sport and Gambling.*

**Carol Stuart** is a freelance journalist and author. She worked for the *Launceston Examiner; Tasmania* and the *Canberra Times.* She now works for *The*

*Age* in Melbourne. She is the author of the article *Rural Life in Australia.*

## PHOTOGRAPHERS

# Explore the World

NELLES GUIDES

## AVAILABLE TITLES

Australia
Bali / Lombok
Berlin and Potsdam
Brazil
Brittany
Burma → *Myanmar*
California
  *Las Vegas, Reno,*
  *Baja California*
Cambodia / Laos
Canada
  *Ontario, Québec,*
  *Atlantic Provinces*
Canada
  *Pacific Coast, the Rockies,*
  *Prairie Provinces, and*
  *the Territories*
Canary Islands
Caribbean
  *The Greater Antilles,*
  *Bermuda, Bahamas*
Caribbean
  *The Lesser Antilles*
China – **Hong Kong**
Corsica
Costa Rica
Crete
Croatia – *Adriatic Coast*
Cyprus
Egypt
Florida

Greece – *The Mainland -*
  *Peloponnese*
Greek Islands
Hawai'i
Hungary
India
  *Northern, Northeastern*
  *and Central India*
India – *Southern India*
Indonesia
  *Sumatra, Java, Bali,*
  *Lombok, Sulawesi*
Ireland
Israel - *West Bank,*
  *Excursions to Jordan*
Kenya
London, England and
  Wales
Malaysia - Singapore
  - Brunei
Maldives
Mexico
Morocco
Moscow / St. Petersburg
Munich
  *Excursions to Castles,*
  *Lakes & Mountains*
Myanmar (Burma)
Nepal
New York – *City and State*
New Zealand
Norway
Paris

Peru
Philippines
Poland
Portugal
Prague / Czech Republic
Provence
Rome
Scotland
South Africa
South Pacific Islands
Spain – *Pyrenees, Atlantic*
  *Coast, Central Spain*
Spain
  *Mediterranean Coast,*
  *Southern Spain,*
  *Balearic Islands*
Sri Lanka
Sweden
Syria – Lebanon
Tanzania
Thailand
Turkey
Tuscany
U.S.A.
  *The East, Midwest and South*
U.S.A.
  *The West, Rockies and*
  *Texas*
Vietnam

## FORTHCOMING
Cuba

*Nelles Guides – authoritative, informed and informative.*
*Always up-to-date, extensively illustrated, and with first-rate relief maps.*
*256 pages, approx. 150 color photos, approx. 25 maps.*